D1219328

THE HORTICULTURAL EXHIBITORS' MANUAL

THE HORTICULTURAL EXHIBITORS' MANUAL

Edited by A. G. L. Hellyer, F.L.S.

LONDON
W H & L COLLINGRIDGE LIMITED
TRANSATLANTIC ARTS INCORPORATED
NEW YORK

1058

Published in 1952
by W H & L Collingridge Ltd
Tavistock Street London WC2
and in the United States of America
by Transatlantic Arts Incorporated
Forest Hills New York
Printed & bound in England
by Hazell Watson & Viney Ltd
Aylesbury & London

Contents

Illustrations

BORDER CARNATIONS

CHRYSANTHEMUMS

DAFFODILS

DAHLIAS

GLADIOLI

PANSIES AND VIOLAS

HARDY PERENNIALS

ROCK PLANTS

ROSES

SHRUBS AND TREES

SWEET PEAS

DECORATIVE CLASSES

FRUIT

VEGETABLES

PREFACE

The Horticultural Exhibitors' Manual

THE PURPOSE of this book may require a little explanation. First it should be explained that it is not intended as a detailed guide to cultivation, but as a compendium of all those special points of cultivation and those refinements of showmanship which mark the difference between the skilled exhibitor and the novice. It is assumed that the reader is already in possession of the elementary rules of good gardening. If he is not he should purchase a book on the subject and study it in conjunction with the present volume.

Every one of the sixteen contributors to the Exhibitors' Manual is a specialist in his or her line. Each has been a successful exhibitor and so writes from actual experience and not from hearsay. It is because of the vast amount of expert knowledge which it contains that I believe this book is bound to be of great value to all exhibitors, whether they are themselves experienced or are still in the apprentice stage.

My own contribution to the work has been simple. It has consisted in the provision of the basic plan for the book and the selection of the authors for each of its numerous parts. In addition I have contributed some observations on the drafting of show schedules which I hope will be of service to those engaged on this very difficult and thankless task. I must make it plain, however, that my chapter is not intended to take the place of the excellent *Rules for Judging*, published by the Royal Horticultural Society, but rather to supplement it by laying emphasis on some of those points which occasion most controversy among exhibitors. *Rules for Judging* must remain the sole official guide on such matters and the final arbiter in all cases of dispute. To introduce any rival or alternative code would only be to make matters more difficult for the judges, the exhibitors, and those who compile schedules intended to satisfy both.

By this I do not mean that there should never be any departure in detail from the suggestions made by the R.H.S. experts, but rather that any such variations should be made with a full and clear knowledge of what is being done and a sensible reason for doing it. In different parts of the country different traditions of exhibiting have been built up, and it is often very desirable that these local practices should be maintained. But when this is so, and when such practices differ materially from those in more general use, redoubled efforts should be made to state the requirements in simple, unequivocal language.

Finally it is my sincere belief that exhibiting provides some of the greatest pleasures that gardening can give, that it acts as a stimulus to breeding and adds considerably to knowledge of the behaviour of plants and to skill in their cultivation. Occasionally a too fanatically held opinion may lead exhibitors into a blind alley, as has happened more than once in the setting of standards of colour or form too narrow for the particular flower to which they were applied. But that is a danger which appears to be far more widely recognized to-day than it was fifty years ago, and I do not think there is much danger now of progress in plant development being checked instead of fostered by the enthusiasm of exhibitors. They are, by and large, grand people, and it is to them that this book is dedicated.

Rowfant, 1952 A. G. L. HELLYER

ACKNOWLEDGEMENT

The tables on pages 224, 228, 266 and 267, showing the scales of points and the number of specimens to be shown for fruit and vegetables, are taken from Rules for Judging (*ninth edition*), *published by the Royal Horticultural Society, and reproduced by kind permission of the Society.*

INTRODUCTION

The Show Schedule

BY A. G. L. HELLYER, F.L.S.

THE FIRST requisite of a good show is a good schedule—and this includes not only the provision of suitable classes to meet the requirements of potential exhibitors, but also the wording of the whole schedule in such a manner as to leave no ambiguities and no uncertainties as to what the exhibitor may and may not do.

Fortunately the problem is greatly simplified by the existence of standard recommendations covering a great many of the questions that must arise when a show schedule is under consideration. These are published by the Royal Horticultural Society under the title *Rules for Judging* and should be obtained by all secretaries of horticultural societies.

Matters upon which disputes most commonly arise are the use of the words 'kind' and 'variety'; the definition of an annual, the distinction between the terms 'perennial', 'hardy perennial', 'herbaceous perennial' and 'hardy herbaceous perennial'; the precise position of bulbous-rooted plants in relation to such headings as those just named; and the meaning of such terms as 'stem' and 'spray'. Disputes may also occur over the size of exhibits and the use of foliage or flowers as a foil to the main part of the exhibit.

A final cause of misunderstanding is ambiguity in the actual wording of the schedule. It is surprising how easily this can occur even when great care has been taken and the best authorities have been consulted. The trouble is that the author of the schedule knows so clearly what he means by the words chosen that he quite fails to note that they could have a different interpretation. One example of this kind of thing may suffice. A schedule contained a class for 'three roses, any variety, one vase.' An exhibitor staged a bloom of Madame Butterfly, another of Crimson Glory and a third of

McGredy's Yellow and won the class. An objection was lodged that this was contrary to the schedule which specified 'any variety' not 'any varieties'. Now this is the literal interpretation of the words and the objection had to be upheld though it was not the intention of the show committee to prevent exhibitors from showing more than one variety. If the society is fortunate enough to number a lawyer amongst its members it is always worth while to have the draft schedule read by him, for his legal training will make him quick to pick out ambiguities of this kind.

Turning now to the other points I have named and taking them in order, 'kind' and 'variety' are carefully defined in the R.H.S. rules, but it may be worth adding to what is there stated that most plants can be identified accurately by *two* names, the first of which relates to the *kind* of plant and the second to the *variety*. Thus we talk of Apple Cox's Orange Pippin, Plum Victoria, Cabbage Primo, Pea Onward, Rose Peace, Chrysanthemum Sweetheart and so on. Apple, plum, cabbage, pea, rose and chrysanthemum are different kinds of fruit, vegetable and flower, whereas Cox's Orange Pippin, Victoria, Primo, Onward, Peace and Sweetheart are the names of particular varieties of these kinds.

The importance of this from the point of view of schedule drafting can be seen if we consider the following two apparently rather similar classes. 'A collection of vegetables, six kinds, to be displayed on a space 3 feet by 2 feet', and 'A collection of vegetables, six varieties, to be displayed on a space 3 feet by 2 feet'. An exhibitor would be quite in order in staging six varieties of one kind of vegetable in the second of these classes; for example, he could put up six varieties of potato (say, Home Guard, Majestic, Arran Banner, King Edward, Red Skin and Dunbar Standard), but he would be disqualified if he did this in the first-named class. In this each of the six items must be of a different kind; for example, potatoes, peas, beans, lettuces, carrots and beetroot would pass muster. It is worthy of note that, as each of these kinds would also and naturally be of some particular variety, an exhibit made up in this way would be as eligible for the second of our hypothetical classes as one made up of six varieties of the same kind.

An annual is a plant which normally completes its life cycle in one season of growth. Seed of the plant germinates, grows without break or rest into a mature plant, flowers, seeds and dies. Usually in the northern hemisphere this life cycle is completed within one calendar year, that is to say, the seed is sown in spring and the plant flowers in summer and dies in autumn, but this is not invariably the case. Many annuals can be sown in autumn, after which they will grow very slowly during the winter, burst into full energy the following spring and flower in early summer. This spreading of the flowering season over parts of two calendar years does not convert the plants into biennials. It is worthy of note that in the southern hemisphere it is normal for the annual to spread its growth over two calendar years, for the spring occurs in September, October or November of one year, and the autumn in March, April or May of the following year. The real test of an annual is that it normally completes its cycle in one unbroken lap. In this it differs from the biennial which starts its growth one year, then takes a rest during the winter and finally bursts into growth again to flower, seed and die sometime during the following year. The Canterbury bell is a typical biennial while the familiar Shirley poppy is a typical annual.

The real confusion, however, arises not between annuals and biennials but between plants which are genuine annuals and plants which are not really annuals at all though they are commonly grown as such. So puzzling is this that my own view is that it is best to eliminate from schedules the simple classification 'annuals' and substitute for it the wording 'annuals or plants commonly grown as such'. This is much fairer to the exhibitor who seldom has a great deal of technical knowledge on such points as this and is apt to take his information from seedsmen's catalogues and the backs of seed packets, both of which are frequently faulty or contradictory in their classifications. For example, the plant frequently known as annual scabious or sweet scabious is not a true annual, but few gardeners know this and it is invariably grown as an annual in our gardens. Trouble arises when some smart judge, anxious to air his knowledge, proceeds to disqualify from an 'annuals' class all exhibits which contain sweet scabious or some similar plant. He may be enforcing the letter of the law but he is certainly not interpreting its spirit. If the formula 'annuals or plants commonly grown as such' is used, disputes of this kind cannot arise.

Confusion between the terms 'perennial', 'hardy perennial', 'hardy herbaceous perennial' and 'herbaceous perennial' have caused many disputes at shows. A perennial is *any* plant which normally lives for more than a year, and flowers and seeds more than once. Some perennials are normally quite short-lived, exhausting themselves after two, three or four years, whereas others may continue to live for hundreds of years. The lupin and the aquilegia are normally short-lived perennials; the oak and the yew are long-lived. The fact that oak and yew are trees does not mean that they are not perennials. They are just as much entitled to that term as are soft-stemmed plants such as lupins and aquilegias. Moreover the term tells us nothing about the hardiness of the plant. An orchid that must be grown in a hothouse is just as much a perennial as a daisy which can be grown anywhere. In fact the term is too wide to be used by itself for classification in any show schedule. It must always be qualified.

'Hardy perennial' narrows the field but not nearly as much as some schedule makers appear to imagine. It still leaves the door wide open to hard-wooded as well as to soft-stemmed plants. For example, if a class is included, as it often is, for a vase of hardy perennials, there is nothing to prevent an exhibitor from including roses or branches from any ornamental trees or shrubs he may possess. This is often done and not infrequently disputes arise as a result, but the exhibitor is within his rights according to the schedule.

'Herbaceous perennial' defines the type of growth of the plants that can be shown but says nothing about their hardiness. A herbaceous plant is one with soft as opposed to woody growth, so any plant that lives for several years, flowering and seeding more than once, and is not of a woody character, is a herbaceous perennial. Lupins, delphiniums and michaelmas daisies are all of this class but so are dahlias, and it is quite usual to find their showy flowers included in classes which are described simply as for 'herbaceous perennials'. Again, it is common for protests to be made on the ground that the class should be confined to plants grown outdoors all the year, and it often transpires that this really was the intention of those who drafted the schedule. But the words they have chosen convey a different meaning and so the protests cannot be upheld.

There is only one way to describe classes which are to be confined to those plants which are herbaceous, perennial and capable of growing outdoors at all times and that is as being for '*hardy herbaceous perennials*'. The first term eliminates all plants, such as dahlias, that need winter protection, the second all woody plants, such as roses, the third all those plants that flower and seed only once, dying thereafter. The description is precise and leaves no loopholes for evasion.

It should be observed that the term 'bulbous-rooted' is not one which contrasts with 'perennial', 'herbaceous' and 'hardy' but which can be used to modify or restrict them still further. In any of the classes which I have just considered it would be quite in order to show plants with bulbous or tuberous roots, provided they conformed in other respects. Hardy lilies and montbretias are frequently included in classes for hardy herbaceous perennials and quite rightly so. If the schedule makers wish to exclude such plants they must state this positively by adding the words 'bulbous- or tuberous-rooted plants excluded'. In small shows I think it is seldom wise to do so, but in large shows which contain a separate class for bulbous- or tuberous-rooted plants, it may be a wise provision to ban them from the 'herbaceous' classes.

Note, again, that bulbous and tuberous are terms which do not themselves define the hardiness of the plant. In consequence a class simply designated as for a vase of bulbous- or tuberous-rooted flowers might well attract dahlias, begonias and other plants requiring protection either throughout the year or at some period of it. If these are to be excluded the word 'hardy' must be added.

'Stem', 'spray' and 'truss' are words sometimes used in schedules and which occasionally give cause for dispute. 'Stem' can almost certainly be eliminated from schedules altogether. 'Spray' must be used for sweet peas, for chrysanthemums when not disbudded to one flower per stem, and for a few other plants that naturally bear their flowers in loose clusters or spikes. Let the emphasis be on that word 'natural' and most difficulties will fall away. A spray is that aggregation of flowers which is the product of one stem. The fact that the flowers are themselves carried on stalks, some of which may be sufficiently long to appear almost like separate stems, does not matter as long as it is quite clear that all these side-growths do, in fact, form part of the same cluster or spray. Where trouble usually arises is when some exhibitor cuts his plant so low down that he severs a main branch carrying two or more stems each bearing its own cluster or spray of flowers. This, of course, is inadmissible.

'Truss' is often used in connexion with rambler roses, and this has exactly the same definition as 'spray'. It might be as well to stick to the one term throughout and so avoid confusion in the minds of exhibitors. 'Truss' is also used in connexion with some fruits. For example, there is often a class for a truss of tomatoes (this will, of course, appear in the vegetable section though the tomato is botanically a fruit), and again it can be defined as all those fruits which are related in one cluster. The truss may branch several times, for this is a characteristic of some varieties of tomato, but it still remains a single truss as long as it is obviously part of the same cluster of fruits. It is not permissible to show as a truss a length of tomato stem carrying two or more separate clusters of fruit.

The size of exhibits, whether this is to be estimated by measurement or by the number of specimens shown, is a frequent cause of dispute. In the case of collections of vegetables or fruits it is almost always wise to state in the schedule the maximum length and breadth of the exhibit; for example: 'Collection of six distinct kinds of vegetables to be staged on a table space not exceeding 3 feet by 2 feet.' In the case of individual dishes of vegetables or fruits, the Royal Horticultural Society has laid down in *Rules for Judges* the recommended number of specimens of each kind required to make a dish. For collections of fruits, the dishes should consist of the same numbers as in the single dish classes, but for vegetables a separate list of recommendations has been prepared. My advice is that these recommendations should be followed wherever possible. In the case of some small shows, such as shows intended primarily for novices or for those with very small gardens, the numbers recommended by the R.H.S. may be too large. In such instance the show committee should decide on its own numbers and print these in the schedule.

The question of 'points' judging often arises. This is a system whereby the desirable features of each kind of flower, vegetable or fruit are analysed and allocated a certain maximum number of points. Then the judge works to this predetermined system, assessing each quality separately and giving it a certain number of points according to its merits. The R.H.S. has recommended pointing scales for a great many fruits, vegetables and flowers, but a drawback of this system is that the total number of points allocated is not large enough to allow the judge sufficient latitude. For example, the R.H.S. pointing for onions is a maximum of 8, to be divided in the proportion of 2 for size, 2 for condition, 2 for uniformity and 2 for form. In a big and keenly contested class it may be quite impossible to separate the best exhibits without giving a number of fractional points and this can become very confusing. To overcome this difficulty some judges adopt the R.H.S. system multiplied by 10; for example, for onions the total would be 80, with 20 for each of the four desirable qualities. This certainly helps, but I think there is a fundamental weakness about all systems of pointing. It is that they encourage judges to look at each exhibit piecemeal instead of whole. They are founded on the fallacy that a flower, fruit or vegetable can be split up into a number of separate features and that the quality of the whole equals the sum of the parts. In fact it is not possible to break up the good features of a plant in this arbitrary manner, and in any case one quality may be so much modified by another that the effect of the whole cannot be arrived at by adding up a series of figures on a points card. Good judges are only made by long experience and they learn to take in the whole of an exhibit so that each quality is seen in proper perspective in relation to all the others. Points systems may be a useful means of leaving a record behind as to why a particular exhibit was regarded as good or bad, but they serve very little other purpose and can seldom be used to clarify a difficult issue.

The only exception I would make to this general dictum is in the case of exhibits consisting of a number of totally distinct items—a collection of vegetables, for example. With these a fresh problem arises, for obviously all the items cannot be placed on exactly the same footing. One vegetable may be worth more in itself than another, quite apart from how much it is worth as a specimen of that particular kind of vegetable. For example, it is generally accepted that celery or onions take more growing, and are therefore worth more if perfectly produced, than turnips or cabbages. In consequence, when judging collections it does often pay to point the exhibits, giving each item the number of points it would deserve in comparison with a perfect example of its kind. The R.H.S. lays down a useful system of points for this purpose. But again I would reiterate that each item is to be looked at and judged whole. The points system in this instance merely serves to give a grand total for all the items when these have been judged separately. Even when that has been done it may still be necessary, in a close contest, to look at the exhibit as a whole, determining how one item has been used to set off another and what the total effect is, before a final and just award can be made.

Unless the schedule makes a specific statement to the contrary, no exhibit must contain any flowers other than those stated, nor any foliage other than that natural to the flowers. Occasionally, exhibitors will attempt to improve the appearance of exhibits by adding garnishings or additions of one kind or another—gypsophila with sweet peas, for example—but this must lead to disqualification unless there is a clause in the schedule saying that it is allowed. In purely decorative classes, as for example, for a bowl of chrysanthemums or roses arranged for effect, it is generally permissible to use other foliage and even, occasionally, berries or other flowers to produce an attractive colour scheme, but to avoid disputes, schedule makers should always make this quite plain by adding the words 'other foliage' or 'other foliage, flowers and berries'. If, on the contrary, they wish to debar such additions, this should be stated in an equally definite manner.

It is not uncommon to include a class for a vase of flowers—it may be a vase of annuals, or a vase of perennials, or it may just be left open for competitors to include any flowers they may have in the garden. The essential point is that the only clue to the extent of the exhibit is contained in that one word 'vase'. In my experience that is too vague a definition. Vases of all shapes, sizes and descriptions may turn up and, more often than not, the exhibitor with the biggest vase wins by sheer weight of the material he has been able to crowd into it. If possible the society should provide its own vases for classes of this type and they should all be of one size and pattern, but if this is impracticable, the maximum height of the vase and its diameter at the mouth should be stated. This will at least start the exhibitors off on a level footing. Some show committees go further and fix definite limits of height and breadth to the arrangement of flowers placed in the vase. I do not think this is essential, in fact my view is that it puts too great a curb on individual ideas of arrangement.

General rules relating to the conduct of a show should be kept as few and as simple as possible. Many rules which appear in this general section would be better incorporated as part of the description of the classes to which they apply. The trouble is that the general rules are frequently read carelessly or not at all and exhibitors then find themselves disqualified for some fault of which they had no knowledge.

Precise instructions should be given concerning the final date for accepting entries for the show and the time by which exhibits must be staged, and these rules should be strictly kept. If such terms as 'open classes', 'amateurs only', 'cottagers classes' are used in the schedule, these terms should be clearly explained. The Royal Horticultural Society defines an amateur as one who does not earn any part of his living by growing plants for sale or for an employer. This is a good general definition for the larger shows but is usually too wide for small shows, for, unless qualified in some way, it permits the wealthy amateur whose produce is grown for him by professional gardeners to compete on level terms with the less well-to-do who work their gardens without any paid help. Where it seems desirable, separate sections may be made for amateur gardeners who employ no labour, those who only employ one gardener, and those who employ more than one gardener.

The term 'open' is sometimes used with the meaning that the classes are open to professional gardeners as well as to amateurs, and sometimes with the meaning that they are open to non-members of the society. Here again the precise intention should be stated.

A 'cottager' may be any amateur who does not employ paid help and is himself engaged in manual labour other than gardening, or any amateur with a garden below a certain size, or a combination of these qualifications. The term is falling into disuse and this is probably a good thing, as the genuine cottagers for whom these classes were originally intended are disappearing.

The rules should make clear provision for the lodging of protests, fixing a time limit for these and making it obligatory that they be made to the show secretary in person. It is often a good plan to fix a small fee to be deposited with each protest, this fee to be returned if the protest is upheld, but confiscated if the protest is rejected. This may protect the show committee from many merely frivolous complaints. In any case all protests should be dealt with promptly by the show committee and not by the secretary only or by any of the judges.

Some of the specialist societies have taken great pains to group and classify their flowers for the purpose of shows. This has been done by the National Dahlia Society, which recognizes eleven separate sections of dahlias, further split up into a number of classes; by the National Chrysanthemum Society with separate classifications for both the outdoor October flowering and the indoor varieties split up into twenty-four sections with numerous sub-sections; by the British National Carnation Society and others. Frequently it is quite unnecessary for small, unspecialized flower shows to follow these classifications in detail as the number of entries to be expected could not justify such a multiplication of classes, but there are other occasions on which the classifications, or some part of them, may be used with advantage. In all such cases it should be made quite plain in the schedule what authority is being followed, and the show secretary should have a copy of the appropriate classification available for the use of both exhibitors and judges. Frequently these specialist classifications are accompanied by very complete lists of varieties arranged according to the classes into which they fall. These must also be available in their most up-to-date editions, as they may prove to be the only means of settling disputes concerning the group or class to which any particular variety belongs. Judges, however expert, cannot be expected to carry all these details in mind, though competent judges will always be familiar with the general principles of the classification of flowers which they set out to judge.

PART ONE

Flowers

CHAPTER ONE

Annuals

BY J. S. DAKERS, A.H.R.H.S.

IN ALMOST every show schedule for the summer exhibitions there will be a class or classes for 'Annuals'. The majority of schedules will ask for 'a vase' of annuals and will probably go on to state exactly what is required. Some schedules may ask for a 'bowl' of annuals. Here is the first point the exhibitor must note; if a vase is stated, then a vase it must be, and likewise, if you are asked for a bowl, it *must* be a bowl. This sounds very elementary, but as a judge, I have on several occasions had to disqualify good flower arrangements of quality simply because the exhibitor had not obeyed the schedule.

The next vital point is to remember that *annuals* are asked for and not those quick-blooming perennials which are grown within the year from seed. The genera exhibited must be from a plant which, having been sown and grown, blooms, sets its seed and dies approximately within a year.

Antirrhinums, for instance, are not annuals, though some schedules state they are 'allowed'. Annual forms (so-called) of carnations are not true annuals and may lead to the exhibit being disqualified. Dahlias, even if grown from seed the year in which they are shown, are not annuals and would certainly be ruled as 'not according to schedule'—but on the other hand, annual chrysanthemums *are* true annuals and, incidentally, ideal exhibition subjects.

There is, I know, a good deal of controversy on this point of what is or is not an annual, but unless the schedule definitely states that plants on the borderline of 'annual-perennial' may be used, then the judge has no option but to disqualify any exhibit which includes even one spike of any plant that is not, from a purely botanical standpoint, an annual.

A few schedules may divide annuals into their two common groups—hardy and half-hardy—and where this is so, one must be careful to obey the rules. To differentiate between the hardy and the half-hardy is not always easy to the amateur. Zinnias are half-hardy annuals, and yet the exhibitor may have sown them outdoors and they may have bloomed without anything in the way of protection or artificial heat in their seedling stages. That, however, does not make them a hardy annual.

The test is whether they will stand up to frost. The zinnia *will not*, in either its young or its mature stage. With regard to the latter, most gardeners will have seen the blackened and dying foliage following the first severe autumn frost. That proves then that it is not hardy. Most seedsmen's catalogues state quite clearly whether an annual is hardy or half-hardy—often by the simple abbreviation 'h' or 'h-h a'.

I would urge that any exhibitor who is not certain whether any particular subject is eligible or not, should ask the secretary of the society a week before the show. It is not fair to wait until the actual day of the show, when the secretary will be very busy.

Another point I would like to make is that where a staging steward or a committee-man sees some ineligible subject being placed in any class, he should, in as tactful and kindly a way as possible, point it out to the exhibitor.

It will be seen from the remarks on half-hardy annuals that a hardy annual is one which will stand frost and will (other circumstances being in its favour) be quite safe in the average British winter, outside. This does not mean that such annuals as are shown must have passed the winter outside. It does not matter when they are sown so long as they are classed as hardy.

For most exhibitors, however, these finer points will not arise, because in the majority of schedules the request is for 'Annuals,' which of course, allows the use of hardy, half-hardy and 'tender' (or greenhouse) annuals. The main thing to watch in such classes is the wording of 'kinds' and 'varieties'. This is one of the main traps for exhibitors, and as it is dealt with elsewhere in detail (see p. 14), I need not go too deeply into the subject here.

Supposing the schedule words a class as follows: 'Three vases of annuals, three kinds distinct', it would mean that the exhibitor could show, say, sweet peas, cornflowers and calendulas, and as there is nothing said about varieties, he can, if he wishes, show mixed colours in each vase, but if the schedule stated 'Three vases of annuals, three kinds in three distinct varieties', then he would have to show one variety of sweet pea, say, Mrs. R. Bolton, one variety of cornflower, say, Royal Blue, and one variety of calendula, say, Radio. Again, if you are not sure, ask the secretary.

Just one more word about schedules. Do not wait till near the show before studying them: rather do this as early in the year as you can get your copy and select the classes that *you know* you have the facilities and the ability to fill. Get the meaning of every class in which you propose to exhibit clearly in your mind and keep this as your aim from the beginning. Where one *has* to use the vases provided by the society, this rule must be rigidly obeyed—for it would not be right for one exhibitor to take an advantage over another by using taller or more ornate vases. The judge will be guided by the schedule, and no matter how superb the quality of the flowers shown, he must follow it and, if necessary, disqualify any exhibit which disregards instructions.

If the schedule allows the use of one's own vases, then the exhibitor is entitled to use those which will help him to make the very best of his subjects. My own prejudice is against any vase (or bowl) that is gaudy or blatant in colouring, and I prefer plain or cut-glass vases where any departure may be made from the usual six- or nine-inch earthenware vase so freely used by show authorities.

STAGING

It may be that some subjects will be difficult to show off to advantage if just placed in the vase without any material to support them. There is nothing against putting a quantity of rushes in the vases, as long as the tops of the rushes are below the top of the vase. This, of course, is universally done in the case of sweet peas, and there are many other annuals which benefit by this method, because it helps to give the impression of longer stems and greater height. I saw this simply illustrated a few years ago. Some clarkias were to be exhibited, but they looked squat and 'dumpy' because the stems (already short owing to a hot, dry season) *would* slip to the very bottom of the vase. The exhibitor had one too many vases ready for his sweet peas, and used this. The effect was improved beyond all imagining.

The use of wires, even if not actually forbidden, does not help exhibitors. Judges take note of the fact that this or that has had to be supported and points are lost.

In setting up even three vases of annuals, the very arrangement of the three will count. Naturally, the exhibitor should make every effort to impress the judge as he first views the class as a whole, and so, apart from anything else, the longer the stems of the subject, the greater the chance of getting a good effect. With your tallest bowl at the back, the two forward ones will be graded in height so that neither obstructs the view of the other.

At most shows the three vases are arranged in a straight line, but I think a triangular arrangement is infinitely better; it is more spectacular, and allows both judge and public to view the exhibits far more easily than when they are in a row. Again, of course, the vase at the apex of the triangle must be tall and bold.

It is sometimes the fault of societies that poor arrangement and poor spectacle result. Take, for instance, one case which came under my notice. The schedule asked for 'three vases of annuals, three kinds, three spikes of each'. Now I ask you—what sort of a show can three spikes of most annuals make in a vase? It might at least have asked for six of each or—better still—left the number of spikes to the exhibitor. After all, annuals are comparatively easy to produce, so why limit them in numbers? Let the exhibitor do the best he can, and in the extra mass the general effect of the show will be much improved.

However, where a certain number of spikes is asked for in the schedule, this must be the number shown, neither less nor more. This is an unalterable show rule!

CULTIVATION

It is not proposed to go into the details of cultivation here, except to suggest some helpful points in the production of quality material. This much I must emphasize—the annual, no less than other plants grown for exhibition, needs just that 'something extra' in the matter of food and treatment to give the refinement, size, texture and colour of flower required, coupled with length and strength in the stem, and richness and cleanliness of foliage.

The exhibitor of annuals must get rid of any idea he may hold that these flowers do not require generous treatment. That such an idea *is* held I am well aware and this may have misled would-be exhibitors at the very start. Frankly, if you are going in for exhibition annuals, treat the site much in the same way as you would for a good crop of onions, parsnips, cauliflowers or other vegetables. Deep digging, not only to ensure drainage, but also to allow and encourage the quick penetration of roots, is essential.

After all, one must remember that the annual has to give its best in a limited period, so, because of this, the grower must be as helpful as he can and, by any and every means, encourage the plants towards an early perfection.

There is also the question of food for the growing plant, and I am a firm believer in putting that food in the soil before the seeds are sown. This means early ground preparation when horse or farmyard manure will be used. It is bad gardening to dig in manure and sow seeds immediately after. If you want high-class exhibition flowers, then you must start with rich soil which has been correctly prepared. Doing this is half the battle.

Tilth is another important factor in the raising of show annuals —that fine and fertile inch or two of broken surface soil in which the seed can germinate and the seedling anchor itself. Remember, it is in the early stages of growth that the foundation of a healthy life is laid, so from the very beginning help the plant all you can.

Thinning. Thin sowing, followed by severe thinning so that each plant has rather more room than is normally given, and this followed by tying and staking, watering and giving liquid food, should ensure perfect flowers.

Reducing the amount of growth on a plant, disbudding in some cases and limiting the production of flowers or flower stems will all mean that those which are left can 'make up' (as the exhibitor calls it) into something that is just that much ahead of the best when given normal cultivation. There is also the time of sowing to be settled but that is one of the things which the grower will have to judge for himself. He must take into consideration the date of the show, the subjects to be grown, the part of Britain in which the exhibitor lives and the type of soil in which the annuals will be planted.

Of one thing you may be certain; the more naturally the subject develops the more likely it is to be of show standard. By that I mean that a plant which is hurried or retarded in an unnatural way will almost certainly give evidence of it and the flowers are not likely to be as good as those which develop normally.

Shading against hot sun may be necessary, or shelter against blustering winds, but this is a normal procedure and will help the production of good flowers.

Half-hardy annuals should be sown about the end of March or beginning of April under glass. The one thing to keep in mind is that they must not be about in boxes or small pots too long before they can be planted out, otherwise starvation will leave its mark on a checked and stunted plant, which will never recover.

All these points must be kept in mind by the exhibitor and if he starts by knowing what is required, it should be of great service all the time.

CHOICE OF SUBJECT

Next comes the most important question of all—'What shall I grow?' Well, that again will depend on the date of the show, though many subjects will be available over quite a long period.

There is one thing certain; the would-be exhibitor must keep in mind that whatever he shows in single vases must be as spectacular as possible; this will lead him to inquire just what subjects attract the judge's eye.

I am going to give a list of what I think are the twelve most suitable annuals for the showman. They all have reasonably long stems, stand well in water, remain in good condition for a day (at least), possess attractive colourings and are not by any means difficult to grow, nor do they make special demands as to soil, site or region. They can, moreover, be made particularly attractive when arranged.

Though I am giving sweet peas as one of my twelve, I shall not attempt to detail their culture here as this is described in Chapter Thirteen.

My choice is as follows:

Calendula	Stocks (annual)
Annual chrysanthemum	Clarkia
Cornflower	Salpiglossis
Sweet pea	Aster
Zinnia	Helichrysum
Nigella	Scabious (annual)

Some of these will not, of course, be available all the season through, but as at most shows the schedule asks for 'Three vases, distinct', this list should provide suitable subjects at any time from June to September.

I now propose to give two more lists, one for the June and July shows and the other for August and September. For the first of these I am choosing subjects which should be in bloom with ordinary weather conditions and having been sown at the normal time. One has to remember that many subjects mentioned may be retarded or hastened by various means, at the whim of the grower. The lists are therefore only intended as guides and are flexible.

For June and July:

Clarkia
Cornflower
Godetia
Stocks (annual)
Candytuft
Nigella
Annual chrysanthemum
Sweet pea
Gypsophila elegans
Larkspur (autumn sown)
Poppy
Phacelia
Phlox Drummondii
Ursinia
Echium
Dimorphotheca
Alonsoa
Calendula
Nemesia
Eschscholzia
Coreopsis
Love-lies-bleeding

For August and September:

Clarkia
Godetia
Stocks (annual)
Calendula
Aster
Cosmos
Statice
Schizanthus
Celosia
Mignonette
Marigold
Larkspur
Viscaria
Dimorphotheca
Scabious
Zinnia
Helichrysum
Leptosiphon maritima
Lavatera Loveliness
Linaria maroccana
Rudbeckia (annual varieties)
Nasturtium
Nemesia
Balsam
Nicotiana Sensation hybrids
Tagetes
Salpiglossis
Sweet Sultan
Ursinia
Venidium

Now all these make excellent exhibition material, whether in large mixed bowls (or vases) or as single vases. They will be ready at somewhat varying times, according to the part of Britain in which they are grown, so again I must emphasize that the various subjects are given only as a guide, and while in the south of England some subjects may have finished their blooming period, the same subjects will still be in bud in Scotland.

Many garden lovers who only grow a few annuals would like to see more classes for bowls of mixed annuals, with the emphasis on arrangement. It would be not only interesting but instructive to see how one's neighbour arranged her (or his) bowls and what was grown to achieve an effect. In such classes there might be a restriction on using any other flowers than those *from one's own garden*, but I would still suggest that the purely decorative classes be so worded as to allow purchased material.

Foliage. May I also add a word of warning here. If the schedule asks for 'A bowl of annuals', do not be tempted to use any but annual foliage. There is such a trap here, for one longs to use some greenery and often forgets that asparagus or fern foliage are not annuals and, while you may use *Gypsophila elegans*, you must on no account use *G. paniculata*.

Actually, you will find quite enough foliage among the annuals. The following will be useful as foliage plants, not only for exhibition but as garden plants as well:—kochia, perilla, humulus, amaranthus, *Artemisia sacrorum viridis* and some of the beautiful ornamental grasses such as *Agrostis nebulosa*, *Briza gracilis*, *B. maxima*, *Coix Lachrima-Jobi*, *Hordeum jubatum* and *Lagurus ovatus*. Add to these the variegated maize (*Zea japonica*) and, I think, the exhibitor will have all the foliage he or she requires.

Cutting. Always cut annuals the night before the show and put them into deep containers filled to the top with water, but do not allow the actual flowers to be in the water. In the morning they will be ready to be packed in boxes, if necessary, to transport them to the show, but if it is possible to travel with them still in the water, do so. Failing this, put the stems into water the moment you reach the show and then arrange them at your leisure.

Lesser-known Subjects. One point more. Do not think I have mentioned all the annuals one could use—not by any means. You should consider the whole range of beauty there is to choose from and then be an adventurer and grow some of the subjects one seldom sees. Having grown them, exhibit them, and if the judge is a good one you may gain extra points and prizes for using initiative and showing the public what they too could do with some of these lesser-known annuals.

What are they? Well, here are just a few for consideration:—*Cotula barbata*, *Collomia coccinea*, *Arnebia cornuta*, *Lupinus Hartwegii*, *Echium plantagineum*, *Anchusa capensis*, *Hebenstretia comosa*, small-flowered dwarf forms of the annual sunflower, *Senecio elegans* (Jacobea), *Trachymene caerulea*, *Zinnia linearis*, *Nolana lanceolata*, *Mentzelia Lindleyi* (*Bartonia aurea*) and *Malope trifida*. There are, of course, many others.

ANNUALS AS POT PLANTS

There is one aspect of growing annuals which cannot be left out of this chapter—namely, the use of these subjects grown for exhibition in pots. During the last fifty years the use of annuals for greenhouse decoration has developed to such an extent, that it is probably safe to say that in most gardens where there is a greenhouse, annuals of one kind or another are grown in this way.

There is much to commend this method of cultivation—even when the greenhouse is not artificially heated. Seed is not expensive, is easy to raise, and seedlings respond willingly to the cool condition all through their young stages and after. If, therefore, a wise choice of subjects is made and these are grown with due care, the result should be a diverse, colourful and interesting collection of useful plants in pots.

With this in mind, surely the time has come when one can expect to find a class in every show schedule for such subjects Such a class or classes would not only stimulate the cultivation of annuals grown in this manner, but would bring out the real skill of the grower. It should never be imagined that no skill is required for the production of such plants, for the truth is that it is—though I hold that such skill is well within the capacity of the keen and careful grower.

True, it will involve the testing of one's initiative in choosing not only the most suitable and attractive subjects, but the growing of them to be at the peak of perfection on a given day. To achieve this means that one is really master of the task, and if successful, it proves that the grower had done his utmost to overcome all difficulties. After all, is not that the basis upon which shows are judged?

Many societies already have classes for 'pot plants,' the number asked for varying from one to six but it is only seldom that one sees annual subjects included. This, in my opinion, should be remedied. It would, to some extent, overcome the all-too-frequent sight of exhibitors attempting to grow plants without being able to give them the conditions which they demand—warm house subjects being grown in cool houses, for instance. Far better, surely, to turn to those annuals which will make attractive plants and yet demand no more than a cool house, plus general care and attention, given by an understanding grower.

Here is a very short list of plants which might well be considered and, incidentally, offers a wide scope for extending not only the summer shows, but those held during spring when the main emphasis is on bulbs: Alonsoa, amaranthus, *Anchusa capensis*, browallia, calendula, *Celosia plumosa*, *C. cristata*, *Celsia Arcturus*, clarkia, godetia, kochia, mignonette, nasturtium, nemesia, nicotiana, *Phlox Drummondii*, schizanthus, scabious, statice, stocks, zinnia.

All these are subjects for the cool house and are but a few of the many possibilities.

To the compilers of schedules I would suggest more classes for annuals, with better prizes, and, to exhibitors, a far wider use of the best and most decorative subjects, grown to perfection. In this way this wonderful range of garden subjects would receive a boost such as they have never yet been given.

CHAPTER TWO

Border Carnations

BY J. B. WELLS

SUCCESS CANNOT be commanded, and it is at the start that we usually determine the measure of it. Young exhibitors are often disappointed that vases are passed over, but these people are apt to depend too much on the fertilizers which they apply when the buds begin to swell, instead of studying the nature of their soil so that the most suitable materials may be incorporated in the initial preparation of the beds.

This is a mistake, for border carnations are not gross feeders. No amount of after-feeding can give the plants the stamina that they require. This can only be steadily built up by the nutriment from well-balanced soil, thus preparing the plants for the time when they will be called upon to assimilate a special diet provided by the particular fertilizer which appeals to the exhibitor. To regard your plants as athletes in training is illustrative of their requirements: but we will return to this later.

EXHIBITION BLOOMS FROM OPEN BORDERS

Growth begins when the weather is favourable in the spring, and April is an important month. Round about the beginning of the month, on a humid day, give the plants a top-dressing of weathered soot, lightly forked into the beds, and then dust it thoroughly over and under the foliage. This is the best deterrent of carnation maggot, sawflies avoiding laying eggs on plants that have been treated in this manner. The valuable tonic properties of soot make it the best preventive of rust.

With genial weather, growth makes rapid progress. Unfortunately, pests are equally prompt, and greenfly are often annoying during east winds. Destroy these by syringing with a suitable insecticide. Do not crush the bodies of the greenfly on the bud unless you wear cotton gloves as the exuding fluid is very injurious, and discoloration or even scarring of the calyx is quite possible.

If a liquid insecticide is used, avoid those which contain soap, for they clog the pores through which the plants breathe and the grass begins to yellow. Syringing with a solution of ninety-eight per cent nicotine, three teaspoonfuls to a gallon of water, once a week and twice in hot weather, from May onwards, is suitable and is the best exterminator of greenfly, thrips and other destructive pests.

To obtain good-sized blooms for show, disbudding is most vital. All abortive small flower stems and useless buds which form at the base of the main shoots should be eliminated as early in the life of the plant as possible. While the crown bloom must always be retained, it is not advisable to disbud too drastically with varieties in which the flower is naturally large, as the extra strength thrown into the chosen buds may result in split calyces. Three buds usually should be left, the crown bud, the third and the fifth, alternate buds being removed, thus leaving an open space for each bloom. This choice is not compulsory and any number of good buds can be selected as desired. After pinching off unwanted buds, slip small flat rubber bands over the others to prevent bursting. This is sometimes found inadequate and any calyx that looks like splitting should be tied round with damp raffia when well colouring; this method takes longer but is one I have never known to fail.

It is permissible to use a cap to protect opening blooms as soon as they start to colour, and then all overhead watering must cease. Prior to this, the early morning or evening should be selected for spraying or syringing, which is very refreshing even to these heat-loving subjects. Never water the beds during the heat of the day, as the sudden shock would be injurious to the plants and so cause a serious setback. Keep the surface soil aerated and friable between the rows with a hoe or handfork, and when watering is required, do it thoroughly. A mulch of decayed cow manure, when obtainable, is beneficial when the soil is light and sandy, preventing too-rapid evaporation which is a source of anxiety during the hot weather.

Do not neglect correct tying as the stems lengthen. Do it so that there is perfect support and at the same time ample room for the stem to develop. It may be necessary, when the bloom is very large, to tie it up straighter than is usual or correct, and in such cases the protecting cap is a necessary device, for without it the flower is fully exposed to rain and heat, and for scalding there is no remedy.

A reminder that border carnations must never be 'stopped' is perhaps necessary. This operation is only practised with the perpetual-flowering types.

Feeding. As soon as the buds begin to swell, feeding, with either liquid organic manure or a suitable fertilizer, according to preference or circumstances, may commence. I prefer to use weak liquid manure but stable manure is not always available. Be consistent in application whichever is used, giving weak doses periodically and not dosing spasmodically in increasing strength as some do, thinking to assist development. Nothing could be more liable to defeat its own object, for the less robust could not assimilate such a diet and the flower stems would become dry and withered, while in those of vigorous constitution the sap will be circulating freely, and if pushed on too quickly the flower would be smaller than if left without added nutriment in the soil and would not only burst its calyx, but prove ill-shaped.

If a proprietary fertilizer is used, apply less than the quantity indicated rather than more, and if no rain has fallen, give a thorough watering before application so that the plants obtain full benefit. If the plant food remains dry it is of no benefit whatever, and there is the danger that another dose may be given before the first has been absorbed. However well prepared, these concentrated materials require more judicious care in application than the comparatively harmless weak liquid manures.

The practice of giving an extra 'pinch' of some chemical or a liquid stimulant, about a week or so before the day of the show in order to induce development and size, is neither advocated nor condemned. It is a matter which exhibitors must decide for themselves, according to their methods and requirements, for in a backward season with possibly limited stock, it may be sheer necessity with some varieties. Lime water is beneficial, and periodical syringing with salt water is tonic and cleansing.

Show Tips. 'Dressing' blooms for showing is prohibited, but it is quite in order to straighten petals by hand after unpacking and to place them carefully to fill any vacant places so that the flowers may show to the greatest natural advantage. Occasionally an otherwise faultless bloom will develop a thin misshapen abortive petal right in the centre. Nip this out, as it is quite superfluous.

Do not neglect any precautions against earwigs, which may burrow into the flowers as soon as they start to open.

Blooms can be retarded if cut, placed in water and kept in a cool, shady place such as an outhouse, but it is a moot point whether this procedure is any more effective than leaving them on the plant and shading. In hot weather, however, it would certainly be better to cut. Normally, cut your blooms in the early morning or evening the day before staging, put them in water, covering the entire stem, and keep in a dim, cool place for at least twelve hours. Any moisture on the petals can be safely and effectively absorbed with small pieces of clean blotting paper.

Staging. In staging the flowers, give yourself ample time; use vases of stipulated size and have stems and foliage according to schedule. Remove all rubber bands and ties, as failure to do so means disqualification. Place cards with the names of the varieties in front of each vase. Stems must not measure less than nine inches from the bottom of the calyx, but the flowers may be arranged in the vases at any desired height.

If the stems are stiff and wiry, it is easy to keep flowers in position, but some are inclined to hang their heads, or turn and show the calyx instead of the petals, both serious drawbacks. As no supports are allowed, small bundles of reeds or other packing—except dyed moss—in the bottoms of the vases will assist stability, the foliage also helping to this end. Judges do not look kindly on untidy, awkward exhibits.

Dyed moss is vetoed because the green dye used in the process of colouring would ruin the blooms.

Where possible, avoid mixing unsuitable contrasting colours in a vase of three selfs of more than one variety. There is no difficulty where only one variety is required, and nothing looks better. If three perfectly grown blooms of different varieties are staged, there is no doubt they are very attractive. Have due regard to placing flowers in the vases, however, and if two varieties are shown in a vase of three, place the odd one in the centre with slightly longer stem, and so give those either side a better chance of display.

The judges will expect upstanding, large symmetrical blooms with substantial, smooth-edged petals, large broad guard petals spread out firmly and horizontally above a perfect calyx. Any tendency to incurve or droop will be considered a defect. The inner petals should lie smoothly and regularly over the guard petals, diminishing in size as they approach the centre. The last two rows may be allowed more liberty of position and stand up slightly as a crown to the flower. A strong, rigid, self-supporting stem, easily capable of carrying its flowers, is absolutely essential.

Uniformity in size should always be considered, for an ill-balanced vase with perhaps one huge bloom and two much smaller is never attractive. Fresh, young blooms which may not quite have reached maturity are preferable to ageing flowers, which, although much larger, are noticeably past their prime and losing their pristine colours.

Good judges can detect failings at a glance, but in judging open border classes they do not expect the same standard of perfection as when judging exhibits from under glass, and they always take into consideration that the flowers have been exposed to wind and weather, except for the protecting cap on opening buds, which cannot guarantee immunity from small blemishes that may occur through causes other than climatic conditions.

EXHIBITION BLOOMS UNDER GLASS

Although grown under totally different conditions, the essential details and treatment required to obtain exhibition blooms under glass are the same as for open border flowers. There is no ban on shading or protection, and they may be handled as desired from start to finish. The highest standard of excellence is expected on the show bench, and flawless blooms are the rule and not the exception.

Disbudding is generally more drastic with indoor plants, and many exhibitors only leave the crown bud. It is advisable to syringe the plants weekly from May onwards against thrips, minute pests in the greenhouse which find their way into the buds when they are very small and cause those white specks on the petals, most disfiguring to the self-coloured varieties.

Scientific methods and new chemicals have in the past few years greatly extended the list of effective insecticides now procurable. Azobenzene and HETP are two of the most suitable for amateur use. The first named is supplied in small canisters of varying size. On ignition a dense volume of noxious, penetrating smoke is emitted. It is essential to follow the manufacturer's instructions accurately, especially as to size of canister, and it is not advisable to enter the greenhouse until the fumes have entirely evaporated.

HETP is for use as a liquid spray. It is highly poisonous and must be handled with the greatest care.

When applying plant food, give a small quantity of weathered soot to each pot weekly, and as in the border, keep the surface soil stirred with a plant label and so avoid caking and souring.

Watering requires the greatest attention and discretion, for some varieties are much thirstier than others, and pots should be examined twice a day. Do not water indiscriminately, for to give where it is not needed provides sodden root conditions, fatal both to plants and hopes of prize flowers. Keep an open tub of water to aerate outside in readiness for watering at any time, the temperature being raised to that of the atmosphere, thus saving all anxiety as to shock. When the plants are again placed under cover, follow the same plan in the greenhouse, where water in an open tank will help to cool the atmosphere if the house is small and apt to be over-warm.

PINKS OF ALL TYPES

A comprehensive pink show is one of the most fascinating displays, owing to the general fairy-like character of the flowers and to the varied colours and types available. Many classes are provided to embrace whatever an amateur is able to grow; the old garden varieties with serrated petals, those which normally split their calyx, or any group of this delightful branch of the dianthus family, which culminates in the happily restored laced pink, the only one with a standard of excellence in the strict sense of the word.

Here the judges will look for a well-built-up circular flower with thick, broad, smooth petals without serration, regularly disposed, and each row smaller than that immediately underneath it. The ground may be pure white or some other colour, and the lacing, whatever colour it may be, from rose to dark red, or lilac to dark purple approaching black, should reach from the inside of the petal far enough outwards to show in front beyond the petals above it and form a rich eye. A narrow, plain, even lacing or stripe of the colour should appear inside the white edge and be just the same width outside the lacing as the lacing itself, and as even. There should be no break or vacancy in the lacing, and the colour inside the petal, as well as the lacing, should be clearly defined, forming a circular coloured eye, or centre, to each row of petals.

In staging vases, the same regulations apply as for carnations. All ties and bands must be removed from blooms, and cards with their names should be placed in front of each vase. Though many of the older varieties are 'bursters', this does not mean that they should not be grown and exhibited as faultlessly as possible, for this is the main object in staging all flowers, and each type requires the same care in cultivation.

The following standards for cultivated pinks are for general

The plant on the right has been re-potted and top-dressed with a good compost in which to peg the layers.

Left: Each stem is severed half through and the cut opened out for layering. *Right:* A layer being pinned in position.

The plant on the left is receiving its first stop, and good breaks resulting from stopping are seen on the right-hand plant.

Left: Making the second stop; the stage of growth for this operation is seen. *Right:* A good plant at the first flower-bud stage.

Left: Secondary buds should be nipped out when quite small. *Right:* Placing a calyx ring over the bud to prevent calyx splitting.

Left: A protecting cone to shield exhibition blooms. *Right:* The judges will examine the back of a bloom so it must not be spoilt by red spider.

Left: An attractive laced pink, variety London Girl. *Right:* Good specimens of the show pink, variety Aristocrat.

Left: Border carnation Limpsfield White, of good form with smooth, rounded petals. *Right:* A white perpetual-flowering carnation, variety Northland.

guidance, but as they represent the ideal, which in many cases no variety fulfils, no amateur should be deterred from exhibiting because his blooms fall short of the requirements set out.

Great size is not desirable, except perhaps in singles, the object being to give an air of daintiness, and outdoor blooms are usually preferred to those which show signs of having been forced, even though the latter may be more nearly perfect in contour. In setting up, foliage can be optional unless specified in the schedule. Stems should be rigid but not clumsy or too big, holding the flower so that it tilts upwards, slenderness then being an advantage. No artificial supports may be used unless stated.

Disbudding is necessary to a certain extent, but preference is given to stems having a number of subsidiary, unopened buds. Perfume is a great asset, and scentless blooms only succeed in exceptional circumstances. A round dainty flower is the objective with the guard petals of a double or all the five petals of a single, lying flat and at right angles to the calyx, overlapping slightly to avoid space between them. In double flowers, the shape conforms more to that required of carnations.

Bicolors should have the boundary between the two colours clear and distinct, with no appearance of 'running'. A bicolor with a sharply defined, very dark eye on a white ground is known as a 'black and white' pink. Selfs must be of one colour, although a very slight shading in the extreme centre may be allowed.

A compost of well-decayed cow manure, wood ash and weathered soot given as a top-dressing in early March and lightly forked in will benefit outdoor plants. Feed with weak liquid manure and soot water, or a plant food as desirable, starting when buds are swelling, which varies according to type. Afford protection to the opening blooms as necessary, the foliage also requiring attention to keep it of a glaucous colour, and showing ample 'wax'. Laced pinks, no less than all other varieties, find well-decayed cow manure very much to their liking, given as a liquid stimulant or dressing, whether under glass or in a border, but wood ashes may be preferred or other material which pink growers have found a suitable food. Show varieties respond very readily to treatment and should not be subjected to undue forcing.

CHAPTER THREE

Perpetual Carnations

BY R. J. MORTON

PERPETUAL-FLOWERING CARNATIONS are ideal subjects for exhibition, owing to the continuous succession of blooms obtainable at all seasons of the year. They can be grown in a light, airy greenhouse with provision for very mild heat in late autumn, winter and early spring. In late spring, summer and early autumn the plants need no heat but all the ventilation possible. They require airy conditions in winter too, but of course, no draughts.

A common fault with many inexperienced growers of this plant is that they overcrowd the greenhouse in an endeavour to obtain as much bloom as possible. This may be reasonably satisfactory where just ordinary blooms are required, but is certainly not the order for the production of exhibition blooms. Most amateurs who grow for show purposes have a selected minimum of plants of varieties covered by the British National Carnation Society's classification chart. This chart covers all the colours which the flower will provide, and enables the exhibitor to know which colours are allowed in each class. It is reproduced in the British Carnation Society Schedules and is found at the end of this chapter (page 50).

CULTIVATION

The amateur grower who decides to specialize in the art of producing blooms for exhibition must of course realize that to achieve success he must obtain the finest stock plants available, or select his own stock by cuttings from the actual stems that have produced worth-while blooms. I emphasize that only by selection and reselection can one build up a fine stock of plants for exhibition work. No plant will pay for this thorough selection more than the perpetual-flowering carnation.

The selection and taking of cuttings may extend over many months, from October to February, when the plants can be watched for the best blooms. The cuttings should be taken from the stems on which these blooms were produced, the best shoot half-way up the flowering stem being chosen. This long propagation period is useful as it permits painstaking selection with no necessity to hurry and it usually results in the building up of a fine stock.

At our shows it is not always blooms that are exhibited but often plants. It may seem easy to produce a plant for the show bench, but if a thorough inspection is made and all points are taken into consideration, few worthy of placing before the judges will be found in a general collection.

I assume that the grower who intends to take up the growing of carnations seriously will without doubt have gained his experience a few years before, so I will not deal actually with all points of cultivation or conditions they require, but endeavour to pass on the benefit of my experience and describe what I consider the finer details of cultivation which help so much towards success on the show bench.

Feeding the nine- or ten-month-old plants in those difficult days of dampness from mid-October to December is always a problem. I consider this to be the worst time of the year, as usually the last of the shows takes place early in November, and many disappointments are caused by blooms damping before then. Top feeding will not make a good plant out of a bad one, and it should be well known that the carnation is not a gross feeder, especially in its young life. However, most pot plants require a stimulant when they are about nine months old, that is, assuming that they have been potted with a suitable compost, such as the John Innes 3 which is as good as anything, provided that the loam is fibrous and not too heavy.

The analysis of the stimulant I use is nitrogen 6·5 per cent, total phosphates 10 per cent, potash 7·2 per cent. This stimulant is not used continually but for top feeding alternately with an organic feed. It is high in phosphates and gives good results.

I use an organic feed with an analysis of nitrogen 5·5 per cent, phosphate 9 per cent, potash 6 per cent, and after each two of the latter feed I use the stimulant the next time. It is important not to over-feed and if possible never feed on a dull muggy day; choose the crisp air, as any feed will tend to soften the stems temporarily. It is well to bear in mind that the judges are always critical of the stem of a bloom, with of course due consideration given to the habit of the variety.

To test the dryness of the soil, tap the pot with a small wooden mallet, and if a high-pitched ring is heard, water will probably be needed, but if one hears a dull thud, sufficient moisture should still be retained in the compost for another day or so. Remember that cracked pots will give no indication by this method, and if these must be used the only way to test them is to take a pinch off the top of the soil and thus ascertain its condition. Never top feed a dry pot, always water the plants one day and feed the next.

EXHIBITING

The difference between prize-winning blooms and others is not always so obvious to the inexperienced exhibitor; many think that the large blooms always walk away with the prizes, but this is not so. Many of our well-known carnations are of the small, firm commercial type, and often at our shows one observes quite a high percentage of these. The other types are the large-flowered or royal. The latter are not always suitable for exhibition, but as a rule any variety, whether commercial or royal, if it has most of the following good points about it, will certainly be fit for the show bench, irrespective of its size.

The necessary points are: good formation of flower with high, proud centre, strong guard petals, strong hard calyx, good strong stem holding bloom erect, good colour for the particular variety, clean foliage and a good long stem (some varieties have stems quite two feet long). Perfume is appreciated by some judges and also method of staging or presentation may gain extra points in a close contest.

The faults that the judges may look for are: weak neck or stem, uneven guard petals, split calyx (although calyx bands are permissible at most shows), hollow or loose centre, thrips-marked blooms, blooms of faded colour, stem cut too short, and blooms that are past their best.

A few hints on exhibiting plants for show may be worth while. Good points are maximum number of breaks, blooms and buds for size of pot. If good cultivation has been given, it may be possible to produce a plant having as many as fifteen flowers and buds, but variety often scores here. The foliage must be clean, with freedom from red spider and aphis. The pot must be clean outside and the soil clean on the top. A card with name of variety and age of plant should catch the judge's eye, as, most other points being equal, it is feasible that they will not pass lightly over a reasonably young plant well grown, if it is against one that may be in a larger pot and perhaps twelve months older.

Season plays a very important part in timing the cutting of blooms for exhibition. For November and early spring shows, it may be possible to leave the bloom on the plant until the day before the staging, but in midsummer, July and August, one has to be careful as, if cut too early and not stored in a suitable place, the blooms may curl and lose their colour. If kept on the plants in the hot greenhouse with very arid conditions, they will curl and fade anyhow, so one has to use a little judgment. If you must cut, put them in water and keep in a cellar for preference. Another tip is to choose the varieties that do reasonably well in hot weather such as those with fimbriated edges; these seldom curl, a common fault with the plain-edged varieties.

For transporting to the show, I do not think that one can do better than pack the blooms in a wooden box, such as is used for sending carnations to market. The size of this box is 3 feet long, 9 inches wide and 3½ inches deep, and commercially holds thirty-six blooms. For show purposes I advise packing only about half or even less than this quantity, as the petals must not touch or rub each other. Supports for the blooms can be made by rolling sheets of newspaper into rolls about half an inch in diameter and a little longer than the width of the inside of the box. One of these is put in, and being long, can be forced into position so that it is more or less firm; only push it about two-thirds down the box and this will leave it about an inch from the bottom. The bloom can now rest on this nicely. Put about three blooms in a row. Then, farther down the box, place another paper roll, and another row of flowers; repeat until about five rows have been packed. Force another roll down on to the bottom of the box to hold the stems tight. Do all this first thing in the morning if possible, and keep the box of blooms in as cool a position as possible when travelling.

Staging. Staging the blooms is important, as bad presentation can bring loss of points. Often when blooms are exhibited it is a condition that no foliage other than carnation foliage may be used. See that this is of good colour with no trace of red spider or aphis on it. Use stiff foliage and only just sufficient to keep the blooms rigid. Give yourself plenty of time to stage your exhibits, and present your blooms well, then you may rest content that the judges will give your exhibit the attention it deserves.

Varieties. It is not possible to give all varieties that may be suitable for the show bench, but here are a few good show types that win the prizes: *White*, Geo. Allwood, Northland, Puritan, White Maytime. *Pink*, Maytime, Minuet, Allwood's Market Pink, Ashington Pink, Royal Salmon, Princess Irene, Peter Fisher. *Scarlet*, William Sim, No. 16 Red, King Cardinal, Robert Allwood, Spectrum Supreme. *Crimson*, Royal Crimson, Wivelsfield Crimson, Topsy. *Fancies*, Chief Kokomo, Ashington Apricot, Doris Allwood, Pharaoh, Marchioness of Headfort, Orchid Beauty. *Yellow*, Miller's Yellow, Lady Hudson, Allwood's Cream.

PERPETUAL-FLOWERING CARNATIONS CLASSIFICATION BY COLOUR

This list is simply a guide for exhibitors, intended to assist them in placing their exhibits in the proper classes. Only a few names of standard varieties are given as examples. No examples are given for white, crimson and yellow, as it is not considered necessary to do so.

It will be understood that under the influence of season, locality and culture, some varieties of carnation change their colour to a more or less pronounced degree.

A. All-white varieties.

B. Pale pink varieties, such as Maytime, Minuet, Allwood's Market Pink, Princess Irene, Elizabeth, Peter Fisher.

C. Pink varieties, cerise and deep rose shades, such as Royal Cerise, Ditchling, Tauntonian, Pink Doris, Betty Lou, Royal Rose, Dark Peter Fisher, Market Rose.

D. Light salmon-pink varieties, such as Ashington Pink, Market Salmon.

E. Deep salmon-pink varieties such as Royal Salmon, Marian Allwood, Charming.

F. Red and scarlet varieties such as King Cardinal, Robert Allwood, Spectrum, William Sim, Red Pimpernel.

G. All crimson varieties.

H. All yellow self varieties.

J. Self-apricot and varieties with orange grounds, such as Tangerine, Chief Kokomo, Royal Maize, Royal Fancy, Lady Hudson.

K. Yellow and buff grounds, such as Bonanza, Golden Wonder.

L. Purple varieties, such as Allwood's Burgundy, Ashington Purple, Wivelsfield Claret.

M. Mauve and lavender varieties such as Cattleya Mauve, Kathleen Stevens, Royal Lavender, Allwood's Heliotrope, Susie, Market Lilac.

N. White-ground fancies, such as Dairymaid, Mary E. Sim, Emily Allwood.

O. Pink-ground fancies such as Variegated Laddie, Royal Tapestry.

P. Varieties, fancy or self, not sufficiently represented to justify a special class, such as Marchioness of Headfort, Doris Allwood, Allwood's Cream, Orchid Beauty, Mrs. Maurice Grant, and all the pelargonium types.

CHAPTER FOUR

Chrysanthemums

BY J. H. GODDARD

GROWING CHRYSANTHEMUMS for market, growing them for cutting for the home, and growing for exhibition are entirely separate propositions. These chapters are designed for the man who is prepared to devote his time to the thousand-and-one jobs demanded when growing for the shows.

And these tasks must be performed, and very conscientiously at that, in spite of the fact that most beginners think there is some hidden secret behind the success that attends many big winners at the shows. No, I am convinced, after over fifty years of exhibiting, that practically every little tip known to a successful grower is available to the general public. It is one thing to know the methods by which success can be achieved, however, and another to practise them, but rest assured, if prizes are to come your way, there must be no half-hearted measures, no procrastination, and no complaints about long days.

The experienced man will recall in the winter the shortage of time in the previous spring, and he will devote many evenings in preparation for the next rush. He will cut and sharpen the ends of his stakes, write his labels, prepare his soil, obtain his fertilizers and pest cures, rearrange his standing ground, paint his lights and perhaps his greenhouse, in fact anything to give him more time for the vital tasks which later loom up before him.

No grower for exhibition should ever get behind with the work or he may find his plants eaten up with fly, or plants wearying with the old root ball asking to be potted. Growths may hang, begging for a stake, to say nothing of those desiring a drink. Watering every plant whether it needs it or not is a great time-saver too, but these methods lead nowhere when one has to face the scrupulously careful grower who stops at nothing to gain first-class honours.

CULTIVATION

A Clean Start. A clean start can be made by going carefully over the stools and burning every single plant known to have had trouble. If any have had a bad attack of eelworm they are as well burnt if clean stock can be substituted. There is a remedy for this of course, but the cure often delays the production of good cuttings, which in turn could make impossible an early stopping to obtain blooms in due time. Very often a variety will tire of the same old treatment year after year and it will be desirable to obtain a new stock. It will display its tiredness by refusing to send up strong healthy cuttings and many of the cuttings will run to a bud.

This must not be taken to mean that every variety whose cuttings end in buds is tired or worn out, as some are very susceptible to this trouble, but when lack of health also creeps in, a change of stock is most desirable. If the cuttings can be had from someone who rests his stock, so much the better; there is more in this changing of stock than many people suppose.

Stools must be kept very cool, 45° F. being ample. They must also be kept clean, by fumigating with either Auto Shreds or tobacco sheets, or by using a nicotine or derris spray. Any coarse ugly growth should be cut right away, as this is scarcely ever any good as cuttings. A little pricking of the soil and an addition of a little light flaky compost will help the production of a good crop of young growth—the type we need for new stock.

Many growers shake out the soil from the stools and replant in light soil. More cuttings are likely to develop in these conditions and to carry on for a longer period, but as it involves some delay in cutting-production, it cannot always be recommended in the case of varieties which need early rooting to allow an early pinch; it is murder to pinch a poorly rooted cutting.

In recent years much of the pleasure of rearing of stock has been disappearing through the advent of the eelworm, and the only time to attack this insidious foe is while the stools are in a comparatively dormant state. There is so much buying-in and bartering of stock that when it gains a foothold the trouble is multiplied to an alarming degree. Up to the time of writing the only cure would seem to be the sterilizing method. One by one the trade has had to adopt this system, tiresome though it is. A rather expensive tank has to be installed, in which, by thermostatic control, the stools are subjected to twenty minutes in warm water up to 110° F. Next, all stools are plunged into cold water for ten minutes before draining and planting.

An amateur grower, or a grower with limited stock, can perform this task with the aid of two baths. One contains water at 110° F. to warm up the stools, and after two or three minutes, when the temperature is falling, all are brought out and are transferred to bath No. 2. As the temperature again declines and bath No. 1 is brought back to 110° F., they can come back to it. As long as the full twenty minutes heating is given—or even thirty minutes will not harm the stools—the eelworms should be dead. It is never necessary to treat one's whole stock as some varieties are practically immune, but it should be done whenever the presence of eelworm is recognized or suspected.

Some of the signs of infection are when the foliage becomes blotched with a greenish-yellow tint, later turning to a browny grey and finally black, when the whole leaf collapses and dies. As the eelworms, which incidentally cannot be seen with the naked eye, work their way up the plant, the leaves become so affected that only bare stems remain. Red blotches and red rings round the stems are sure signs of trouble, and if these are scratched and damped, the tiny insect can be seen through a microscope.

Rooting Cuttings. Much has been written about the best composition of soil for rooting cuttings. Personally, I have never had any trouble in this connexion. They seem to root in any light gritty compost whatever the proportions. One I use is one third each of loam, leaf-mould or peat, and sand. The sand may even be the washed variety, which is ridiculously cheap in some districts, or it may be silver. To this add a dusting of bonfire ash if handy, or a light dusting of superphosphate.

Soil should never be sticky, but if anything rather on the dry side. When watered, such a soil swells up to the cutting; if too damp it recedes, leaving a gap which will cause many losses. Nurserymen usually use boxes or beds for cuttings, but the exhibitor must remember that from start to finish there can be no allowance for checks.

So the man with an eye on a cup decides to take no chances and uses a 2-inch pot and places one cutting in each, and as rooting takes place, they go undisturbed into the 3½-inch pots. This is good practice. For anything short of exhibition stuff, four or even six may be inserted round a 3½-inch pot, and there need be very little disturbance if the rooted cuttings are divided with care. But remember, we are growing for shows.

A slight covering of sand should be placed on the soil surface, and when the hole is made to take the cutting—usually with a lead pencil—the sand will roll down into the hole and make a slight mound on which the cutting will rest.

The type of cutting we desire is one of clean growth, medium in thickness and about 2 to 2½ inches in length. Only about three leaves should be left on, as more are an additional strain. If there is any fear of fly or any other pest, it is advisable, before insertion, to dip the cuttings into a pail of insecticide and then rinse in clear water. A very sharp knife or even a razor blade should be used for the cut, for there must be no bruising.

When one is compelled to use very tiny cuttings, which might easily be washed out when watering, overhead spraying should be avoided by placing the pot in a bowl of water two or three inches deep; the water will seep up the soil, and, when settled, the cutting will stay put.

There is no need to write a page on whether a propagator should or should not be used for cuttings of show plants—the extra protection should be given every time. The rooting time is shortened, the moisture is appreciated, and the vitality kept unchecked. Watering is unnecessary up to almost the time when rooting has taken place, but I like to leave on that little chink of air at an end or corner to keep down excessive moisture, and I give an hour a day with the glass off.

What little flagging there is under this method will do no harm, but if it should persist, just run some water on the peat at the bottom of the frame and put the glass on quite close for a day.

As the plants root they will take on a new look and get quite perky, and it is then that a little more air can be given. This may be increased every few days until finally it will be advisable to take the glass right off.

There will be no need to hurry the cuttings into a 3½-inch pot, as each is self-contained, and also there should be no question of starvation, but there is a limit. The pots must be spaced out to encourage sturdiness, and if it can be done, a spread of ashes or peat under them will be very helpful. As near to the glass as possible should be the watchword, and the amount of air given must be increased gradually.

From now onward a weekly spray of insecticide should be given. Remember, on show work there is no allowance for fly or leaf miner, and it can come as a thief in the night. Should there be the slightest sign, dip the whole of the plant in a pail, but if the spraying is faithfully carried out, there will assuredly be no pests.

Potting On. When the roots have filled the 2-inch pots, a shift will be necessary and dates cannot be stipulated; neither should a plant be made to wait until the whole batch is ready. Very little in the way of food is desirable at this time as the object will be to consolidate the plant with a firm but not too thick stem.

The soil for potting on should consist of 3 parts loam, 1 part leaf-mould or peat, ½ part sand or mortar, and a dusting of bonemeal, wood ash and superphosphate. This will be put through a ½-inch sieve and the size of pot will be 3½- or 4-inch. Always see that the compost is thoroughly mixed. A good plan is to run it through a sieve; I find this method is quick and effective.

After potting, see that the batch is well spaced out and that each plant has a stake. A lot of air should be given on sunny days and only sufficient heat at night to keep the plants steadily growing.

Second Potting. A normal batch of exhibition plants should be ready for another shift during March. This time 5½-inch pots will be needed. A stronger soil will be desirable now and could consist of 4 parts loam chopped to the size of a walnut, or pulled to pieces is better if there is time, 1 part leaf-mould or peat, 1 part rotted manure, ½ part sand or rubble, ½ part wood ash. Add to this a 6-inch potful of soot, a 6-inch pot of bonemeal and a 3½-inch pot of lime to the barrowload. Brick dust of the medium type used on hard tennis courts has been in favour instead of sand in many nurseries.

For a week before this shift it is best to keep the greenhouse temperature down to the minimum needed for safety, as the plants will then be due for the frames.

Transferring to Frames. It is amazing what rubbish a set of frames can collect when not in use, and it will be necessary to spring-clean inside and out thoroughly. Fork up the ashes lightly and give a strong dose of insecticide. If the frames are deep it may be advisable to raise the back row or two of the pots by placing them on boards resting on a few pots. The nearer to the glass the better the plants will like it, but the tips must be well clear of the lights. They might be placed pot thick for a week or two, if space is scarce, but they will soon need more room. If a plant has little room for development it will draw up, and that is not desirable.

Very little water will be needed until the sun gives more heat, and individual watering with a rosed can must be practised, for a plant goes sick more quickly through overwatering than through any other cause.

Sacks or mats must be available for covering the frames at night, for it is a far easier task to cover and uncover these than it is to thaw out a batch of plants, to say nothing about the damage done. See that every plant has a stake of some size.

During this critical frame period, ventilation will be of vital concern, and it must be remembered that while due attention is being given to the comfort of the plants, there must be a hardening-off process for a few weeks in order that they will not suffer during May when full air has to be given. On a bleak cold day only just a chink of air can be left on, but on a warm spring day quite a lot may be given, but it will always be necessary to shelter against the wind. As the pots get filled with roots, a couple of doses of liquid feed will help to bring the plants into a suitable condition for the final potting, but it must be on the weak side, say weak soot water.

Final Potting. Early June is the recognized time for the final potting, but under no circumstances must this take place if the pots are not well filled with roots. If one gets fidgety it would be better far to take a week's holiday by the sea and forget the plants. I know well that it is difficult to keep plants upright when spaced out, and that final potting cures the trouble. A good plan, however, is to place the 9- or 10-inch pots in squares or rows four abreast and place a plant in each; they at least cannot be blown over and do damage, but they must carry a good stake.

Most exhibitors are aware of the fact that potting composts are better if prepared a few weeks before they are used. I emphasize this. A mixture I have used for fifty years satisfies me still, and I certainly see no reason why I should change it. This is it: 4 parts good fibrous loam pulled to pieces about the size of a cricket ball, 1 part partly rotted horse manure, 1 part leaf-mould (oak or beech), ½ part mortar rubble or sand, and ½ part wood or bonfire ash. Add to each hundredweight or barrowload a 6-inch potful each of bonemeal, soot and fertilizer, and a 3½-inch pot of lime. The fertilizers I like best are Bentley's No. 1, Thompson's, Clay's and Eclipse, but Eclipse is of no value in water.

The size of pot is a much debated point, but root action should really be the guiding point. When turning out the old stools, notes should be made of the rooting capacity, and action should be taken accordingly. Sizes 8½- to 10-inch are usual; many large exhibition varieties prefer a 10-inch, and also many of the more robust incurves and decoratives. Singles are nearly all best in 9-inch, and quite a lot of decoratives are well satisfied with 8½ or 9. In any case, an observant gardener can generally see that a vigorous plant in a rather small pot will need a feed earlier than one which is plodding along in a 10-inch, and it is a case of intelligent discretion.

All pots must be well crocked as drainage plays a big part in a plant's welfare, and it is just as important to have a good coating of rough fibrous material over the crocks. This must be made firm, and might consist of the lumpy parts of the compost or a little strawy horse manure, a mixture of 3 parts to 1 part of hop manure; a sprinkle of bonemeal can be mixed with all.

Whatever the variety, or whatever compost is used, the soil should be made very firm and a rammer should be used. The soil round any variety scarce of petal can be made quite hard, while varieties which carry hard buds too full of petal can have less ramming. It is generally recognized that harder ramming produces more petal. This question is, of course, closely related to that of timing the bud, which is often a determining factor when dealing with difficult varieties.

About two inches should be left at the top of the pot for water and future top-dressing and a good flat surface of fine soil will complete the operation. If the stock was watered well before potting and the soil was not in too dry a condition, water will not be needed for five to seven days, according, of course, to the prevailing weather. After the first watering the plants will almost have to ask for the second drink, as the roots enter the new soil much more quickly if the conditions are not too wet.

Canes may be inserted at once, and for the time being a raffia tie can encompass the whole plant. While the plants settle down they can be arranged in squares, being some protection for each other. A few sprays over with water will assist the stock while the plants are settling down.

An adequately large standing ground is a vital asset to an exhibitor, though I have often been amazed at blooms grown on only a tiny piece. Most men know from experience what open space means to a plant, and the urge to take no risks with those growing for exhibition is ever present. Personally, I would rather grow fewer plants than subject a stock to unnatural crowding, and the prize list would not suffer.

There is no need for the cumbersome posts we used years ago, and a few old iron boiler pipes will be plenty strong enough. The wires we used too now give place to a few lengths of partly worn rubber-coated cable. And how much more comfortable this is to manipulate! The tall varieties needing a 5-foot cane will need two strands of cable, but for the smaller varieties, one strand should suffice. Slates, tiles or board should be used on which to stand the plants, as ashes alone will never keep the worms out; the ashes are useful, however, when spraying after a hot summer day.

Watering. It has been said that when a gardener has mastered the art of watering, he has gone a long way towards success. This is true. We see so much of what I term sloppy watering that it is inevitable that there is a big percentage of 'also rans'. In many gardens every plant is watered—or none. This is not, and must never be, an exhibitor's method. In an open garden where water can get away it does not matter so much, but on pot plants—no! There is no need to labour this point, except that we must remember that a reckoning time comes. If a plant needs water it wants a good drink, and if it is very dry and the water runs straight through, it needs another, and perhaps another. And if one poor specimen is hanging limp, don't go in for tea and leave it in its desolation.

And when you go to the bathroom for a swill and a refresher after a day's work, always ask yourself if the plants would appreciate a spray too.

Feeding. Feeding is a process which the beginner conjures with more than the old hand. He stakes his life and stock on the feed, but an experienced gardener, who knows how little food is necessary, is very little concerned.

If the potting soil was in good heart, nothing is necessary for some five or six weeks, and then the first two or three feeds must be very weak.

Personally, I like to kick off with two feeds of Clay's, used rather weak. Next, I come on to Bentley's No. 2, or perhaps Thomson's, whichever is handy. If the weather is wet, I would use just sulphate of potash at an ounce to the gallon, but I would never think that even these excellent foods would in themselves bring the cups home. My belief is more to attend, very religiously, to the daily tasks of watering, weeding, spraying, staking, etc., all at the right time; then it does not matter much what is used. It is over thirty years, however, since I used animal manure.

Fertilizers can be used in different ways, but where time is precious it is most convenient to make up a solution in a tank at an ounce to the gallon. Many prefer to mix with some fine soil and then top-dress with this. Another way is to water the plants, then give a sprinkle over the soil, washing it in an hour or so afterwards.

The practice of giving a top-dressing of about half an inch of soil once during August and once in September is most necessary. Fertilizers and bonemeal can be mixed with this, and no other feed must be given during the week that it is applied.

A couple of doses of sulphate of iron will provide a good stimulant during the season, and it can be used at the rate of one ounce to three gallons. This can be supplementary. The final dose before housing can be sulphate of potash at an ounce to the gallon, to give hard and firm petal. Then all feeding should cease. When housing, water with a solution of lime—a few pounds in a tank of water—to sweeten the soil.

Bud Taking. From early August all buds must be retained as they come. There is no immediate hurry to get away the side shoots, in fact there is great danger of damage if one gets among this tender growth too early. It is better to let the growth go to about an inch long and then take off the laterals gradually. In cases where buds are too early, one or two growths can remain until a few inches long and no harm will result. There is a limit of course.

At this stage the whole collection should be overhauled. The large exhibition plants should be reduced to two shoots, each containing one good bud. The incurves, singles and decoratives, should carry four shoots, each with a good bud, and everything else should be taken away. This is for exhibition blooms, but for smaller work one will have to use discretion.

A very sharp knife must be used so as to ensure a clean cut. No bud should be allowed to chafe continuously on a stake, and in some cases lengthening stakes must be used.

Housing. One of the most pleasant operations, though one of the hardest perhaps, is the housing. In the first place the house should be fumigated with sulphur candles, after which all woodwork and crevices should be scrubbed clean and the whole place made sweet.

Then there is the spraying of the plants. I have always found it best to lay each plant over a bath, with a box and a couple of bricks at the end on which to place the pot. Liver of sulphur at a quarter of an ounce to the gallon is placed in the bath and with the aid of a good syringe the solution is shot through the plant back into the bath. To avoid the dreaded mildew, the undersides of the leaves must be well soaked. At half-way the plant can be rolled over to ensure a perfect drenching.

No one can give tips on arranging the plants without seeing the

Left: The tip of a young plant showing the first break after stopping. *Right:* A disbudded head where the small side buds have been nicked out.

A substantial protecting screen for early blooms can be knocked up from rough material. Stout paper has been used for the roof.

Left: Protecting exhibition blooms with paper bags. *Right:* Packing blooms for taking to the show.

A stout packing case in which large blooms are carried to the show. Blooms are tied individually to a wooden framework which slides into grooves in the box sides.

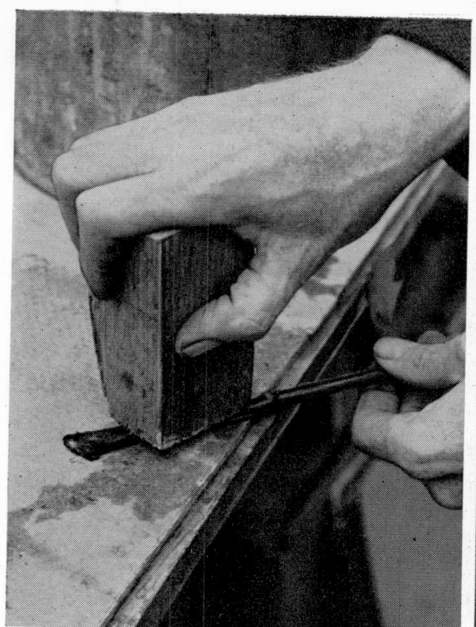

Left: Bruising the end of a chrysanthemum stem to assist it to draw up water. *Right:* Fixing a wire support for the stem and head of a heavy bloom.

Left: Tying a stem and foliage to a large exhibition bloom. *Right:* Arranging a vase of three first-class specimens.

The first-prize winner in a class for six vases of early flowering chrysanthemums.

A winning exhibit of eighteen varieties of large exhibition blooms.

house, but they are best arranged so that every bud can be seen at a glance. In no case, however, should the plants be packed tightly, as then no plant can do itself justice and many otherwise good buds are spoiled; every plant must have breathing space.

If inside shading is practised, now is the time to apply it before the plants are housed; much depends on the condition of the buds. A good idea is to shade one side and place those early buds beneath it, and the later ones to receive all the help possible from the unshaded space. Butter muslin tacked to the rafters is as good as anything and catches the drip, if it should possibly be present; most exhibitors do any necessary repairs before housing.

Earwig traps—hollow bamboo lengths—should be placed among the foliage from the very start and be blown into hot water every day; in a week this will usually reduce the infestation, though the traps are best left in use.

Full air must be given for the first two weeks, and as the weather deteriorates, the ventilators will be gradually closed. Top ventilation should never be quite closed, even when damp or cold weather forces one to fire, except of course, when the fumigating is done, and as much air should always be given as circumstances permit so that the glass is never steamy.

Neglect of fumigation is just about the most serious blunder one can make, and no grower should wait for the greenfly to make a start first. Strike the first blow and use the lamp or the shreds as soon as the plants are housed, and every seven days afterwards. Choose a mild night if possible, and try to manage without a fire because of having to close the house.

Very little water will be needed now that the plants are inside, as there is a vast difference between the stagnant air and that of the outside. Water only the plants that need it, but never let them get bone dry. The morning is the best time to water, never at night.

STOPPING

There are two distinct reasons for the stopping of chrysanthemums. One is to cause a multiplication of growths for the increase of the number of blooms which the plant must carry, and the other to ensure that the buds should produce blooms to fit the date of the show. It is the nurseryman, of course, who is interested in stopping more for quantity, the show man only if for a special purpose he needs smaller blooms.

Some varieties will make a natural break every four or five weeks, while others will only break once in that number of months. In the first case it is comparatively easy to ensure that there will be a bud at the best time to conform to the needs of either the trade or an exhibitor. But the others must be systematically timed to obtain buds and blooms at a specific date or the plant will be wasted.

Taking the large exhibition section, one first calls to mind such varieties as Jas. Bryant and Duchess of Kent, and it is absolutely essential that these be pinched by March 1 in order to produce a bud early in August, that is, a period of five months. If the plant is not rooted in time for a pinch, say, April 15, the bud will be six weeks too late and the bloom correspondingly so, and naturally will be too late to develop its bud to a sufficiently great extent for show purposes. Beside being too late, it will be much too small. So what it boils down to is, that missing this pinch is like missing the last train home.

The same thing happens with some easy kinds such as the Majestics. These may make a natural break in early June and give us a bud in September. In normal seasons a pinch about May 1 will cause growths that will produce a bud about early August, that is, three months from the pinch. Such varieties as H. E. Trueman, Duke of Kent, Edith Cavell, Conference, Mrs. B. Carpenter, can be bloomed on any crown, first or second, because if they miss the first by being too early, they will invariably hasten to catch up by making quick growth towards the second crown. The buds develop very fast when once secured, and though the blooms are inclined to be smaller, they are generally full of refinement which counts very considerably with good judges.

Of course, these are more reliable if produced by design rather than by accident. If a plant of Trueman makes its own natural break early in May, it can be delayed a week or two by cutting back a few inches in order to compel it to make its break off harder wood, which naturally takes longer. On the other hand, it may be better to reduce the number of growths at once for it to race onward towards the next crown, and if the plant is still in the 6-inch pot, it can be assisted by a couple of feeds, say, of sulphate of ammonia, weak, or sulphate of iron, or even nitrate of soda, at intervals of a week.

Fortunately, most specialists give a key for stopping and timing, and this is quite a good guide. But there are times when exhibitors get puzzled. Quite a lot are given as natural first-crown varieties, but this natural break does not always come when it should.

When cuttings are inserted at the end of November or early

December, there should be no difficulty in getting a plant into a pinchable condition in time for pinching or to enable it to make a natural break round about the third week in May. This would be a good normal procedure, but a lot depends on the time of taking the cuttings.

A January-struck cutting will naturally be later in making a natural first crown in time, and may have to be pinched.

With these borderline cases it is distinctly better either to root early for a second crown, or to root late for a first. If the plant refuses to give a natural break by the end of May, it can then be pinched. The pinch will then be only just removing the tiny point, as this is the quickest method of obtaining laterals. By examination it may be seen by the thickening of the apex of the growth that a break bud is nearly there; this will be preferable to a pinch or a cut back.

In any case, I might repeat that it is never advisable to get at these tiny growths or the bud too soon. If the bud has to come out, well, a few days presence will make no difference anyway, as it will come to nothing in consequence of the growths monopolizing the sap.

Many growers whose desire is for two blooms to the plant will allow three to grow for quite a while, some right up to the time of bud production, then, when two good buds are assured, the top two-thirds of the growth not needed is cut away. I practise this often, but confine it to where foliage is thin or scarce as I believe foliage is a great help to the plant.

The timing of the incurves is done in much the same way, but two, three, four or five growths can be run up from the first break, afterwards allowing four to emerge from the first crown. Where the growths come evenly, the four or five can be kept, but in case of bad placing, it would be better to run two up then break into four.

Some few, such as the Curry family, will give six blooms quite easily; in fact the best blooms I ever had were at seven to the plant. They unfold more easily that way.

Very little ever goes wrong with the timing of singles; they seem to know their job, and whether one relies on natural first crown or stops twice, they try to oblige.

Decoratives are sometimes awkward, but we exhibitors have brought that on ourselves. Many fine varieties intended for December blooming have been brought forward by two stoppings—April and June 1—in order that they may be seen at the November shows.

I plead guilty to avoid argument and recrimination. As long as the variety does not suffer by the alteration in the flowering date, there is no harm done, but in many cases the blooms are likely to lose some depth in the colouring and to be rather on the rough side. Quite a lot are better on the first crown than on the second, but the number of breaks will be too few for the professional flower grower. The exhibitor can usually get his four or five to the plant.

THE OUTDOOR SECTION

The outdoor chrysanthemum section is not quite as involved as the indoor, and it is surprising what blooms can be grown in quite a small garden. The point can often be exemplified by remarks one hears when judging, such as 'he's only been at it two years'. Of course, all exhibitors will know well that it is not always the quantity grown that counts, it is a question of how they are grown and the amount of labour put into them. And while some can spend an unlimited amount on frames for protection, the back-yard grower merely employs a dozen or two shades and some paper bags.

Any old rough piece of land can be made to produce exhibition blooms in a very short space of time. A winter dressing of basic slag, if the soil is heavy or lumpy, and a good dressing of manure too, will do a lot. Incidentally, no land will go many years without a dose of this commodity. The compost heap is as good if it is sufficiently large. A dressing of bonemeal, soot and hop manure will help. If double digging is practised in the autumn, the lime can be spread in the spring just prior to the fork-over before planting. I would strongly recommend pots in preference to boxes for exhibition work as the plants are bound to get away better when roots are undisturbed.

Careful hardening-off will be our first consideration, as early May is very fickle, but if an early start is made, there should be sufficient time for the plants to grow and harden at the same time in a frame. Most of the varieties noted for being late will need to be pinched while in the frame, about mid-April. No small puny stock, however, should have this treatment before they have made good growth and are some six inches tall. If only exhibition purposes are being considered, every decent plant will respond to the pinch, as really only four or five growths will be needed. It is no use attempting to get exhibition blooms at nine to a plant. Later on only four should be kept.

I like to get the positions settled first and then insert the stakes and plant right up to them. Three- or four-foot canes, according to the expected height, should be used. The plants, of course, will be planted with the aid of a trowel and the ball covered by an inch of fine soil. No watering will be necessary if the soil is in a fairly moist condition, but to plant in mud is calamitous. If rain is long delayed it would be better to give water rather than that the plants should become distressed.

Tying up should be practised from the start, as a lot of damage could ensue from swaying. Each row should be labelled at both ends and a chart made out in case any labels get lost.

When buds appear, a top-dressing of fertilizer once a week should be given, as this increases size, health and colour. A fortnight before the shows, two doses of sulphate of potash at an ounce to the gallon will materially stiffen the blooms.

Most of the reflexed type will run rain off easily, but incurved varieties such as Empire White, Geo. McLeod, and Golden Circle really need some protection. In many northern districts, where soot and smoke abound, practically everything has to be covered or there would be no shows.

The hoe should be used right through the season, taking care not to injure the roots, and water should be given at feeding time before the fertilizer is applied; then this may be lightly watered in. All basal growths are cut off as they appear and all side growths must be cut out. Keep the stems tied up to the stakes, and when a number of promising buds materialize, it is best to give each a thin stake. In this way all blooms will avoid chafing, foliage will remain intact, and the stems keep straight.

Many growers treat their plants in a carefree manner through the growing season and rely on feeding to pull them through, but this should not be the exhibitor's way.

PREPARATION FOR THE SHOW

Now we come to the preparation for the show itself. The day prior to the show is a rather exciting period for all growers, young or old. Those who are blessed with a wife who shares the sport are lucky men. Buckets, pails, bowls, indeed, everything that will hold blooms, come into action.

Cutting the blooms is a satisfying occupation, especially if they are good, but what is a good bloom?

A large exhibition bloom should be both broad and deep and well shouldered. It must be full in the centre. The colour should be rich and possess no damped spots. Petals must be firm and of good substance. There should be nothing resembling coarseness and no dents or tufts. The eye should scarcely be noticed, and two or three eyes are fatal. Cups or wires are allowed, but a three-inch ring or cup is the limit.

An exhibition incurve should be quite globular; petals must be smooth and of good quality, incurving very regularly all over the surface, very firm and close. Faults could be staleness, showing an eye, roughness, an uneven outline, and breadth without corresponding depth.

Reflexed decoratives should be deep and broad, fresh to the tip, devoid of an eye. Petals must be brilliant in colour, fresh and hard without a single dead or damaged petal, and the whole bloom very symmetrical in shape with evenly formed petals right through the bloom. Foliage should also be fresh and undamaged.

Incurving decoratives should be quite deep in formation with a globular outline, full of petal, good substance, clean and clear in colour and fresh throughout. Again, no damped or damaged petals.

Singles should possess no more than five rows of florets. These should be broad, firm, and flat. Avoid any bloom going past its best, with stale disk florets.

Cutting and Packing. This is what we want, so look for those blooms best fitted for the job before commencing to cut. We have spoken of the marks lost by damaged blooms and damaged foliage. To avoid damage, never lay a bloom down after cutting. Have plenty of buckets handy so that the stems can go straight into water. When once the cells of the stem have healed—and it does not take long—water will not enter quickly; cutting or breaking under water is often beneficial where hard wood is concerned.

In the case of the large exhibitions, where foliage can be added, it is best to strip the stems of leaves at once; this reduces the strain quite a lot. The incurves, decoratives and singles might be stripped to half way. The stems of all should be bruised for an inch or two at the base in order that water can be taken up more easily. And may I repeat, never leave a bloom lying about out of water.

It takes quite twelve hours or more to charge a stem with water, but then blooms are suitable for packing and they will easily stand a long journey to a show. Large blooms are usually carried upright in a case specially adapted so that the blooms do not touch each other or chafe the sides of the case; this latter trouble has lost many a cup. Incurves, decoratives and singles can easily be accommodated in flat cases, but they should be a couple of inches or so deeper than the florists' boxes. Cushions of rolled paper can be placed across the case to come under the neck of the bloom.

From the time of leaving home take good care that the cases are never out of your sight. Lorrymen and railway porters can do a lot of damage by rough handling. Keep all cases level at all costs and watch that the boxes are not jarred or dropped heavily. In other words, do it all yourself if you can.

Staging. On reaching the show, get a quiet corner if you can, and quiet concentration will be the watchword. Get a plentiful supply of vases charged with water and, as speedily as possible, get the blooms into them before commencing to sort out.

An exhibitor usually knows which class he is going out for and, of course, he will sort out the best he has of each variety for the purpose. If you want to win a certain cup, make no bones about it and let each bloom be a winner. Many a mess has been made by trying to win too many classes.

If you have a dozen to put up in single vases on a table space, see that good deep blooms occupy the back row, as this position shows up the depth. The two corners should also have good breadth too, but the places for two weak blooms, if you have them, are the outsides of the middle row. The front row is the place for those devoid of depth as they will not be quite so noticeable. Of course the judges, if they are worth their salt, will spot all or any weak blooms and any shuffling will be more for the general public. The only way to get round this is by having no weak specimens.

If the blooms are good, keep them well up so they will look important. Short stems often lose points by appearing squat even though the blooms may be good; about twenty-four inches is usual. Where vases are concerned most societies have many classes for three blooms. I find it best to have one higher at the back and two at the front. They can often be wedged in this way, by moss or even paper, but it is much safer to put a short lengthener to the back bloom in order to keep the blooms rigid. Always use a bit of moss for the vase top—paper is ugly.

A three-day show is a big test for blooms, and I would strongly advise an exhibitor to go over his exhibits with a watering-can during the second day and fill up the vases.

And just one friendly word on exhibiting. Always be a good sport whether you win or lose. Never complain about the judges or the judging.

We often think we did not quite get justice, but taking a long view this evens out.

I recall my first visit as an exhibitor to the National Show in London some thirty-six years ago. I took the prizes all right and received the congratulations of the other competitors, and was agreeably surprised when at the end of the show they assisted me to pack up. That evening I made a host of friends, many have passed on, but others remain faithful friends to this day and my life would have been poorer without them.

Exhibiting will be what you make it, so always look for an opportunity of assisting beginners by a little kindness and encouragement. This also applies to visitors from other societies.

CHAPTER FIVE

Daffodils

BY C. F. COLEMAN

MANY OF the qualities essential for a successful show flower are not within the control of the average exhibitor, though there are, of course, a few people who raise their own seedlings. It may be useful to consider, for a moment, the qualities a daffodil breeder will have had in mind when selecting new varieties for exhibition from amongst his seedlings. The new blooms must have a proper balance between all parts, good form and poise, clean colour, smoothness, substance without coarseness and, of course, strong constitution as well as showing some improvement over existing varieties. In fact, they must approach that elusive quality, perfection.

This search is one with which normally the exhibitor has no immediate concern for he must make his personal choice as to which varieties to grow for exhibition from amongst those varieties offered for sale. The selection is wide for there is no sure and certain winning variety in any class. The exhibitor may, if he is so inclined, pay as many pounds as pence for a bulb, but let it not be thought that 'new and expensive' is the easy road to success. Many a well-grown and well staged older variety has eclipsed an indifferently grown or poorly staged expensive novelty, and the judges are not influenced by cost or names except in so far as correct naming may tip the scale in close competition.

Planting. Exhibition daffodils are usually grown in beds three feet six inches to four feet wide and as long as may be convenient, leaving paths eighteen inches to twenty-four inches wide between the beds. The exact width of the bed has no special merit and is governed by the stature and reach of the grower; it will, however, be found that beds of the sizes mentioned are the most convenient, for both cultural and picking purposes. On some soils, especially those of heavy and close textures, these beds should be a few inches higher than the paths; this is easily done by lowering the paths and placing the soil dug out on the beds after planting the bulbs. Quicker and better drainage is thus provided, for though daffodils must have a sufficiency of moisture during growth, stagnant water is harmful, and weeding, hoeing and general cultivation can be done at times when these operations would otherwise be impracticable.

The bulbs should be planted not later than the end of August or early in September in ground that is in good heart and well supplied with humus. Following a crop, such as potatoes, for which the ground was heavily manured is ideal, but otherwise old and well-decayed compost should be dug in. Bonemeal or steamed bone flour should be given, at the rate of two to three ounces to the square yard, at the time of planting.

Space the bulbs six to eight inches apart in rows nine inches from each other, marking the rows at each end by a cane or stick; the necessary hoeing can then be done without damaging the pushing shoots before they have emerged. Each variety should be suitably labelled and, as frost often ejects the labels, a measured plan will assist in the proper replacement. Those whose acquaintance with new varieties has not yet reached a stage where they can correctly associate flower and name must be careful with this label problem, for, as has previously been mentioned, in a close contest, correct naming counts.

The beds must be kept clean, so hoeing should be carried out as often as conditions allow, and on light sandy or gravelly soils that dry out rapidly, watering may be necessary to bring the flowers to perfection; one very thorough watering is usually sufficient and should be done before the buds turn down.

Protection. Rough windy weather is the great hazard at flowering time and on exposed sites this can wreak havoc, breaking the stems or bruising the flowers. A very good protection is the coarse mesh coconut-fibre netting, used by hop growers to surround the hop gardens. Some well-renowned exhibitors also protect their flowers, against hail and direct sunlight, by a top covering of calico or similar material—white where the flowers will not fade or are improved by exposure to bright light and green or light brown if the flowers are inclined to lose colour or burn when exposed to brilliant sunshine. This protection must be very securely fixed to strong supports and wires, and stretched as taut as possible to prevent it flapping on to the

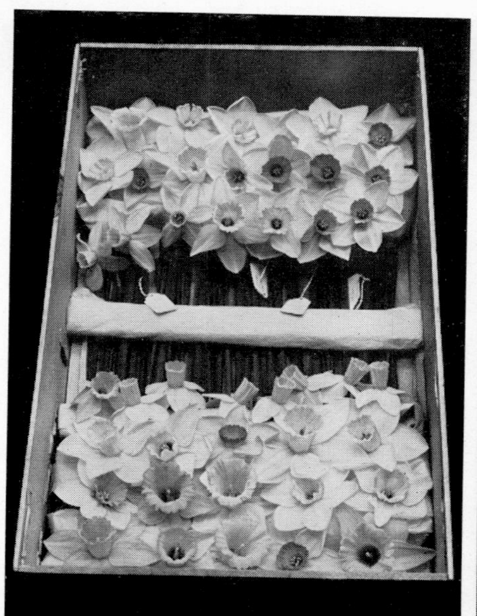

Left: A box of specimen blooms labelled and packed for carrying to the show. *Right:* Unpacking the blooms and plunging them into water.

Staging the individual vases after separating the blooms for the various classes.

Left: Gently ironing a 'petal' to flatten it and improve its set. *Right:* Choose blooms where the apical perianth segments are in line with the stem, as the one on the right.

A class for three vases of three distinct varieties with pink colouring in the corona, three blooms of each.

blooms. It cannot be too strongly emphasized that the whole structure must be very securely erected; gales have been known to cause such protective cages to collapse and the havoc is better imagined than experienced. The top covering must not be put on before the flowers are about to open and should be removed as soon as possible after it has served its purpose, otherwise it will draw the plants and weaken them. This top cover is perhaps justified when large quantities of impeccable flowers are required, but for the smaller exhibitor whose time is limited, there is an alternative (described in the section on cutting the flowers) which also gives scope for a large degree of control in retarding or in advancing the flowers.

Cutting. Most daffodils can be cut any time during a period of up to ten days before the show, if there is sufficient length of stem, for although the flower will open, no further lengthening of the stem can take place. The best age to cut them is just as the flower has opened and the conditions under which they are kept will depend on the date the show is to take place. Those likely to be too early and so past their prime can be retarded by keeping them in a cool, shady room or shed or even a cellar; the laggards can be cut just as the flower is about to open and hurried on in the warm moist atmosphere of a greenhouse or in the living room, and in extreme cases, on the kitchen mantelshelf. Some varieties do not respond to this last-mentioned treatment and in any case it should only be tried as the last resort. If the flowers are cut during a warm spell, do not put them at once into a cold place but acclimatize them gradually as otherwise they may be chilled and spoiled. During this 'storage' period, change the water every day and cut a thin slice from the bottom of the stem. It is better to allow the trumpet varieties to mature on the plant, but red cups which may burn or fade in the sunlight are best cut as soon as they have opened.

The blooms should be cut, not plucked or pulled, with as long a stem as possible above the white part at the bottom. It is imperative to put them into water immediately they are cut, and a suitable receptacle, such as a pail or jug, with sufficient water for the bottoms of the stems to be immersed, should be carried for this purpose. The ideal time for cutting is early morning, failing which choose the cool of the evening and never do it during the heat of the day when the sun is brilliant. The flowers should stand in water for at least twelve hours and, if possible, longer, before being packed in their boxes; they will then travel for many hours without harm and, moreover, they enlarge and improve astonishingly after this immersion.

Label each flower, either before cutting or immediately afterwards, with its name and the class in which it is to be shown. One of the simplest ways is to use the small tie-on price labels which can be easily attached to the neck of the flower, by slipping the label through the cotton loop. These may be as quickly removed on the show bench by cutting the loop, and no disturbance of the arrangement is caused.

Selecting Show Blooms. Every individual specimen of any variety differs slightly in form and detail, and great care and discrimination is called for before cutting it. Each flower must be critically examined, as will be described later, and the temptation to cut any that just fails to reach the standard of its type, or is flawed in any way, must be avoided. Many sub-standard 'spares' are a hindrance when you finally choose and set up your flowers at the show hall where, in any case, there is seldom time for too much deviation from prearranged plans.

The perianth is the dominant feature and in the modern show flower should almost invariably be flat and set at a right-angle to the corona; there are, however, two outstanding exceptions in the *N. cyclamineus* and *N. triandrus* hybrids where it should be well reflexed. This then is the first part to be examined and, viewed from the back, defects such as twisted and badly placed petals—faults which never can be remedied satisfactorily—are easily seen. Look now at the front and choose those with the smoothest segments, discarding any with nicks or split edges, but slight roughness of texture or ribbing can sometimes be smoothed out. It is seldom that the perianth opens perfectly flat; the segments tend to lean forward, or one of the segments only, usually one of the inner ones, has this tendency; gentle pressure with the thumb at the base of the segments will correct this and they will usually remain in position. This is sometimes caused by the dried sheath pressing on a petal, in which event lift it before pushing the petal back.

It will be seen that the six perianth segments form two triangles, but whereas some flowers have the apical segments vertical and the two points are in line with the stem, in others they will be found to be in a horizontal line across the stem. Choose the vertical form if possible as they look 'smarter' than the horizontal ones, and though this is a detail not generally appreciated, it does help to make the exhibit more attractive and outstanding.

The corona is the next part to scrutinize. A fault sometimes found, especially in those with a rolled or flanged edge, is what might be termed a hanging under-lip on the bottom side; the rolled flange is flattened and protrudes. It is quite impossible to correct this, but slight irregularities in the symmetry of the roll can often be rectified. The corona should be circular in section; if it is not, careful pinching is the remedy. The periphery of the corona in those without a roll is often divided into six domed segments or crenations; the sides of these sometimes extend too deeply or the adjoining crenations overlap, giving the flowers a coarse appearance; avoid them if possible.

The anthers should not be too large or prominent and should fit tightly around the style; the starfish effect of loose anthers spoils the appearance of the flower. The style should not project too far or be too prominent, though this is generally found in the short cup varieties.

Brilliance of colour is of paramount importance; it is a transient quality, rapidly lost in hot sunshine, and the edge of some of the red cups is liable to melt, hence the advice to cut them as soon as possible or shade them. The whiteness of white varieties, however, improves in sunlight, especially with those varieties in which the corona opens a yellow or lemon tone. Finally, the flower should look you squarely in the face and neither hang its head nor lift it much above the horizontal. At this stage slight mud splashes, rain spots and fly marks can be ignored as they can easily be washed off later.

This general examination is not the lengthy operation it may seem from this detailed description; the experienced eye will cover all the points in a comprehensive glance and decide whether a flower is worth further consideration.

Packing. For packing and carrying the flowers to the show, light, strong wooden boxes, with a base of soft wood into which drawing pins can readily be pressed, will be found to be the best receptacles. Line the boxes with soft tissue paper and at one end place a pillow, formed by rolling a sheet of tissue paper into a roll about two inches in diameter. Arrange a row of flowers with the necks resting against the roll, the upper perianth segments lying on top of it. Another pillow is then gently pushed under the lower perianth segments and another row of flowers then put into position. Repeat this operation, until the stems reach the other end of the box, securing the stems at every third row or so by a length of tape fixed to the base of the box with the drawing pins. The operations can be repeated from the other end; two or three rows can usually be fitted in, but care is required in slipping the stems under the pillows and between the stems of the other flowers. The whole is then securely fixed with a length of wood, covered with tissue paper, about an inch square, and slightly longer than the internal width of the box. This is gently pressed down on to the stems. Finally, place a sheet of tissue paper over the flowers and secure the lid.

Leaves and moss must be provided. Inexpensive varieties should be grown for the leaves, wide ones for the bold flowers such as the trumpet varieties and narrow ones for the daintier kinds. Cut enough to allow not less than three for single blooms, four or five for the three-bloom classes, and proportionately more for those classes that call for more blooms in a vase. Put the leaves in water as soon as cut, as was recommended for the flowers. Moss is the best material to use to keep the blooms secure in the vases; sphagnum or any other long moss is suitable and it should be used damp.

Dressing and Staging. The first thing to do, upon arriving at the show hall, is to find a convenient place where you can dress your flowers and, if possible, also obtain a seat. Water is invariably available and sometimes buckets are also provided. Unpack the flowers and stand them in the bucket, then collect your entry cards and name cards from the show officials. It is wise to inspect the lay-out of the staging and the positions of the classes so that you can reach them by the shortest route from your dressing table.

Having filled the vases with water and placed the moss and leaves in a convenient position on the table, put the chosen flowers loosely in the vases. It is at this stage that the flowers undergo their final inspection and grooming. Hold the flowers in the left hand and examine each one individually for defects. Dust is removed by careful brushing with a dry, large sable- or camel-hair brush of 'Swan' (No. 8) size; mud splashes or fly marks are removed with the moistened tip of a smaller brush of 'Crow' or 'Duck' (No. 1 or 3) size; these brushes can be bought at an artists' materials shop. Firmly but gently hold the neck and stem of the flower with the thumb and little finger in front and the first three fingers behind so that the flower faces you, and carefully press the petals back to form a right angle with the corona. Gentle pressure at the base of the petals with either the thumb of the other hand or the large brush is usually sufficient. If the set of the petals is not quite vertical or horizontal gently twist the flower round, holding the neck in one hand and the seed pod in the other. The petals should be flat, but sometimes the edges curl either up or down: this can often be remedied by 'ironing' the petal, using the first finger as the 'ironing-board' and rolling the large brush up and down the petal. This action will also improve the set of any rebellious petal that will not stay in position. The corona, if not naturally symmetrical, can be gently squeezed into shape and defects in the roll of the trumpet can be corrected by a touch from the large brush, while the short cup varieties are sometimes enhanced by slightly flattening the cup, but do not overdo this or the cup will split. This brush work and manipulation can be carried out with confidence and will not harm the texture of the surface if done with care and in reason. It is surprising the degree of strong manipulation to which the thick-textured modern daffodil will submit without damage.

Put the required number of leaves in the vase, hold the flower, facing you, just in front of the leaves and pack the top of the vase tightly with moss. Take up sufficient moss to carry this out in one operation and do not push it too far down the neck of the vase. The flower sometimes looks better if the stem is very slightly tilted back, especially if the flower hangs its head, but do not overdo this.

When setting up three flowers, arrange them in the form of a triangle, close together but just not touching, and put the best bloom at the top.

More than three flowers call for a different technique and though classes for five are seldom wanted, they can be placed in the vase in two ways: (*a*) three in a triangle with two below, or (*b*) two at the top and three below. For seven flowers put two at the top, three in the middle row and two underneath. Nine flowers are not often required, except when submitting a flower to the Royal Horticultural Society for an Award of Merit. In this case put two at the top, four in the middle and three at the bottom. The flowers must rise in tiers from the lowest row in the front and, to keep these multiple numbers in position, put the back row close to the leaves with some moss in front, arrange the next row against the moss with more in front, then the front and bottom row with the final packing of moss. The stems can be adjusted up or down through the moss and the spacing can also be adjusted by pressing small balls of moss between or against the stems.

When arranging the vases on the staging in a collection of mixed varieties, always put the best flowers on the top row, or at the back if the staging is not tiered, and adjust the flowers in each row to the same height. If possible, place the vases so that two of a colour are not adjacent, using the paler varieties as a foil for the highly coloured ones, which are generally best placed at the ends of the rows, and towards the top of the exhibit.

It is well to remember that more awards are lost through poor setting up and staging than through deficiency in the quality of the flowers and that the neater and smarter exhibit will usually receive its reward. Never allow the flowers to sprawl in the vases; a single stem must be truly perpendicular when viewed from the front and though the stems of the outside flowers in a multiple vase must of necessity lean slightly outward this should be only sufficient to separate the blooms so that they do not overlap. Be sure that all the blooms truly face the front.

Finally, give yourself ample time to set them up and place them in the correct classes and to give them that final 'touch up'. Then if you are not successful, examine the winning exhibits to see where they excel and the next time modify your own entries accordingly.

CLASSIFICATION OF NARCISSI

Such great advances have been made, in the form and colour of daffodils, in the past twenty-five years that it was thought that the system of classification in use during that period was inadequate. The Royal Horticultural Society, after consultation with the General Bulb Growers' Society of Haarlem and with specialists in the Commonwealth and the United States of America, has recently reclassified them. There are now eleven divisions; the classification is logical and easier to understand and makes provision for the evolution of the flower. Most good bulb catalogues include the revised system in full and the correct classification of the individual flowers offered is also shown.

Exhibitors should obtain the classified list of daffodil names published by the Royal Horticultural Society. This list gives the names of over 7,000 varieties with much interesting and historical information about them, as well as the revised classification, which is here given in full.

Revised system for the Classification of Narcissi which came into force on January 1, 1950:—(i) 'Coloured' means yellow or some colour other than white. (ii) 'White' means white or whitish. (iii) The length of a perianth segment is the extreme length measured on the inside from its junction with the corona along the midrib to the extreme tip, and the length of the corona is the extreme length measured from its junction with the perianth to the end of its farthest extension when the edge is flattened out,

Division 1—**Trumpet Narcissi.** Distinguishing characters: One flower to a stem; trumpet or corona as long or longer than the perianth segments. (*a*) Perianth coloured; corona coloured, not paler than the perianth. (*b*) Perianth white; corona coloured. (*c*) Perianth white; corona white, not paler than the perianth. (*d*) Any colour combination not falling into (*a*), (*b*) or (*c*).

Division 2—**Large-cupped Narcissi.** Distinguishing characters: One flower to a stem; cup or corona more than one-third, but less than equal to the length of the perianth segments. (*a*) Perianth coloured; corona coloured, not paler than the perianth. (*b*) Perianth white; corona coloured. (*c*) Perianth white; corona white, not paler than the perianth. (*d*) Any colour combination not falling into (*a*), (*b*) or (*c*).

Division 3—**Small-cupped Narcissi.** Distinguishing characters: One flower to a stem; cup or corona not more than one-third the length of the perianth segments. (*a*) Perianth coloured; corona coloured, not paler than the perianth. (*b*) Perianth white; corona coloured. (*c*) Perianth white; corona white, not paler than the perianth. (*d*) Any colour combination not falling into (*a*), (*b*) or (*c*).

Division 4—**Double Narcissi.** Distinguishing character: Double flowers.

Division 5—**Triandrus Narcissi.** Distinguishing characters: Characteristics of *Narcissus triandrus* clearly evident. (*a*) Cup or corona not less than two-thirds the length of the perianth segments. (*b*) Cup or corona less than two-thirds the length of the perianth segments.

Division 6—**Cyclamineus Narcissi.** Distinguishing characters: Characteristics of *Narcissus cyclamineus* clearly evident. (*a*) Cup or corona not less than two-thirds the length of the perianth segments. (*b*) Cup or corona less than two-thirds the length of the perianth segments.

Division 7—**Jonquilla Narcissi.** Distinguishing characters: Characteristics of any of the *Narcissus Jonquilla* group clearly evident. (*a*) Cup or corona not less than two-thirds the length of the perianth segments. (*b*) Cup or corona less than two-thirds the length of the perianth segments.

Division 8—**Tazetta Narcissi.** Distinguishing characters: Characteristics of any of the *Narcissus Tazetta* group clearly evident.

Division 9—**Poeticus Narcissi.** Distinguishing characters: Characteristics of the *Narcissus poeticus* group without admixture of any other.

Division 10—**Species and Wild Forms and Hybrids.** All species and wild, or reputedly wild, forms and hybrids.

Division 11—**Miscellaneous Narcissi.** All Narcissi not falling into any of the foregoing divisions.

CHAPTER SIX

Dahlias

BY A. T. BARNES

WHERE THE art of exhibiting dahlias actually commences, it is difficult to say, but I think it is correct to assume that the selection of varieties is of major importance. It is most valuable to note the names of those varieties that appear consistently in the prize lists, and I advise the newcomer when making his selections to use these lists as a guide.

It is essential to consider very carefully which types of dahlia you intend to grow for competition, as on this will depend the number of plants that will be required. Take the giant decoratives section as an example. A grower wishing to stage six blooms, distinct varieties, is well advised to grow nine distinct varieties of giants. It might seem that six pairs would be better, but each variety seems to have its own flowering period and it is quite likely that the pair would be either going over or breaking bud at the wrong time. Nine distinct plants disbudded to five buds each should furnish six equal-sized blooms during any period within three weeks. To extend this period a further two weeks, one of the axillary buds can be selected instead of the crown bud.

It is interesting to note that at the time that the crown buds are taken they will mostly appear to be in the same stage of development, but it is quite possible for some to be fully developed a week to a fortnight before the others. Apparently root development has a lot to do with this, as has the number of undisbudded lower shoots left on each main stem.

Timing a dahlia to within a few days is very difficult, many factors contributing to this. Some varieties take weeks longer than others to build up a structure sufficient to support huge blooms. Even when the buds show colour there may be a difference of a week or ten days before the flower is ready for cutting. For instance, a giant like Rita Betty will develop fully under normal conditions in about ten days, whereas one of the very full petalled types like Queen Elizabeth may possibly take three weeks. Other factors that upset timing are weather conditions, the number of blooms the plant is allowed to develop, the supply of moisture and the time of year. It will be found that dahlias develop much more slowly at the end of July than at the end of September, this being governed by root development. It is practically impossible to lay down any hard-and-fast rules in this respect, but individual study and the keeping of records will serve the exhibitor in good stead for future occasions. It is always advisable to keep in mind that the growth of no two dahlias is alike.

Let us consider the numbers that one would need to plant to produce sufficient exhibition blooms in other classes. If one proposes to stage a dozen distinct giants, then at least eighteen distinct varieties should be grown. For a class of six bunches distinct, three in each bunch, it is advisable to grow nine varieties, three plants of each. By growing three plants of a kind one can usually depend on cutting three evenly matched flowers at the required date. On some occasions it may be found possible to cut three good blooms from one plant, but I do not advise the keen exhibitor to rely on such slender chances as these. It is too chancy cutting only the exact number of blooms that are to be staged; there is bound to be damage in some form or other. Some flowers will shake out badly in transport, others may get bruised or refuse to take up water, in fact a dozen things can go wrong at the critical moment. Therefore always aim to have some spares.

The greater the distance the blooms have to travel, the more will be the damage when they are taken out of the cases. This applies especially to the large and giant decoratives. The cactus types can be packed with their petals more woven together, i.e. loose but firm, and this method of packing ensures a fairly safe journey. (The packing of all varieties is more fully described on page 102.) An exhibitor who has only a small distance to go can cut his flowers on the morning of the show, and he has the advantage over the competitor who has to travel a long distance.

Many years ago I made a record of the number of plants required for providing the requisite number of blooms in any particular class, and this planting chart has been of great service, usually working out very accurately in normal seasons. It is a peculiar thing that however many dahlias one plants, one variety or another will fail; that is why a good number of reserves should be included.

EXHIBITION PLANTING CHART

Variety	*Blooms in Class*	*Number of Plants required*
Large or Giant Decoratives	12 distinct vars.	18 distinct vars. 3 each
	9 ,, ,,	12 ,, ,, ,,
	6 ,, ,,	9 ,, ,, ,,
	9 bunches distinct vars. 3 in a bunch	15 distinct vars., 4 each
	6 bunches distinct vars. 3 in a bunch	12 ,, ,, 4 ,,
	3 bunches distinct vars.	6 ,, ,, 3 ,,
Giant and Large Cactus all as above.		
Medium Decoratives	6 bunches distinct vars. 3 in a bunch	9 distinct vars., 3 each
	3 bunches distinct vars.	6 ,, ,, 3 ,,
Small Decoratives	12 bunches distinct vars. 6 in a bunch	18 ,, ,, 3 ,,
	6 bunches distinct vars. 6 in a bunch	12 ,, ,, 3 ,,
	6 bunches, 3 in a bunch	9 ,, ,, 1 ,,
Medium and Small Cactus all as above.		
Show and Fancy	12 distinct blooms	18 ,, ,, 2 ,,
	6 ,, ,,	9 ,, ,, 2 ,,
Pompons	12 bunches distinct vars., 10 in a bunch	18 ,, ,, 3 ,,
	12 bunches distinct vars., 6 in a bunch	15 ,, ,, 3 ,,
	6 bunches distinct vars., 6 in a bunch	9 ,, ,, 2 ,,
	6 bunches distinct vars., 3 in a bunch	9 ,, ,, 1 ,,
	3 bunches distinct vars., 3 in a bunch	6 ,, ,, 1 ,,
	9 distinct blooms	9 ,, ,, 1 ,,
Collarettes	6 bunches distinct vars., 3 in a bunch	9 ,, ,, 2 ,,
	3 bunches distinct vars., 3 in a bunch	6 ,, ,, 2 ,,
	9 distinct blooms	12 ,, ,, 1 ,,

For the classes of dahlias with smaller blooms, the number of plants required will be less, but in all cases at least two of a kind should be grown. Old exhibitors know only too well that although it may look as if dozens of good flowers will be just right for the day, when they are cut and matched up for size and colour very few are left to take their place on the show bench. Pompons can be a great delusion. To stage a dozen vases of six blooms each one has to cut and grade hundreds of blooms. These neat little button dahlias become more difficult to match as the size of the class diminishes. Curiously enough, it is the nine-bloom class that requires the greatest care in matching; each imperfection and variation in size seems to be magnified.

Other varieties, such as the anemone-flowered, star dahlias, peony-flowered, etc., can be planted under the same numbers as the pompon. In the above table it will be noted that a good reserve is included, sufficient to offset any normal failures.

STAKING

Many factors contribute to the production of perfect exhibition flowers: one of these is adequate staking. Too much stress cannot be placed on the use of strong efficient stakes, especially when growing the large and giant varieties. In a good growing season, some of these huge dahlias may easily reach six to eight feet, and it is very disheartening to see magnificent blooms broken down by heavy rain, or blown over by strong winds. Wherever possible, the grower is advised to use five stakes; this number will allow of good control over the leader and the four laterals. Two or three rings of strong string round the four outer stakes will keep the plant secure until the end of the season.

It is as well to ascertain the height of each variety before planting. This will be helpful in two ways: the number of the various-sized stakes can be ascertained, and the planting lay-out can be so plotted to ensure that no variety is dwarfed or overshadowed by its neighbour. It is advisable to grade the dahlias so that the dwarfest-growing varieties are near the path, an arrangement which, as well as allowing for a better flow of air, will ensure that the plot forms an attractive rising bank of colour.

In selecting the size of the stakes it is better to allow a little extra height when using new stakes such as hazels. These usually go two years without breaking, but after that they break off a foot each season, so that a little extra length at the start may well mean an additional year's service.

The choice of wooden stakes grows more limited each season. Occasionally one can pick up a few bundles of ash saplings which will be found more durable than hazel. The best wood of all is split chestnut. These stakes cost a little more at the outset, but if treated with a wood preservative, they will last for many years. Metal stakes can be made from three-quarter-inch electrical slip tube, or, if a heavier gauge is required, use that known as screwed tube. These tubes are easily cut with a hacksaw and one end should be flattened and the other stopped with putty. Finish off with a coat of leaf-green paint and you have an unbreakable and inconspicuous stake that will last a lifetime. Another method is to cut down the metal tubing into 30-inch lengths, flatten one end, and in the tops use up the canes that have become too short for normal staking; it is an economical way of using up odd materials, especially in making up any desired length of stake, different top lengths being used as required.

A quantity of 2- to 3-foot thin canes should always be available; they can be used for training lateral shoots to the outer stakes, and later in the season used for securing the opening blooms. Long-stemmed dahlias are more vulnerable to wind and rain damage than the short, sturdy varieties, and, to offset this, canes should be tied to the various stakes, taking care to see that they are higher than the finished flower will be. Soft string looped round the cane and tied at intervals, the top tie being just below the bud, will usually prevent damage.

Square wooden stakes are useful where a small number of dahlias are grown, but these are not recommended for plants where a lot of tying is required. All dahlia ties should be first looped round the stake to maintain the tie in position, and it will be found that where square stakes are used the tying material will not move freely round the squared edges and this results in a considerable loss of time. Soft string in balls is the most economical material for tying. If the end is taken from the inside, the ball can be placed in the coat pocket, thus leaving both hands free for tying and cutting. Scissors are the best for cutting string, and if a tape loop is taken through one of the finger holes of the scissors they can be hung on the wrist and this will save much time foraging in pockets; after a little practice one becomes adept at catching and dropping them. If raffia is used for tying it should be damped first as otherwise many of the ties will work themselves loose; even reef knots will do this with raffia.

Assorted stakes are best in lengths of 4 to 6 feet; in well-dug soil they will probably push in to a depth of 18 inches, leaving 3 feet for pompons and other varieties that do not exceed 4 feet, and 4 feet 6 inches for those that grow above that height. Many of the taller-growing varieties will require 3-foot canes spliced to the outer stakes later in the season. When a dahlia is known to grow extra tall (as is found with Searchlight, General Eisenhower, Gunyah Glory and others), the stakes should be at least 5 feet 6 inches out of the ground to start with. Where possible the use of five stakes is advocated for the giant exhibition varieties, taking care to select the strongest for the centre. Three stakes will suffice for the less heavily flowered varieties such as the small decoratives, cactus and pompons. To prevent the plant flopping to one side, strings should be looped round each stake and taken round the centre of the plant and tied at the back of the stake; these strings need not be too tight as their purpose is merely to keep the plant in position. Two lots of strings, the first at 2 feet from the ground and the next at 3 feet 6 inches, are generally sufficient. The whole plant is kept compact by a few individual lateral ties and three string loops taken round the stakes at intervals of 18 inches.

Where long rows are planted for cutting or market, a different type of staking can be employed. One of the most popular methods is to give each plant a strong centre stake and then place additional stakes at 4- to 6-foot intervals in two lines which are marked out 18 inches either side of the centre stakes. Round the two lines of stakes, government surplus rubber-covered wire is looped and pulled tight, thus enclosing the plants in a yard-wide strip. The first line of wire is placed 18 inches from the ground, followed by two more at intervals of a foot, making the top line 3 feet 6 inches from the ground. This height is sufficient to maintain the average cutting variety. From each end of the row two more lines are spaced at foot widths inside the strip and these are stretched tight. With long rows it may be necessary to place a few extra stakes to prevent sagging of these inner lines which should be at the same heights as the side lines. Connecting cross lines should be made from each pair of stakes with strong string or covered wire. This criss-cross support of strings and wires, similar to that used for carnation beds, will usually be found sufficient for ordinary requirements. Where extra care is needed, more strings can be placed across the lines at suitable intervals. Loop the string round each line in the process and see that the whole string and wire meshing is pulled tight.

This method of support can be fixed at the one time early after planting, or as the plants make progress. The dahlias will grow through the mesh and all lateral growth will be supported. It is essential that the central leader is tied several times to the centre stake, but no other tying is needed. When a number of rows are planted, the space between each should be 4 feet 6 inches; this will allow of more freedom when carrying the water containers. Note, if the rows are very long it is advisable to break them into blocks,

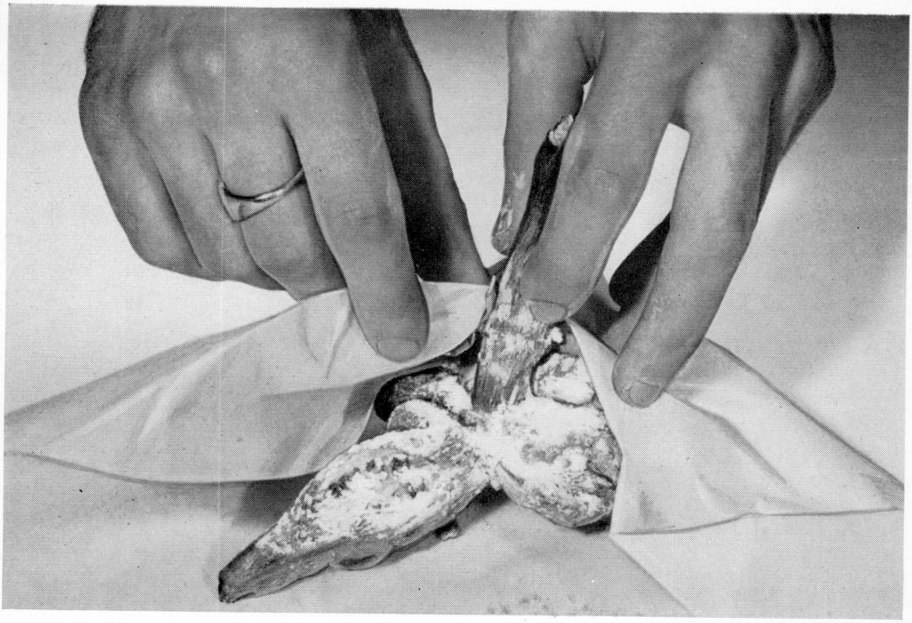

Tubers, having been dusted with flowers of sulphur, are wrapped in tissue-paper for winter storage.

Two rooted cuttings struck at the same time, showing the difference in growth which illustrates the need for a five-inch pot.

Left: A young plant being tied loosely. *Right:* Showing the method of tying to support a plant with three stakes. Normally the ties are made as the plant makes growth.

Left: Method of placing five stakes. Strings show the ultimate positions of the ties. *Right:* Showing the angle to place a training cane.

otherwise one may have to walk half the length of the plot to get to the far side of a neighbouring row.

CULTIVATION

Planting. The giant varieties are best planted about 4 feet apart—the more space a plant is given, the less it is inclined to draw. Medium varieties do well at 3 feet and the smaller dahlias at 30 inches. Pompons are best grown in a double row—if possible, with a path all round; they do well if planted 2 feet apart in rows 1 foot 6 inches apart.

Before planting, the plot should be dressed with a metaldehyde slug killer, paying special attention to parts that border on fences and shrubberies. The best time to dress the ground is after a shower, when the conditions have become warmer; late April is a very effective time. To facilitate planting, the plot should be lined out and the centre stakes placed into position. Staking after planting may result in tearing off part of the roots, and can easily set the plants back a fortnight.

Planting dates must vary with the district. In the south, it is usually safe to commence planting during the first week in May, but in the north it is best delayed until the end of the month. No district is really immune from those nippy spring frosts which can usually be expected in the middle and also during the last few days of May. Keep a good supply of protective materials to hand; straw, sacking, pots, etc., all serve a useful purpose. A piece of newspaper wrapped round the plant and held with a pin at the top will ward off many degrees of frost. Early planting is best done in a shallow depression about three inches deep, the slight wall of earth acting as a good protection. See that the young plants are behind the stake and facing west. This may seem a trifling item, but a thick stake can prevent a lot of searing when east winds are prevalent.

All plants should be tied by first looping the string round the stake and then tying loosely to leave sufficient space for expansion. This first tie should be closely watched, for once the dahlia gets going it grows fast, with the result that an unnoticed plant may soon become strangled. In all cases it is advisable to make a thorough check a month after planting. Special varieties can be given added protection by placing a few pieces of shrubby material round the plant; these can be held together with a couple of turns of string.

When the plants are about eighteen inches high the tops should be pinched out. This will cause the side shoots to break out and so build up a compact bushy plant. If the giant varieties are required for early August shows, however, the leader should be allowed to grow naturally. This means that the laterals will be slower in breaking out and somewhat later in flowering. When a dahlia has been stopped it is usual for two shoots to develop at the top. In dealing with the giant varieties only one should be allowed to remain to form the central leader and to keep the plant balanced. The leader and the laterals should be de-shooted, leaving one to take the place of the bloom that is cut.

It is important to note that a good deal depends on which shoot is selected to form the new leader. A shoot near the top will flower much earlier than one several joints lower down, but at the same time the false stem will be much shorter. I use the term 'false' to differentiate between the actual flower stalk and the added stem which is part of the leader and the length of which is governed by the position of the shoot selected. If the retained central leader threatens to flower too early, then one of the axillary buds should be selected in place of the crown. The ideal is to have the second leader showing colour at the time the first bloom is cut, thus providing a series of blooms in quick succession.

Later in the season when the roots have built up a vigorous system, more laterals can be allowed to develop. Some varieties will easily carry eight leaders, while others with poorer root systems will have difficulty in maintaining three; so much depends upon the variety. As the size of the flowers diminishes, less thinning will be needed. In the case of small decoratives, cactus and pompons, practically nothing but the removal of the axillary buds is necessary. If these are left to develop they spoil the flower stem, so the most practical thing to do is to nip them out as soon as they get to any size. If the blooms seem to be going too small, the plants will be better for thinning and a feed of liquid fertilizer.

Lateral Supports. Dahlias that have been pinched back will direct their energies to the production of side shoots, and very often these may be quite low down and growing out almost horizontally. As they grow and thicken out rapidly, it very frequently happens that the weight causes the lateral to drop, and being fleshy and brittle, it may break off at the base or 'jump its socket'. To prevent this a training cane is brought into use. The cane is pushed in sideways by the side of one stake and across the centre stake and is secured to both. It should be so placed that the side shoot can be tied to it without straining. When the side shoot has grown long enough to be secured twice to the outer stake, the cane can be dispensed with. The more upright shoots can be supported by hazel and other twiggy material.

Where a lateral has dropped and partially sprung out of its socket it should be given prompt attention. First, a piece of cane is pushed in behind the lateral, making sure that the fracture is tightly closed. The shoot is then tied lightly to the small cane and this cane tied to the centre stake to prevent the lateral falling back. Complete the operation by placing a pad of turf or a small heap of soil to act as a cushion underneath. In a short time the fracture will heal and so save a valuable leader.

When dealing with the giant varieties it is advisable to place the first string loop in position a month after planting. This should be placed a foot from the ground and looped round each stake in the process. Fast-growing laterals will be supported by the string until the grower has time to secure them to the stakes. As the five leaders make growth they should be secured to the stakes with roomy string ties. To keep the dahlia compact, two further string loops should be taken round the stakes, one in the middle and the other six inches from the top. The lateral selected to take the place of the first leader should be watched; it will grow fast, and should be tied back to the stake at the first opportunity. The smaller varieties may be less prone to wind damage if a few extra stake supports are given as the plants make progress.

POMPONS

Size is an important point in an exhibition pompon. A near-to-perfect flower should average one and three-quarter inches, but as no two varieties are identical in size, the production of evenly matched blooms is a matter that can, to a good extent, only be controlled by the grower. Some varieties are rampers, others are better for a larger breathing space. It takes a season or two to know the peculiarities of each variety. Those that grow tall and produce large flowers should be planted in the same bed, the more moderate growers in a separate bed and with more distance between each plant. Usually the first flowers come a little large on all varieties, but if the axillary buds are left on, also the old flowers, the size will soon go down. Pompons must be carefully watched. Disbud and feed plants whose flowers are going small, while those that are too large should not be disbudded, neither should the old blooms be removed until the following flowers show a tendency to come down to the required size. As the season advances many more laterals will be thrown up, and this added growth will in turn help to reduce the size of the blooms. In the case of the less vigorous varieties it may be necessary to take out some of the weaker growth to prevent exhaustion, such as is prone to happen in hot dry summers.

PESTS AND CONTROLS

Dahlias are vulnerable to such pests as slugs, earwigs, capsid bugs, green and black aphis, cutworms and occasionally, wasps. The majority of these insects are night feeders, and the damage that is done in one night can easily result in a ruined flower three weeks later. Some, such as the capsid bug, are at work all the time. This insidious pest closely resembles a large greenfly; it lives right down in the heart of the tender growing shoots where it thrives by constantly sucking the sap. If allowed to persist it will in time retard growth. Shoots that have grown out of a capsid bug attack are riddled with holes and can serve no useful purpose to the plant. So quietly does this pest work that very often the damage is done before the grower realizes what is happening. To prevent a first attack, spray with nicotine or liquid DDT a week after planting, follow up by two further sprayings at intervals of three weeks, taking care to get down into the base of the shoot. Dry dusting is effective for a time, but the advent of heavy rain soon washes the plant clean.

Earwigs. Earwigs are very persistent, with two broods each year. One can often find some sixty young insects in a small piece of old stem or hollow cane left over from the previous season. If this batch is not checked, they will in turn breed by the end of the season. The damage done by this pest is enormous. Feeding during the night, they eat out the tiny growing points, checking the growth of the plant. In some cases they take out every particle of future growth above the ground, and the plant has to send up a new shoot from a joint below the ground. In some instances a plant has no secondary shoots, and the only thing to do is take it up and replant, usually resulting in a month's delay.

No liquid insecticides seem to have any effect on this insect, and control can only be obtained by trapping, poisoning and the raking up and burning of every piece of material that is likely to afford cover. Watch for hollow canes, split stakes and curled leaves. Take off and burn the leaves and stop up the canes, etc., with putty or clay. Note that canes may be perfectly sound at planting time, but the advent of hot days will cause them to split and so afford protective cover during the hours of daylight. All split canes should be taken out and replaced with solid stakes.

Too much cannot be said regarding the earwig. As it works on young plants, so will it work on the opening flowers, and the effect of one night's work can completely ruin an otherwise perfect exhibition bloom. Trapping can be carried out with any materials that will afford cover in daylight. Matchboxes, crushed pieces of paper, bits of hollow stems or the old standby—inverted flower pots—will take care of a good number. The traps should be examined each morning and the insects shaken into a container half full of water. Dahlia growers who keep poultry will find their birds relish the earwig. In bad cases of infestation, a ground bait composed of 2 lb. of bran, 2 ounces of sodium fluoride and 1 ounce of treacle well mixed in a quart of water should be placed in small heaps in the most infested parts. Note that sodium fluoride is poisonous and poultry should not have access to it.

Red Spider. This pest is most prevalent in dry seasons. The leaf tissues of infected plants look a dried-up greyish-green. This is caused by the mite rasping the underneath part of the leaf and absorbing the sap. Bad attacks can be so damaging as almost to stop growth. The best method of control is by spraying the undersides of the leaves frequently with derris or with a strong soapy solution to which a quantity of nicotine sulphate has been added.

Cutworms. These smooth, grey-green caterpillars can cause a lot of damage, working at night and hiding by day, at the base of the main stem, usually about two inches under the soil. Like most other pests, the cutworm has two methods of attack, biting off young plants just below the ground and later in the season crawling up the plant and gnawing the florets or the centre out of developing blooms. At this stage the cutworm does not always go back to the ground. If a damaged bloom is examined the pest may be found curled behind the calyx, and in some instances, inside one of the large outer petals. Blooms that have been gnawed in the centre are best cut off and the nearest shoot allowed to develop as a replacement. Spraying the base of the plant as well as the foliage with a solution of nicotine sulphate will give a good measure of control. To make sure of keeping exhibition blooms free from damage it is advisable to fluff out a piece of cotton wool and tie it lightly on the flower stem about six inches below the bud. If the edges of the wool are lightly touched with paraffin the bloom will be safe from the majority of crawling insects. Another method is to prepare the wool by sprinkling it with naphthalene and rolling it up for a few days when the odour of the chemical will be absorbed so that the wool is ready for use without any additional treatment. Naphthalene-treated wool has many uses. It can be wrapped round the stem of a dahlia that has been gnawed by wasps or placed round the base of the plant to deter the ascending cutworms.

Wasps. These do not attack all types of dahlia indiscriminately but they have a preference for a variety whose sap contains a large amount of sucrose. This sugar is used for feeding the newly hatched wasps, the cellular tissue being chewed into a papier-mâché-like substance with which the cells of the nest are constructed. Carbolized vaseline smeared on the gnawed stems will check their activities as will the naphthalene wool described for cutworms.

Green and Black Aphis. These aphids are easily controlled if the plants are sprayed at the first sign of infestation. Like the capsid bug and other sucking insects, they are carriers and spreaders of mosaic and virus diseases. Black aphis can often be found wintering on the shoots of the spindle tree (*Euonymus europaeus*), and early in the spring the branches can be seen black with the pest. It usually takes several strong sprayings to combat the attack. It is also advisable to watch the industrious ant, for if these insects are seen running up and down a plant, one can usually find that they have carried a colony of aphids to the top. By tracing and destroying the ants' nest, a lot of future spraying will be averted.

MULCHING AND FEEDING

Much labour of watering can be avoided by mulching the dahlias with strawy manure, chopped straw, grass cuttings, compost or other moisture-retaining materials. The mulch should be laid down when the plants are from 18 inches to 2 feet high, and it should be at least 6 inches thick. During the season it will break up and rot, so that by the time the tubers are lifted it will be in the right condition for digging in. By this method a sufficient supply of humus is maintained and no other manuring is necessary. Dahlia roots do not forage deeply, usually the fine feeder roots will be found just under the surface; if these are allowed to dry out, the plant will suffer a setback. Mulching prevents this, and it also ensures a more equal distribution of liquid fertilizers. The giant dahlias suffer the most in hot dry summers and care should be taken to see that the roots are kept moist for at least a yard round the main stem.

The plants will derive much benefit from a good overhead spraying in the evening after a hot day. The foliage should have occasional drenchings, especially of plants whose flowers are to be cut the following morning. Light applications of water to the roots can be harmful; the result is to bring the finer roots to the surface where they end by being sun-dried, and this is a serious matter to a big dahlia whose root system can hardly keep pace with the heavy transpiration that takes place during very hot weather.

Feeding. Care should be taken in the choice and application of liquid fertilizers, especially those with a high nitrogenous content. A dahlia can only absorb a limited quantity of food, and this must be in a highly diluted state. Too much nitrogen will only result in coarse, soft foliage and few, flabby-petalled flowers. The effect of too much nitrogen is often indicated in blooms that go soft soon after cutting, and also in the resultant tubers rotting during the resting period. If the ground is in good heart the dahlia usually makes plenty of strong healthy growth. Should any plant develop thin, pale-green foliage, it can usually be corrected by applying potassium salts in solution—usually in the form of sulphate or muriate of potash at the rate of one ounce to a gallon of water.

It is when the plants are in full production that liquid feeding can be an advantage. Such manures as poultry and pigeon droppings, guano, soot and pig manure are very strong. Quantities of these materials should be placed in a piece of sacking tied up and suspended in a tank or tub for ten days to a fortnight and the liquid used well diluted to a pale straw colour. Fresh horse and sheep droppings can be used in a much stronger solution, and both give splendid results. Some fertilizers such as soot and soluble dried blood give wonderful results in the production of more brilliancy of colour. Colour feeding should commence a week before the bud shows colour and applications should be at the rate of half a gallon of liquid per plant for the ensuing three weeks. Care should be taken to see that the ground is thoroughly moistened before liquid manures are applied. The application of small quantities of this type of fertilizer is wasteful; the best method is to give one heavy watering to each dahlia if the best results are to be obtained. To maintain healthy balanced growth it is essential that liquid containing some form of potash should be given at periods in between the application of nitrogenous liquid fertilizers.

SHADING

Shading is of great importance to the exhibitor. It can make all the difference to an otherwise perfect bloom. Some colours, such as gold, fawn and yellow will stand up to the hottest sun, but dahlias in the red, scarlet and purple range bleach badly. As it is not possible to shade all the blooms required, preference should be given to those that are known to fade. The type of shade is a matter of individual choice; there are many odds and ends that can be used with advantage, but care should be taken to see that any material used does admit a good proportion of filtered light. Too dark a shade will have the effect of paling the natural colour, sometimes making it difficult to be certain of the variety.

In districts surrounded by houses, soot can be very damaging to white, cream and the pale-coloured varieties. Heavy rain will bring down soot particles, and when these fall on well-opened blooms the minute amounts of sulphuric acid produce little rusty burns. In such surroundings it is advisable to screen or shade all pale colours.

For individual flowers the foolscap type of shade is very practical. Some are made of calico with loose bottom rings, and others of varying materials stretched over rigid frames. A cheap shade can be made from stiff white paper made into a cone; the joint should be stapled and the complete cone given a coat of varnish. When dry, a thin piece of wood about $\frac{3}{4}$-inch square is placed over the joint and nailed through to an outer piece about 20 inches long. This allows a stalk of about 8 inches which can be wired or tacked to a separate stake. Some growers fix their shades to the actual flower stake, but this is not recommended. Using a separate stake, the shade may be more freely moved from one bloom to another. Shades and blooms must be rigid, otherwise wind damage will be as bad as sun bleaching.

Scrim or fine open sacking can be used for screening rows of dahlias; this should be stretched well over the plants on either side and secured by strong string to outlying stakes. At intervals a taller stake should be pushed up high in the middle of the scrim and tied round the top. This will prevent sagging in rain and ballooning during heavy winds. See that all blooms are well below the scrim or more damage will ensue by the constant movement.

Shading is best commenced when the first two rows of petals have developed, and should be maintained until the flowers are cut. Some varieties are better without shades, particularly the show and fancy types and those with hard or green eyes. Where possible this type of dahlia should be held with cross-string ties, keeping the centre facing upwards.

A semi-permanent shade that can be quickly run over a dozen plants in a row is easily erected. Four 7 foot 6 inch iron supports are required. These can be made from $\frac{3}{4}$-inch iron pipe usually obtainable from a scrap merchant, or from pieces of $1\frac{1}{4}$-inch angle iron. If the latter is used, $\frac{1}{4}$-inch holes should be drilled through, 1 inch from the top, to take the wire runner. These supports should be driven 2 feet into the ground with a width of 5 feet in between. The length can vary according to the requirements of the exhibitor. Next, a quantity of scrim or loosely woven sacking should be cut into the width of 5 feet and the length required and small brass rings sewn on at intervals of 2 feet along each side of it. The final material required is a small quantity of No. 12 gauge galvanized wire. Cut off two lengths a yard longer than the distance between the posts and twist one end tightly round the top of the end support. Thread on the ringed material and strain and twist the wire round the other stake. It takes very little longer than when dealing with the fixed shading, but it has more advantages. It can quickly be slid back on a dull day or vice versa. Special plants can be shaded without affecting others, and, although not designed for the purpose, it can give a good measure of protection to fully developed blooms during heavy rain. If the plot is permanent, the irons may be left in position. Untwist one end of the wire, slide off the material, coil up the wire and tie to the opposite support. See that the material is thoroughly dry before storing away.

There are many other materials such as old umbrellas, cellophane, cotton-reinforced paper, etc., that can be usefully employed as shading or protective materials. An exhibitor's garden is not designed simply to please the aesthetic taste, it is in the nature of a workshop, and everything that will help to produce the perfect flower should be usefully employed.

ROUTINE SUMMER WORK

By the middle of July the dahlias will have made a great deal of growth; any that appear mottled or dwarfed must be suspected of virus and should be pulled up and burnt, otherwise valuable healthy stock may become infected. A plant newly infected with virus appears quite normal until the end of the season; it is not until cuttings are being propagated or even later that symptoms of the disease may appear.

Check the stakes; some may have rotted and these will quite likely snap in the first high wind. It is advisable to tie three loops of string round the stakes at intervals of a foot or so; it makes for added strength, and should a stake go, the lateral will be held until repairs can be effected. Where plants have made very heavy growth, additional stakes should be used.

Much scorching and fading is prevented by shades, but the exhibitor should see that the shades are firmly fixed to their stakes and the blooms to be protected rigidly fixed to theirs. It is not necessary to place the shades on too early; it will do quite well when the flowers have partially opened.

Long-stemmed giants are best supported by tying thin canes to the stakes and then securing the blooms by two ties, the top tie being made behind the flower near to the calyx. If a pad of cotton wool is placed round the stem before making the tie it will prevent damage and stop the upward trend of earwigs and cutworms.

Hot drying winds play havoc with finishing blooms. Shading will prevent colour bleaching, but it will not offset the amount of water lost by transpiration in a plant that is approximately ninety per cent water. Keep the mulching material wet and remove unwanted flowers at the earliest opportunity.

CUTTING, PACKING AND TRANSPORT

It is advisable to go over the plot a few days before the blooms are required and make a note of those that will be ready for the day. If the days are hot, an overhead spray during the evening will freshen and plump up the flowers. The evening before cutting is a busy time, when the packing cases should be lined with clean soft paper, those to carry pompons padded with cotton wool, leaving a reserve quantity in each case for separating the layers. A quantity of paper will also be required for making ring-pads for the giants. See that plenty of containers are ready for the morning drink; florists' buckets are ideal, as are 7 lb. sweet tins and clean paint cans. On no account use the household bucket, for many an exhibitor has come to grief through the use of this receptacle; the sides slope too much, with the result that the larger blooms are top-heavy and tip out. 1 lb. jam jars or tins will accommodate the pompons and a dozen blooms in each is sufficient if damage is to be avoided. Make a check list of your entries and see that the labels are correct. Spare sets will have to be carried and labels should be written for these; include a few blanks which may have to be written at the show. Get an assistant to help with the cutting, which should be done early in the morning. Flowers may then be damp from dew or overhead spraying, but if placed in the receptacles without crushing, they will slowly dry out and suffer no damage—the trouble comes when flowers are packed damp.

Let the assistant carry the containers round with you, and as each flower is cut, hand it to him to be placed in deep water at once. If the blooms are held too long in the hands, air passes up the stem and often creates air-locks. This is one of the reasons why some flowers will not take up water. Always cut just above the joint; it allows the inter-nodal space to take up water much quicker. Short-jointed blooms will benefit if upward slits are made with a razor blade through the lowest joints, one on each side being sufficient. Some growers seal the ends of the stems in a flame or by placing them in boiling water for a minute or two. When the ends are seen to be shrunken, the blooms should be placed into deep water immediately. As each container is filled, it should be removed and placed in the shade. When the cutting has been completed, the blooms should be stored in a cool, dark room or cellar.

Packing. One must admit that the exhibitor from a distance competes under a handicap; he may have to cut his blooms one to two days before the show, and, because of damage in transit, more spares are required. This means more packing cases and more cost in transport. Whenever possible, long-distance exhibitors are advised to pack late and travel through the night. After many experiments, I find that a great number of flowers tend to sleep, and in this comatose condition they travel firm and fresh, out of water, for a much longer period than during the hours of daylight. I found that dahlias will open and close in a darkened room just as much as they do in the light, and, at the same time, this suggests that the flower is controlled by some emanation from the sun without coming into contact with actual light.

Round or ball-type flowers, like the shows and pompons, often travel badly and, where possible, I advocate the competitor taking complete sets of spares; there is nothing more disheartening than to see a complete vase of pompons blowing, which usually happens when the blooms are fully up in the centre. With a good set of spares the trouble can be easily remedied. In all cases where an exhibitor is showing six vases of six blooms, he should take three spares of each variety and one extra set. In the dozen class the same number of spares and two extra sets should be carried. The small cactus types usually hold their backs well, and it is usually sufficient to take single spares only. Where the giant and large cactus varieties are shown in threes, it is advisable to take extra threes instead of spare blooms; often spare blooms from discarded threes can be used to make up a vase of six distinct varieties. In fact, quite a lot can be accomplished with a little ingenuity. When staging a dozen distinct giant decoratives, it is good policy to pack fifteen distinct; by doing so, the exhibitor is assured of a dozen distinct without duplication, and, as before, the spare blooms will come in for other classes.

Blooms to Avoid. When sorting blooms for packing, discard those with pendent stems, off colours, cross eyes or long eyes, those with green or weak centres and odd sizes. Bicolors should be evenly marked on each petal. Stage each flower with care; when a number are placed in the same vase they should be evenly spaced, with the centres facing level. Judges usually look at the centres first, followed by the stems and backs. All vases being equal in this respect, the flowers are again scrutinized for slight off-colours and odd sizes; trifling items, but sufficient to peg an exhibitor down in keen competition. All vases should be labelled with the name of the variety marked or 'unknown', as the case may be.

Boxes. There can be no hard-and-fast rule as to what constitutes the correct size of a packing case; much depends upon the variety to be carried. Among the giants, one can find blooms of all depths and, by packing flowers of like nature together, quite a lot of room can be saved. For varieties of great depth like Queen Elizabeth, a box 40 by 24 by 8 inches would be necessary to accommodate six blooms. Flatter flowers of the Rita Betty type would pack quite well in a box of the same dimensions, but only 6 inches in depth. Some exhibitors use a dual-purpose box from 10 to 12 inches deep, and by the use of wire brackets these boxes can be adjusted to carry blooms of varying depths, i.e. one deep and one medium set of blooms or two medium sets and a tray of pompons on top. The brackets are made from 12-gauge wire, which can be easily bent with a pair of pliers. Sets of varying depths should be made so that the trays will fit in at 6 inches or 4, as the occasion demands. The brackets can be made to hang over the sides of the box or taken through holes drilled below the lid. When the latter method is adopted, the wire should be cut level with the sides of the box to prevent scratches. The pompon trays are made from chicken wire fastened on light wooden frames about 1½ inches by ¾ inch in depth. They should be of a suitable size to lift in and out quite freely. Pompons will travel well if packed in cotton wool in boxes averaging 30 by 15 by 5 inches.

Arranging the Blooms. Time will be saved if the giant varieties are prepared for packing the previous evening. The stems should be plugged with cotton wool over which a small square of rag should be placed and held in position with a small rubber ring. As each bloom is plugged, it should be immediately put back into water. Do not remove damaged petals before packing, as these will save others being damaged during transit. As each bloom is packed, the surplus water should be squeezed from the stem, and then a thick ring of cotton wool should be ready and the stem taken through this, and then the pillow worked up so that the back of the bloom nestles evenly on the cotton wool. This is a valuable asset to blooms that have to travel long distances.

Cactus varieties travel comfortably if the flowers are lightly and firmly packed. The best method to do this is to have a helper at hand to pass each bloom as required; the first bloom should be laid in with the petals upright against the side of the box. Hold up the petals of the opposite side with one hand and place the next flower with the petals upright against the first, completing one row at a time. It is surprising how many blooms of this type can be packed into one box without damage.

Pompons being the smallest, travel the best; a box averaging 30 by 15 by 5 inches will carry up to eight dozen blooms. Lay a sheet of cotton wool over the bottom of the box and lay in the first row. Place a piece of fluffed-out cotton wool between each pair of flowers and, having completed the first row, lay a strip of wool across the stems just below the blooms and follow with a second row, and in this manner complete the box. All dahlias should be packed from both ends, commencing with the longest-stemmed flowers and gradually working in the shorter ones into the centre. Complete the box by wrapping up a piece of cane in tissue paper and wedging this across the centre; this will prevent any movement.

The ball types, such as the show and fancies, small decoratives and pompons, are the most difficult to pack; the larger the variety, the more the weight will flatten out the backs, and once this happens the spherical form is lost. The larger ball types will require considerable care. There was a time when all show and fancy varieties were cut short and fixed into a cork, wedged and then placed into a short tube, after which they were dropped through holes in their carrying trays or sliding show boards. In some parts of the country they are still exhibited in this manner; in others they have to be staged in vases. For years I tried to find the solution to carrying this type of flower because only about three in each dozen were fit to be staged on arrival.

The best method I have found, so far, is to nail in pieces of wood 6 inches apart through the middle of a box about 6 inches deep. A good size would be about 40 by 24 by 6 inches and a box this size would carry three dozen blooms. The sticks lying across the box should be well padded with cotton wool, neatly bound and tied. A number of strong wires cut from 10- or 12-gauge wire will be required; these should be straight and as long as the flower stems. The dahlia is held with the top of the bloom in the palm of the hand and the wire gently pushed up through the calyx, just sufficiently to hold it rigid; next, the blooms should be tied to the wire, the top tie being as near to the calyx as possible, followed by another tie at the bottom and one in the middle. When all the blooms have been wired, they should be placed in the box carefully by sliding the stem beneath the carrying pieces and tying each bloom firmly to the padded rest. It is necessary that these blooms should be fixed into position from both ends. There will be some space to spare in the middle and if this is covered with wool a number of pompons or collarettes can be accommodated in the same box. It is a job that takes time and patience, but one does get the blooms to the show in a good condition. The ends of the stems are best plugged or covered with a piece of moist wool as for the larger varieties. Never try to pack more blooms than the box will comfortably hold and on no account pack one row of flowers upon another; if this is done, the weight of the top layer will crush the bottom set and most of the contents of the box will be ruined.

On arriving at the show, blooms whose stems have been scorched, or treated by immersion in boiling water, should be placed in a bucket and two inches of stemshould be cut off under water; by this method no air rushes into the vacuum which has been created by the heat treatment, but the stem becomes filled with water which results in the flowers keeping stiff and fresh. Old flowers do not respond as well as those three parts out, and it is good advice not to include old blooms unless these are necessary to make up a bunch of three. Quite a lot depends upon the weather a few days preceding the show. If conditions are cool, oldish blooms will probably last out the day, but the effect of heated tents soon creates flagging in these older flowers. To be safe, it is best to depend on dahlias three-fourths out when the colour is better and the tendency to wilt is not so risky.

There are occasions when three of a kind are required and one usually finds a weak bunch which must be made up with an older flower; this bloom is usually larger than the other two and so creates an unbalanced effect. Removing a few of the larger back petals will help to reduce the size, or it can be so placed in the vase that the adjoining variety will have the effect of making it appear smaller or, by colour contrast, much fresher than it really is. The art of staging well repays close study.

STAGING

The first task on arrival is to get all the blooms into water immediately. The exhibitor is advised to take a number of cans with him, as, in many shows where vases are provided, there are only sufficient for the competitors' exhibits, and exhibitors who take more than their share make it difficult for later arrivals to stage their blooms. The giants should be taken out of their cases first, the plugged ends cut off, and the stems placed in water immediately. Remember, the larger the flower, the more it drinks and the sooner it should be placed into deep water; this is especially so after a long journey. If the sets of flowers are placed in water in their order of size, not much wilting will occur.

When all the blooms have been cut and placed in water, check up and collect the requisite number of vases for staging. Those vases that are to hold pompons should be filled with privet or some shrubby material which should be cut off level with the top of the vase. Some of the other, thinner-stemmed varieties may require wedging, but this is best done as the flowers are being placed in position. One of the difficulties in exhibiting dahlias is having to stage three huge giants in a 10-inch vase; even when these have been coaxed into position, there is not enough water to keep up with the transpiration that is continually going on, and the effect of this is quickly seen on a hot day. I know of one exhibitor who placed small cubes of ice in his vases, and one must admit that his blooms kept better than most. I also noticed he brought the ice in a vacuum flask —a case of ingenuity rewarded! During staging, do not go round comparing exhibits with other exhibitors or let others talk to you; doing this may cost you a prize. There will be plenty of time for discussion after judging.

Show schedules are usually issued a few months in advance of the show and intending exhibitors should be fully conversant with the framing of the various classes. It is easy to trip up over the words 'kind' and 'varieties'; also the word 'distinct' can frequently cause trouble. Here is an example: 'Giant Decorative Dahlias, three vases distinct, three blooms in each vase', and another, 'Three vases, three blooms in each vase, distinct varieties'. The first means three blooms of the same variety in each vase, in the second case nine distinct varieties are required.

To help the framing of schedules, the National Dahlia Society has compiled a sectional classification list (see page 114) and also a classified list of dahlias in which, as far as possible, all listed varieties have been placed in their correct sections; each year the list is checked and the necessary revisions are made. Exhibitors at shows held under the auspices of the society must stage blooms that comply with this classification list, but this rule is not enforceable at other shows unless this is definitely stated in their schedule. When this is the rule, it is the duty of the secretary to have copies of the classification list on hand for intending exhibitors to study. All members of the National Dahlia Society receive copies of this list, but there are many dahlia growers who do not know of it.

In some schedules the classes for smaller dahlias contain a size rule such as 'not over 5 inches across,' or 'not exceeding 5 inches in diameter'; this does, to some extent, indicate what is required. Experienced exhibitors usually know the correct blooms to stage, although one cannot be too rigid when it comes to the small, borderline and medium varieties; often one type overlaps the other and confusion arises in shows not abiding by the classification list. The exhibitor should be careful in staging blooms where the size is given, especially if young flowers are staged on the previous night. Dahlias grow rapidly in water and many an exhibit (mine included) has been disqualified for being over the requisite size.

Artificial Supports. When a show schedule makes no mention of artificial support, it is up to the exhibitor to use any artifice that will enable him to stage his blooms to the best advantage; for instance, pompons make a splendid exhibit when placed into wire frames. I know of no better sight than that of twelve bunches of pompons on their triangular wire frames, exhibited against a black background. Cactus varieties in bunches of three when placed on wires are very effective on a tiered stand with a backcloth. Wires are made in strength according to the size of flower they are to accommodate, the giant decoratives and cactus requiring extra stiff wire.

Packing pompon dahlias to take to the show. The heads are placed on cotton wool.

Show dahlias are tied firmly to horizontal struts padded with cotton wool.

Left: A looped wire is tied in position to support the heavy head of a large bloom
Right: A well-staged vase of small decoratives.

The winning exhibit of a dozen giants. Kelvin, the best giant in the show, is the second bloom, top left.

For giant decoratives, which are usually exhibited as single specimens, use a straight piece of wire with a circular or square foot an inch long. Footwires should be made in various lengths; any too long can have a piece cut off the top. To wire a bloom, one merely pushes the support up into the calyx in front of the stem and ties it in three places. For giant cactus, a loop wire with a foot makes the best support; the stem of the flower is put through the loop, and the calyx is also taken through and tied tightly to the horizontal piece of wire that ends in the loop. By tying the calyx firmly, the head is prevented from jumping the stem; this can easily happen when stems are strained to fit a three-wire which requires semi-angular bending to fit a vase.

Pompon frames are constructed from birdcage wire; they should be made to a given size and neatly soldered. All the wires are quite easy to make. For long, thin-stemmed flowers, a loop spiral wire with a round foot is a very useful gadget. First, a small loop is made at the top, then comes a straight length, followed by a spiral or several loops in succession; these should be made in various sizes so that the loops are towards the bottom of the vase. It is not necessary to place all the flowers in wires. For instance, if six blooms were being staged, the top back flower and the two in front could be in wire loops. With these in position, it is quite easy to fill up the vase with wedging material, trim off level, and place the remaining three blooms in position without supports. Wires without some sort of feet are apt to keep swinging round, but this simple bent-wire device will prevent this happening. All wires will look better for a lick of pale green paint.

The words 'no artificial support' means that no form of wiring, wire frames or thin canes is permissible to support the flower stems above them, neither should any vase-packing material stand so high that it supports an otherwise semi-pendent bloom. The use of privet, fine reeds, or any shrubby material is useful for packing vases, but all these materials must be trimmed off level with the top of the vase. All fine-stemmed dahlias can be arranged to advantage when the vases contain packing materials.

There are occasions when exhibitors find that some of their flowers are too short in the stem, and in this case a method must be devised to wedge them in the vase and still comply with the rules. The pompons and small decoratives will usually stand rigid with only an inch or so of stem in the vases, but the heavier flowers will be better for a stronger bottom support. A piece of wire can be pushed up a thick, fleshy stem or a thinner-stemmed bloom can be inserted into a thicker piece of hollow dahlia stem; both these supports must be cut short enough to allow of the natural stem being an inch or so in water. This complies with the rules and does not constitute artificial support, any more than if the blooms were wedged into the top of a packed vase—it is merely a stem lengthener.

Some rules state that dahlia foliage only is to be used; for this I suggest the foliage from pot roots; it is harder and will stand up and last better than the natural foliage. If the natural foliage is left on the flower stem, it uses up water which could with advantage be taken up by the flower; long-stemmed blooms and the giant varieties are best trimmed of foliage when cut. If foliage is left on giants, it soon goes limp and all the time it is making heavy demands on the intake of water; this results in the flower wilting much more quickly than would have been the case if the bloom had been trimmed. Never allow dahlia foliage to become submerged, as it quickly gives off poisonous compounds, which also leads to the dahlias flagging.

To prevent water becoming stagnant, place a few pieces of charcoal in each vase. Aspirins will not prolong the life of the dahlia, but they will make the life of the exhibitor a little more pleasant when things go awkwardly—usually just before judging—when things are most hectic and when a little extra concentration might well bring the coveted prize. Sugar and glycerine have their adherents, the latter being the better of the two. It seems to work well with autumn foliage. So why not with dahlias? One ounce to a gallon of water is recommended. A solution much favoured by American exhibitors is made from hydrazine sulphate in the proportion of one ounce to a quart of water. When applied, it is diluted to one to two tablespoonfuls per gallon, to which is added the same quantity of sugar in solution.

STAGECRAFT

Many a prize has been lost through lack of stagecraft, i.e. colour harmonizing one variety with another to accentuate their beauty instead of creating colour clashes. Avoid placing two reds together, but, where possible, separate them with white or pink; purples and mauves are enhanced by cream and yellow; deep maroon will throw up scarlet, orange and yellow; white is always safe to split dark colours. It is not always your particular exhibit that is likely to create a colour clash; very often it is caused by the neighbouring exhibitor. Watch what is being staged on both sides of your exhibit.

Maybe an extra large bloom has been placed next to one of your weakest. Get busy and make a change round. In doing so, you might try to turn the tables on your neighbour. It is quite possible that he has noticed your vase of crimsons and, to make them look more dull, has placed a vase of bright scarlet blooms on the edge of his exhibit; this, of course, accentuates the colour in his. Counter this by changing your crimsons for a vase of bright yellow; to do this may mean rearranging several vases both for size and colour, but it is worth the extra care.

Try to place the coarser blooms in the back row, especially in classes for a dozen giants or nine bunches of cactus; although the distance is only a few feet, it creates the illusion of more even-sized flowers. Try to stage your most perfect blooms at eye level—in tiered staging this would come in the centre row. When making changes, do so a few minutes before the bell rings; otherwise the other exhibitor may get wise and decide to do likewise. Years ago, when show dahlias were the chief exhibits, it became a habit to place several weak or smaller blooms on the boards, the exhibitor keeping several of the best still in the travelling box until just before judging, when quick changes would be made. Usually the newcomer fell for this trick; not so the old hands. Often during the last quarter of an hour it looked as if a kind of dahlia chess were being played. Even after the hall had been cleared, a competitor would find he had left his lunch-box behind. I think stagecraft is the correct term.

No showman went to a show without taking a bunch of elderberry piths; these were short pieces of elderberry stem about six inches long and the same thickness as the ordinary dahlia stem. When a show dahlia is set up it is pushed through a cork, pulled fairly tight and held in place with a wedge made from another piece of dahlia stem. Other blooms would grow larger, causing some to separate from their stems, and when this happened first-aid was given. First, a piece of pith was sharpened, next the dahlia was held with the centre in the palm of the hand and with a sharp penknife the residual stem behind the calyx was neatly cut out; after this operation the sharp end of the pith was pushed up firmly, and so the flower was given a new stem; water is taken up through the pith interior, and flowers on false stems will last as long as the natural ones. This was an aid, and not faking; shows and fancies were judged on form, texture and colour; no stems were ever seen; at times I have known six out of the twelve blooms to be on pith stems. The same applies today where this section is still shown on boards.

JUDGING DAHLIA BLOOMS

In trying to standardize judging, the National Dahlia Society has worked out a system of points. This should be a guide to both judges and exhibitors at future shows.

	Points
Freedom from blemish	20
Freshness	20
Form-symmetry and perfection of centre	20
Stem—a good stem must be long and rigid enough to carry the blooms naturally at a suitable angle, about 45 degrees. Length and quality of genuine foot stalk as distinct from stalk and stem will be a consideration	20
Colour—perfection of tone according to variety	10
Size—the bloom to be true to character according to its class	10
	100

All things being equal, arrangement of exhibit will be taken into consideration.

Finally during the hours of staging do not go round comparing points with other exhibitors, and do not let others talk to you. Distraction at this period may cost you a prize. There will be plenty of time for discussion after judging. Be sure the name and competitor's card have been correctly placed and make a final check on the number of blooms staged. Many times I have found vases with a bloom short or one too many.

Do not blame the judges because their verdict disagrees with yours; it is far wiser to have a talk with one of the adjudicators and find out what pegged you down. Accept the results in a sporting spirit; defeat is often the quickest way to learn.

CLASSIFICATION AND DESCRIPTION OF DAHLIAS

The following revised classification and description of dahlias has been drafted to assist exhibitors in making their entries in the classes in which they are desirous of competing. Reference should also be made to the Society's Classified List of Varieties.

Revised 1951

Section I. SINGLE DAHLIAS

Single Dahlias should not exceed 4 inches in diameter and have a single outer ring of ray florets; the centre forms a disk.

Class Ia. Show Singles should have smooth ray florets, broad and overlapping, forming a perfectly round flower.

Class Ib. Singles. In these the ray florets do not so completely overlap and the tips are separated.

Section II. STAR DAHLIAS

Small, with two or three rows of somewhat pointed ray florets, not or scarcely overlapping at their more or less recurved margins, and forming a cup-shaped flower with a disk.

Section III. ANEMONE-FLOWERED DAHLIAS

Anemone-flowered Dahlias have an outer ring of flattened ray florets surrounding a dense group of tubular florets, which are longer than the disk florets in Single Dahlias.

Section IV. COLLARETTE DAHLIAS

Collarette Dahlias have one or more rings of flat ray florets with a ring of small florets (the collar) approximately half the length of the ray florets.

Class IVa. Collarette Single Dahlias have only a single row of ray florets and one 'collar' with a central disk.

Class IVb. Collarette Peony-flowered Dahlias have two or more rows of ray florets and 'collars' with central disk.

Class IVc. Collarette Decorative Dahlias are similar but fully double.

Section V. PEONY-FLOWERED DAHLIAS

Peony-flowered Dahlias have flowers consisting of two or more rows of more or less flattened ray florets with a central disk.

Class Va. Large Peony-flowered Dahlias with flowers over 7 inches in diameter.

Class Vb. Medium Peony-flowered Dahlias with flowers between 5 and 7 inches in diameter.

Class Vc. Small Peony-flowered Dahlias with flowers less than 5 inches in diameter.

Section VI. DECORATIVE DAHLIAS

Decorative Dahlias have fully double flowers, showing no disk. The ray florets are broad, scarcely revolute, more or less flat or slightly twisted and usually less pointed.

Class VIa. Giant-flowered Decorative Dahlias with flowers over 10 inches in diameter.

Class VIb. Large-flowered Decorative Dahlias with flowers over 8 inches and not exceeding 10 inches in diameter.

Class VIc. Medium-flowered Decorative Dahlias with flowers over 6 inches and not exceeding 8 inches in diameter.

Class VId. Small-flowered Decorative Dahlias with flowers over 3 inches and not exceeding 6 inches in diameter.

Class VIe. Miniature-flowered Decorative Dahlias with flowers not exceeding 3 inches in diameter.

Section VII. DOUBLE SHOW AND FANCY DAHLIAS

Double Show and Fancy Dahlias have fully double flowers, over 3 inches in diameter, almost globular, with central florets like the outer but smaller; florets with margins incurved, tubular, short and blunt at the mouth.

Section VIII. POMPON DAHLIAS

Pompon Dahlias have flowers like those of Double Show and Fancy Dahlias, but smaller.

Class VIIIa. Large-flowered Pompon Dahlias with flowers over 2 inches but usually not exceeding 3 inches in diameter.

Class VIIIb. Small-flowered Pompon Dahlias with flowers not exceeding 2 inches in diameter.

Section IX. CACTUS DAHLIAS

Cactus Dahlias have fully double flowers, showing no disk. The ray florets are usually pointed, narrower than those of Decorative Dahlias, revolute for a part of their length, and either straight or incurving.

Class IXa. Giant-flowered Cactus Dahlias have flowers over 10 inches in diameter.

Class IXb. Large-flowered Cactus Dahlias have flowers over 8 inches in diameter but usually not exceeding 10 inches in diameter.

Class IXc. Medium-flowered Cactus Dahlias have flowers over 6 inches in diameter but usually not exceeding 8 inches in diameter.

Class IXd. Small-flowered Cactus Dahlias have flowers over 3 inches but usually not exceeding 6 inches in diameter.

Class IXe. Miniature-flowered Cactus Dahlias have flowers usually not exceeding 3 inches in diameter.

Section X. MISCELLANEOUS DAHLIAS

Any Dahlias which do not fall into one of the foregoing sections, e.g. Orchid-flowered Dahlias.

Section XI. DWARF BEDDING DAHLIAS

Plants do not usually exceed 24 inches in height. The flowers may belong to any of the foregoing sections.

CHAPTER SEVEN

Gladioli

BY ROLAND IKIN

THE GLADIOLUS is a very popular flower, and the number of amateurs who are interested in its culture increases each year. It makes an admirable exhibition flower, as it can be grown well in a great variety of soils and responds to that little extra care which makes the difference between the produce of the real enthusiast and that of the ordinary gardener. Moreover, there is so much variety in gladioli that many different classes can be devised, and this adds greatly to the interest of a gladiolus show.

CHOICE AND PREPARATION OF CORMS

First, let us give some consideration to the corms from which the exhibition blooms are grown. Corms are developed from seed, and hybridizers may grow thousands of seedlings, from which probably one or two worth-while varieties are selected for propagation as named varieties. Once a variety is selected for this purpose, propagation proceeds by the growing of the cormlets, which are lifted with the corms. The life of a variety varies very considerably, some varieties becoming extinct in a matter of fifteen years or so, while others of a more robust constitution have a life of over thirty years.

Corms, as supplied by the retailers, differ considerably as regards both size and shape, and it is not correct to imagine that the bigger the circumference of the planted corm, the better will be the resulting bloom. Many of the corms with a large circumference are rather flat and pancake-like. This generally denotes old age. The younger corms are quite different in shape, and often the height is greater than the girth. They have a neat, plump appearance. The intending exhibitor is strongly recommended to plant the latter type as being more reliable and more likely to produce the desired results. Do not let me mislead anyone. I do not wish to imply that any small corm which is plump-looking will give a perfect show bloom. I would say that the diameter of young corms should be at least one and a quarter inches. Below this you cannot expect the best of results.

Good blooms are obtained at times from the largest of corms, but it is essential that all the eyes, with the exception of one, be removed before planting, so that only one bloom is allowed to develop. This may appear a very drastic measure to some readers, especially where expensive corms are concerned. In such cases it is recommended that rather than allow two eyes to develop on the corm, the corm be cut into two parts, and each part be allowed to grow one bloom. When this procedure is adopted, the corm should be cut through the centre, leaving an equal portion of root base on each part. After cutting, the cut portions should be treated with charcoal or allowed to dry in the sun before planting.

While on the subject of corms, let me add that all should be thoroughly inspected and disinfected before planting. For inspection it is necessary to remove the outer coverings or husks so that the solid corm may be seen. Disease, if any is present, cannot otherwise be detected. The ideal, of course, is a corm free from any blemish whatever. Not all corms, however, are found in this condition, and the most common disease encountered is scab (*Bacterium marginatum*). This is quite easy to identify. Small brown or reddish-brown spots having a glazed appearance, with the centres generally darker in colour than the outer edges, will be observed on the corm. These may easily be removed with the point of a penknife, after which it is safe to plant the corm.

Another disease which may be found is dry rot, when dark-brown or black lesions, which are sunken and have very hard surfaces, will be seen on the corms. This disease, once established, may progress very rapidly, and it is advisable to destroy any corms affected.

All corms should be disinfected before planting, and two safe mediums for this purpose can be recommended, lysol and the mercurial preparation Aretan. Lysol should be used by adding one teaspoonful to a quart of water and immersing the corms for six hours. This may be done at any time within a period of six weeks before planting. Where Aretan is used, this should be done in accordance with the maker's instructions.

Quite recently another disease has shown up very much on the gladiolus horizon, which, for want of a more specific name, is referred to as 'premature yellowing'. As this name indicates, the leaves of affected plants turn yellow; this is the first stage of the development of the disease, and, as it progresses, the whole plant turns a brownish colour and becomes quite dead.

The first signs of yellowing usually appear about mid-June, when faint traces appear on the outer leaves of the plant, and there is, at present, no known cure. It is wise to lift the plant and burn it in its entirety. Before doing so, however, the root system should be examined, as traces of the disease will be found there. The roots appear to be under-developed, but, if closely examined, it will be observed that the root tips are apparently dead. They have been attacked by the disease which is the cause of the condition of the plant above soil level and have, in fact, died back from the tips of the roots for quite a distance.

In America gladiolus growers have been troubled for many years with a disease known as Fusarium Yellows, and, from book knowledge only, some interested persons concluded that this disease had reached this country, and that in fact, 'premature yellowing' was Fusarium Yellows.

Experiments since carried out have proved this contention to be correct to a point, it being established that this disease is the cause of the yellowing in some instances, but not in all.

Readers should be on the look-out for further information on this subject as it becomes available, and in the meantime not take any risks. Destroy all affected plants, and do not grow gladioli in the same ground each year if this can possibly be avoided.

CULTIVATION

Soil. We cannot possibly choose the soil we would like, and it is therefore a matter of making the best use of what is available. Gladioli, however, are very accommodating subjects, and will grow in most soils. Any soil which will produce a good, clean crop of potatoes may be regarded as one from which good gladiolus blooms may be also produced. The ideal is probably a good medium loam. Whatever the kind of soil, ample drainage is an absolute essential, for although gladioli are moisture-loving plants, they do not appreciate stagnant water in the region of the root system. Heavy soil may be made more amenable by the incorporation of strawy manure, and sand or peat. Deep digging is advisable and should be done wherever possible in the autumn or early winter.

Where manure is available, it should be forked into the bottom of the trench at a minimum depth of, say, nine inches. The corms should never be allowed to come into direct contact with manure. As a substitute for manure, peat or compost may be used, and a liberal dressing should be given at the time of digging as with manure. The use of artificials is a question on which opinions differ, but bonemeal and fish manure are generally accepted as being very beneficial. Either of these may be worked into the soil a few weeks before planting is commenced. At this stage, too, the soil should be broken down until a fine tilth is obtained. Time should always be allowed after this operation for the soil to settle down, and it is advisable to have it completed by the end of February.

Site. In choosing a site for the gladioli, the one essential thing to remember is that they must be given the maximum amount of sunshine. Avoid shade at all costs, whether from adjacent buildings or from trees or tall shrubs. For exhibition purposes, one should not endeavour to grow gladioli in a herbaceous border. Provide them with a sunny, open position, and plant the corms in beds; do not attempt to grow any other flowers along with them. The size of the beds must vary, and must be governed by the amount of space available and the shape of the plot. The beds should be, wherever possible, three to three and a half feet in width and of the maximum length obtainable. The corms should be planted in rows, leaving, if possible, one foot each way between them. This measurement I consider represents the maximum distance between the plants, and may be reduced to nine inches each way where the amount of space available is very limited, provided good treatment is given during growth.

Planting. It is not possible to give a specific date for planting, nor is it desirable that all the planting should be done on a single occasion. The best method to adopt is to plant at fortnightly intervals, from about the third week of March to the end of May, if it is intended to exhibit at various shows. I have personally successfully exhibited in a season from the third week in July to the last week in September from plantings which commenced on March 26 and continued at intervals until the first week of June. I keep records of both planting and blooming dates for all varieties, and this provides a very reliable guide over a number of years. It is a practice strongly recommended to all exhibitors.

The methods of planting may vary somewhat, according to the number of corms to be planted and to the personal preference of the individual. A trowel or a dibber may be used for planting. The depth of planting is dependent to a certain extent upon the nature of the soil. Where it is light, a depth of six inches to the base of the corm is not too much, and for heavier soil, a depth of from four to five inches may be considered as the most satisfactory.

Whatever the nature of the soil, or the depth of planting, it is recommended that at the base of each hole some damp sand or a mixture of sand and fine ash be placed. A personal preference here is for the use of sand only. After inserting the corm, further sand may be placed on it, but this is not absolutely essential. It will, however, ensure the corm lifting in a nice, clean condition. The advantages of using the sand or the mixture underneath the corm are to ensure that its base is resting firmly on the ground, and that it has a good start into growth. The fine, rather tender roots will appreciate its presence very much. Some growers rather object to the use of a dibber for planting, inasmuch as it is deemed by them to leave an air-pocket at the bottom of each hole. Where sand is used, as here recommended, this objection is obviously overcome.

Since at exhibitions either it is essential to name varieties, or exhibitors are requested to do so, care should be taken at the time of planting to see that the whole planting is correctly labelled. As a safeguard too, and also for one's personal satisfaction, it is strongly recommended that a plan of the beds be made, and kept, in case of necessity. Many unexpected things may happen between planting and blooming time, and this extra precaution will often be well repaid.

After planting, there is not much that can be done until the growth appears above the ground, and for a time after this happens the chief operation is regular and frequent hoeing. This is very important for keeping weeds in check and the soil aerated. Care should be taken not to cause any damage at all to the growing plants by the use of the hoe, and it is safer to remove by hand the weeds found in very close proximity to them. Moisture plays a very important part in the development of the perfect spike, but generally speaking, it is not necessary to begin watering during the early stages of growth. Should, however, an exceptional spell of dry weather come early in the season, water rather than have the plants struggle along in a very dry soil.

Feeding. The question of feeding is one which calls for special consideration, and it is a mistake to think that a lot of top-dressing is necessary in the early stages of the plant's development. It should be remembered that the purpose of feeding during growth is to help to give size and quality to the bloom, and that it cannot possibly have any effect on the number of individual flowers on a spike. This factor is decided very early in the life of the plant, and the importance of having a good, rich medium in the bed before planting cannot be overstressed.

When five leaves have developed on a plant, one may feel the flower-spike within the main stem, and from this point onwards its growth is quite rapid. This is considered to be the most appropriate time to commence feeding. Fertilizers with a high nitrogen content should not be used at this stage, for they are quick acting and are rather in the nature of stimulants. Applications of weak liquid manure or a good brand of fish manure will be found much more beneficial. Where liquid manure is used, it should be diluted until it is the colour of weak tea or lager beer, and when the agent used is fish manure, this should be applied between the rows at about the rate of two ounces per yard run. Whatever feed is used, it should be applied when the soil is damp, and, if possible, well watered in.

After this initial dressing, further applications may be left until the flower spike reaches the top of the main stem and is ready to burst through. From then until the bottom bud shows colour, applications should be at ten-day intervals. Frequent dressings of small quantities are much to be preferred to a single large one which may be an overdose and do more harm than good.

If a stimulant is required to give additional length to the stem, and with some varieties this is a decided advantage, then it should be applied when the spike has completely appeared through the stem. A weak solution of nitrate of soda or sulphate of ammonia will serve the purpose well. Alternatively, a proprietary brand of this type of stimulant may be used in accordance with the maker's directions. A day or two after any application of fertilizer, the hoe should be used over the plot. I have mentioned previously that at the fifth leaf stage, feeding should commence, and from this stage until the bottom flower on the spike is open, the plants should not be short of water.

Water should be applied in generous quantity; really good doses at weekly or ten-day intervals will do good. Small quantities applied frequently will not benefit at all. Get the water well down below corm level so that the roots will receive direct benefit.

Staking. When the flower spikes are showing, the plants should be staked so as to keep them straight and also to prevent damage to the root system, which may be caused by wind swaying the plants about. It is about this time of the growing season that a promising-looking bloom may be ruined overnight by a caterpillar attack. This risk may be eliminated by several applications of a nicotine insecticide spray given at fortnightly intervals and commencing at about the same time as the first feed is given.

To produce exhibition blooms from plants grown as I have now suggested, should not be difficult, but care must be taken to ensure that the spikes develop along the right lines. Occasionally, as the bud pushes its way between the sheaf-like leaves, it becomes stuck. A keen look-out should be kept for any such happening, and, if found, the spike should be released. Neglect to do this may result in a stunted or misshapen bloom. As the flower heads develop, too, a watch should be kept for any buds which are growing out of shape, and these may be gently handled and induced to face as required for the perfect symmetry of the flower.

Shading. The question of the shading of blooms is one on which opinions may differ. At most shows, shading is allowed, but at some it is not. Certainly, more blooms may be opened while the bottom one is quite fresh if shading in some form is resorted to. The most popular method adopted by amateur enthusiasts is the boxing of the blooms. This is done by means of a box, say, three feet long, ten inches wide and about six inches deep. Remove the front and one end, nail to a stake of the required length, which must be a strong one, and place over the flower head when the bottom floret is showing colour. As the florets continue to open, strips of strong paper or cloth should be placed across the front of the box to protect the bloom from either rain or hot sun.

Fine blooms are obtained this way but there is a tendency for many blooms which appear perfect on the eve of a show to carry one or two wilted blooms by the time they are judged. Personally, I do not use any boxes for shading, chiefly because of lack of time. I grow between two and three thousand corms and exhibit at as many shows as possible. My method is to have the blooms cut when the bottom flower opens and to keep in water in as cool a place as possible.

Lifting and Storing. Once the blooming season is over we come to the time for lifting and storing the corms. The importance of this operation cannot be over-stressed if the corms are to be wintered satisfactorily and in a sound condition when the planting season arrives once again. The time for the lifting may be from four to six weeks after blooming. Weather conditions must be considered in fixing the actual date, however, for the soil should be reasonably dry when the lifting is done, and it is better to delay a week or two rather than attempt to do the work when the soil is in a very water-sodden state. The drier the corms are when lifted the easier will it be to complete the drying-out process afterwards.

With regard to the actual operation of lifting, this should be done very carefully, the aim being to ensure that the corm and all the cormlets attached, are taken from the ground without leaving any of the cormlets behind, and without doing damage. A simple and effective method is to use either a spade or a garden fork, digging down about six inches from the plant and to a depth sufficient to get well underneath the corm. Then gently lever the tool which is being used so that the plant is lifted and the surrounding soil loosened. The stem of the plant may then be pulled gently, and the whole will come away from the soil intact. Some people still like to tie the plants in bundles and hang them up to dry. The better way is to cut the stem about one inch above the top of the corm immediately, and place the corms with as much soil as possible removed and with the primary roots trimmed, but with the cormlets still attached, in flat boxes in single layers, for them to dry off. The boxes in which tomatoes are imported are easily obtained and are most suitable for this purpose. Where only a few corms of a variety are grown, divisions may be made in the boxes by the use of either thin wood or stiff cardboard. They should be placed in position as each variety is lifted, rather than beforehand, so that the fullest use is made of the boxes.

When the weather is fine the boxes should be left in the open for the contents to dry, as sun and wind will do the work very effectively. From time to time the corms should be inspected, and turned over when necessary. Once lifted, care should be taken to ensure that they are never exposed to rain and when the weather is unfavourable the boxes may be stacked in an airy shed or cool greenhouse. It is most essential that this drying is done thoroughly, and it should not be hurried. About a month after the time of lifting take hold of a corm above the cormlets and then, holding it in the left hand, take hold of the old corm which is at the base of the new one, with the thumb and index finger of the right hand, and give it a twist, when it should easily be detached from the new corm. If it does not come away easily it may be taken for granted that further drying off is advisable. When one is satisfied from this test that the corms are really dried off, they should all be treated in this manner. Make sure that they are all sound but do not at this stage remove the outer husks, but wait until the early spring inspection as advised at the beginning of the chapter.

This operation completed, the corms should be replaced in clean dry boxes where there is no possibility of damage from frost, but where air can circulate freely among them. Any room where there is a temperature averaging 50° F. with a minimum of 40° will be quite suitable. It is, however, better to have a temperature slightly above this average than one which is below it. The cormlets may be kept in paper bags and placed in the boxes along with the corms.

Unless the season is a very abnormal one, lifting may start towards the end of September and finish in early October. In the south of the country these dates may be about a fortnight earlier. By the end of October the cleaning-up process should be well under way.

The corms should be inspected in the store at intervals of from two to three weeks to make sure that they are remaining in a sound condition. Each one should be handled and, if any show signs of becoming soft or shrivelled, they should be removed and burnt.

Propagation. Where it is desired to plant the cormlets for increasing one's stock, they should be peeled before planting. This is rather a long job but may start in January, and is quite a good way of spending some of the long winter evenings. Quite a good way of doing it is to place a cormlet between the thumb and finger and gently squeeze, when the husk will be heard to crack. From this crack it is quite easy to remove the whole covering.

The cormlets may be planted at the same date as the earliest planting of the corms and they should be placed in very fine soil at a depth of about two inches with a similar distance between each one.

EXHIBITING

Too great care cannot be exercised in the packing of blooms for transport to a show. Many exhibitors have wooden boxes specially made for the purpose. These have racks or trays in them which enables each bloom to be securely tied. This is, I believe, the best method to adopt; ''tis far better to be sure than sorry'.

'What points do judges look for in an exhibition gladiolus', one is often asked. Well, from observations made over a number of years it would seem that opinions differ. However, I state that a good exhibition spike should have a straight stem and flower head, a minimum of five flowers open and should be well balanced—the flowers being similar in size and distributed equally on the stem. The flowers should all face forwards so that the stem is practically

Left: Supporting a young plant with a bamboo cane. *Right:* Tying an older plant. Wires down each side of the row also help to give support.

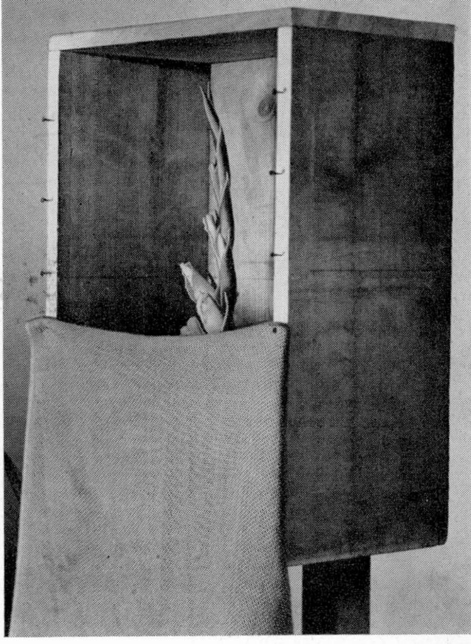

A specimen spike should have as many blooms as possible fully open. To achieve this a hessian shade holds back the lower blooms (seen right).

Left: An exhibit of primulinus gladioli showing the slender arching spikes and drooping heads. *Right:* A first-prize exhibit of six first-class spikes

hidden when the blooms are fully developed. The spike should be at least up to the average for the particular variety, as regards both the length and the size of the individual flowers. The whole should be of a fresh and clean appearance.

Faults to be strictly avoided are: bottom flowers wilted or removed; flowers damaged or with the edges torn off; flowers badly placed; flowers not true to colour due to flecking or streaking, and bent or crooked stems. All flowers should be shown without artificial supports and should be correctly named, whether the schedule specifically calls for it or not.

Finally, let me remind readers that not all the varieties on the market are capable of producing blooms of exhibition quality. Some are useful for decorative purposes only. I cannot here give the best varieties for exhibition. Lists are often given in *Amateur Gardening* and will be found very helpful. Also, as exhibitors, readers will have opportunities themselves to see what is winning at the shows. In addition, they will benefit by experience and by the keeping of detailed records of the performance of all the varieties they themselves grow.

CHAPTER EIGHT

Pansies and Violas

BY HOWARD H. CRANE, F.L.S.

ALTHOUGH IN the south specialization in the growing of exhibition pansies and violas as such has waned, in the north there is still considerable interest in their cultivation. Probably owing to conditions generally, there has been a falling-off in the propagation of the good old named varieties (both bedding and exhibition), and few worth-while new ones have come to the fore in recent years. Propagation by seed has become more popular, but no trouble has been taken to propagate outstanding seedlings by cuttings. It would seem that many growers do not appreciate what constitutes a good type of pansy or viola.

The FANCY PANSY of the florist of many years ago had to conform rigidly to certain well-defined standards. It is opportune to mention the attributes which a good type of exhibition fancy pansy should possess.

Form. The bloom should be nearly perfectly circular, flat and smooth, without wavy or crinkled edges, the bottom petal almost covering the lower half of the flower and with its top edge horizontal.

Texture. Petals should be velvety and of stout substance, lying closely over each other.

Colour and markings. The 'blotch' should be dense, covering the whole of the three lower petals, with the exception of a narrow belt of colour on the margins, the top petals the same colour as the blotch or the margins, and sometimes diffused.

Eye. Bright orange, distinct and without rays or markings.

Size. Not less than two inches across.

At one time there was another distinct type of pansy known as the SHOW PANSY. The standards and markings to which blooms had to conform were different from those of the fancy pansy. With the exception of a very few varieties, which can still be found in the north, the show pansy is almost extinct, and it is not proposed, therefore, to deal specially with it.

In an EXHIBITION VIOLA, the points to be looked for are as follows:

Form. A well-proportioned bloom with large petals, the bottom one of good size forming nearly half the flower.

Texture. Petals should be of stout substance, lying flat on each other.

Colour and markings. Any colour or combination of colours.

Eye. Yellow or orange in colour; neat, and preferably without rays or markings.

Size. As large as possible without undue coarseness.

Plants of pansies and violas grown with the object of producing exhibition blooms need careful culture and attention. It is necessary, therefore, that they should be grown in well-prepared beds of a formal character so that attention may be concentrated on them.

CULTIVATION

Site. A convenient width for the beds is four feet or thereabouts; the length depends on the number of plants grown and the layout of the garden. Space should be allowed for a path of adequate width along at least one side of the bed.

A reasonably open situation should be chosen, but if a position where some shelter from hot midday sun is available, this will be an advantage. In very exposed situations it may be possible to afford some shade from a row of sweet peas or runner beans planted for the purpose. Such filtered sunshine is very suitable. Otherwise artificial shading can be resorted to, as explained later.

Soil. Pansies and violas thrive in a well-drained, free-working loam; if the available soil is not of this type, it must be improved. The bed should be deeply dug at least two spits deep or bastard trenched—preferably some weeks before planting—so that the soil may weather and be in a friable condition at planting time. If spring planting is to be carried out, digging should be carried out during the winter. A generous dressing of bone-meal or well-rotted horse manure at digging time can be recommended.

If the soil is a heavy one, incorporate plenty of grit, composted material, burnt earth, old manure and any substance calculated to make it more easily workable. A dressing of lime is advantageous, both mechanically and in setting free plant foods. The bed should be raised some six inches above ground level. With a light soil, the addition of cow manure, compost and other humus-making material will do much to improve it.

Should the soil be very unsuitable, it would be well worth while to import a few loads of good loam with which to make up the bed. When using new loam, keep a sharp look-out for wireworms; in the circumstances it would be well to apply a volatile fumigant at the base of each trench at digging time and so destroy these and other pests.

Planting. In deciding whether to plant in the autumn or the spring, not only will local conditions of soil and climate be important factors, but the time at which the blossoms are to be ready will also have to be borne in mind. Plants put in in the autumn will in the ordinary way flower earlier the following year than those planted later on in the spring.

If autumn planting is decided on, it will be necessary to plan so that the soil will settle down and be in a workable condition by the middle to the end of September. It is highly desirable for the plants to become established before severe weather sets in. A good mulch of a sandy compost applied a week or two after planting adds to the well-being of the plants during the winter months. Equal parts of loam, peat or leaf-mould and sand make a suitable compost.

On heavy soils and in gardens not well drained, it is safer to wait until the spring before planting. Some varieties of pansy and viola are very intolerant of cold, wet soil conditions, and it would be almost useless to plant them in such unsuitable quarters.

With spring planting—which can be done at any time from the middle of March onwards, when weather and soil conditions are favourable—once the plants have begun to throw out new roots they soon make headway, particularly with the advent of the more genial weather expected as the season advances. Avoid planting too early in March if there are bitter east winds and the weather is generally uncongenial.

In order that the plants may be given as good a start as possible—and this applies particularly to plants packed and sent from a distance—it is well worth while making up a sandy compost to have handy for use at the time of planting. The John Innes potting compost is excellent for the purpose.

Each individual plant—usually consisting of one rooted growth with perhaps a small side-growth—should be planted with care. Take out with a trowel a hole of adequate depth and place in it some of the sandy compost. Adjust the plant so that the roots rest on the compost; then work in more compost round the roots and

Left: The basal cutting seen on the right is more suitable than any part of the flowering stem for propagation. *Right:* Using a short stake for support.

Exhibition violas arranged with foliage in glass tubes inserted in small buckets of sand.

Exhibition violas staged on white paper collars on a black board.

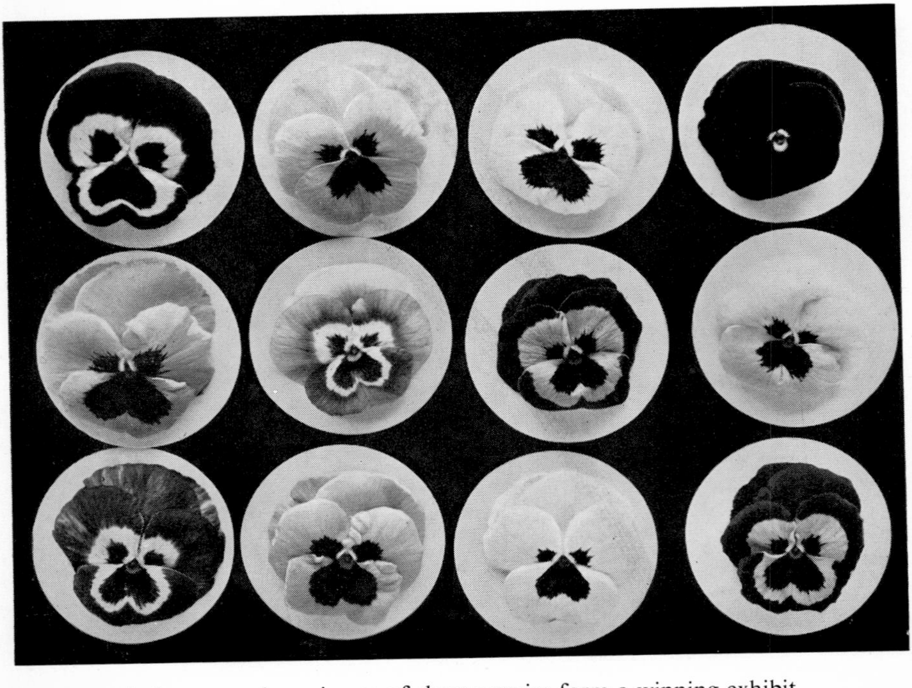

A dozen good specimens of show pansies form a winning exhibit.

base of the plant, at the same time filling in the excavated soil. When this work is completed, the stem should be firm and erect. Plant firmly at all times and finish off neatly.

Allow at least one foot between each plant. Thus a bed four feet or so across will accommodate several rows—according to the number of plants grown—each containing four plants. Label each variety as planting proceeds. Water the plants in gently if the soil is dry.

Protection. After planting, remove all flower-buds, thus allowing the energies of the plant to be concentrated on growth. With autumn planting, once the plants have become established little protection will be needed in most districts. In very exposed situations the plants may with advantage be given shelter from strong and cold winds; boards and inverted flower pots are useful in this connexion. Plants inserted in the spring may need similar attention in rough boisterous weather. In certain parts of the country, with autumn planting, it may be necessary to erect a temporary frame and lights to ensure adequate protection during a hard winter.

For a time, as the plants begin to grow in the spring, an occasional light hoeing and the drawing up of soil round the crowns of the plants will promote their well-being. Flower-buds should be removed as they develop until the plants are growing away well.

Be sparing in the use of the watering-can in the ordinary way, but in very dry weather, a thorough saturating of the soil in the cool of the evening will be beneficial. The application of liquid manure about once a week in the growing season will keep the plants in vigorous condition with the consequent prospect of enhanced size of blossom. A proprietary manure may be used, otherwise a useful stock solution can be made by immersing a quarter-bushel bag of horse or sheep droppings in a thirty-gallon vessel of water for a week or two. This should be used at the rate of about one part to two parts of water. As the season advances, mulch each plant with a compost made up of loam, leaf-mould or peat and sharp sand.

Show Blooms. For the production of large blooms, the growths on each plant may be limited to five or six, or even less. A further concentration in blossom development may be obtained by rubbing out some of the side-shoots on these growths. This should be done with circumspection. With many pansies and exhibition violas, long growths on which flowers are borne may with advantage be either pegged down or supported by short sticks. Later on in the season the basal shoots should be allowed to develop.

Some two or three weeks before a show, according to weather and growing conditions, all blooms should be picked off the plants. The second crop of flowers after this disbudding will usually be of high quality and good size. On no account should spent blossoms be allowed to remain on a plant, otherwise the plants will deteriorate.

In very hot and sunny weather, the blossoms should be shaded from the intense heat of the midday sun by covering each plant with a cone-shaped shield such as is used for roses, or the whole bed can be shaded by stretching a length of some very thin light material over it. Rings attached to the edges of the material and run along wires about two feet six inches above the bed on each side, enable the shading to be easily withdrawn. Remove the shading every day at the earliest moment it becomes unnecessary. It can also be used as a protection from heavy rain.

EXHIBITING

The best time to pick the flowers, particularly after a long spell of hot weather, is the early morning on the day of the show. If this is not feasible, however, pick them as late as possible on the previous evening. Break off the flower-stalk at its junction with the axil of the leaf on which it arises, and place the flower at once in a vessel of water.

Until comparatively recent years, the usual methods of exhibiting pansies and violas were as follows:

Pansies in metal trays, each flower lying flat and sometimes with a paper collar at the back.

Violas set up on boards or easels, in formal sprays of three to ten blooms, each individually wired—with the addition of wool or moss to hold moisture—and spaced out to show each specimen.

A method of exhibiting which has become popular, especially for violas, is the setting up or arranging of the blooms in pans containing wet sand, sometimes with foliage. The stems are either inserted directly into the sand or into narrow tubes filled with water and set up in the sand. Where tubes are not used, care should be taken to see that the sand is thoroughly saturated; if tubes are used, they must be filled to capacity with water.

With blossoms exhibited in pansy trays it is a good plan to place a sheet of clean thin glass over them for some little time prior to judging; they are thus kept flat and free from dust.

In classes for several blooms of a variety or varieties, stage them in such a manner as to give the best colour effect. See that as a whole the individual blossoms are as uniform as possible, as regards both size and characteristics. Make certain that each exhibit is strictly according to schedule; and for the information of the public, label each variety where possible.

Always gather more flowers than are required under the schedule and have these in readiness as reserves in case any of those first selected show signs of wilting.

Where large numbers of blooms are being exhibited in pans—as is often the case if there are classes for bedding varieties—each variety can be carefully bunched and placed in a small vessel of water, the whole then being enveloped in tissue-paper and placed in a shallow stout box. Or if it is not possible to take them to the show in water, the flowers can be placed on a thoroughly moist cloth in a shallow wooden box and then covered with sufficient sheets of tissue-paper to ensure as little movement as possible. They should be placed in water immediately on being unpacked. In very hot weather a few small pieces of ice in appropriate places in the boxes will assist in keeping the blooms cool and fresh.

The following are some recommended varieties for exhibition purposes.

Exhibition Fancy Pansies. A. Watson, Dan Cochrane, David Duncan, Elizabeth McCallum, George A. Close, Hector McFarlane, Herbert Cheetham, John Hynd, John Whiteford, John W. Forrest, Mrs. Sam Knox, Tom Hunter.

Exhibition Violas. Dorothy Stein, Fred Denton, Harlequin, Harry Merrifield, Helen Cochrane, Jean Lister, Lizzie Irving, Madge McKnight, Milton Jumbo, Mrs. Dan Cochrane, Mrs. M. B. Wallace, Mrs. Bates.

CHAPTER NINE

Hardy Perennials

BY J. G. VAUTIER

With a wealth of beautiful subjects available, the hardy flower classes at summer shows should be one of the most arresting and attractive features, but experience proves that these classes are too often poorly supported. There are exceptions, and some societies by tradition have become noted for magnificent displays of hardy flowers at their shows. One reason for poor support is the difficulty of packing and transport; another obstacle is the ambiguity of schedule classification in some cases. These points will be dealt with in the course of this chapter.

Some gardeners may be deterred from exhibiting by a feeling that there are secrets to successful culture; this is a mistaken impression. To be a successful exhibitor needs hard work, enthusiasm, patience, and above all, common sense. One must be ready to take advice, and, contrary to general opinion, this will be given readily by the old hand. It may be felt that growing for show purposes will conflict with the maintenance of an attractive garden, but, although cultivation in certain aspects must be on more elaborate lines than the care of a normal flower border, there is no reason why the garden should suffer if the exhibitor uses discrimination in his plantings. In fact, culture of chosen subjects to a high standard will lead to a finer display than haphazard growing of poor material.

The exhibitor himself will derive great pleasure and learn much from his association with other exhibitors and the shows. The possession of only a small garden should not deter a prospective exhibitor, for, with energy and enthusiasm, many amateurs with but limited space have proved highly successful on the show bench.

CULTIVATION

Preparation of Site. The hardy perennial is in the main a good-tempered plant and easy to grow; unfortunately, as a result, its culture is often neglected. This is not good enough for the exhibition table where thorough cultivation is essential to success. Where there is a choice of position, select a sunny, open site, if possible with a fence or hedge to give protection from prevailing winds. Most perennials enjoy good living. The ground must be dug at least two spits deep and organic manure incorporated throughout by forking it in and not placing it in layers, sandwich fashion. Keep the manure about six inches below ground level; add a dusting of bonemeal at four ounces to the square yard through the top spit as digging proceeds. Where there is difficulty in obtaining stable manure, compost or hop manure will prove efficient substitutes. On light land, cow or pig manure can be used advantageously.

Digging should be carried out in time to allow the soil to settle before planting. It is advisable to dig heavy land early in the winter in order that the frosts may break down the soil to a good tilth for planting. Most soils need lime, and the keen plantsman will discover the lime content of his garden soil and decide on the quantity required; in this connexion the County Horticultural Education Officer may be approached for an analysis.

Thinning. The exhibitor must pay close attention to routine culture, and a matter to be dealt with early in the growing season is thinning. For good results this is of great importance, and this reduction of growth is beneficial to a wide range of hardy plants. For those who fear that such thinning will spoil garden effect there need be no qualms; the higher quality of the remaining growth will more than make up for the stems removed.

Division. The exhibitor must be alert to the necessity of dividing certain subjects at intervals, usually every two years, and among these are heleniums, rudbeckias, erigerons, solidagos and veronicas; unless this is done, actual deterioration is possible. There are, of course, a number of plants which may be left undisturbed for some years, and will give good quality blooms if they receive judicious routine care. Peonies are an example.

Staking. Staking, too, needs careful attention. Perennials making light branching growth can be staked effectively with hazel boughs set in among the plants early in the growing season. For the kinds with stiff, heavy stems, there is nothing better than three stakes to a plant, set in near the crown, leaning outwards, successive ties round the triangle of stakes at intervals of about one foot being made as growth proceeds. Carry out hoeing regularly during the growing season, but do not work too near the crowns of plants like phlox and heliopsis, whose feeding roots are near the surface.

Mulching. Many plants, in particular delphiniums, phloxes and heliopsis, will benefit from a mulch in early summer to conserve moisture; well-rotted stable manure, garden compost, granulated peat or spent hops may be used. Keep mulches moved with the hoe. In very dry spells, watering will become necessary, and thorough soakings must be the rule—sprinklings are useless, and, in fact, can be harmful.

Feeding. The basis of good culture is effective preparation of the soil, but to obtain that 'something extra' which brings success to the exhibitor, supplementary feeding is needed. It is difficult to give precise advice as so much depends on weather conditions, the type of plant which is receiving attention, and the character of the soil.

Commence feeding when growth is moving freely. A varied diet must be the aim, given at intervals of ten days or a fortnight. Compound fertilizers of good proprietary brands can be recommended—they must be used strictly in accordance with the makers' instructions. Under showery conditions the fertilizer may be applied directly round the plants and lightly forked or hoed in. Under dry conditions, the ground must be watered prior to the application of fertilizer, which, in its turn, is then watered in.

When ringing the changes on diet, fertilizers may be applied advantageously in liquid form. For this purpose, compound proprietary fertilizers may be used. In addition, use dried blood and stable or sheep manure by steeping a bag of the chosen material in a tub and applying it as a weak solution. Soot water will also help to intensify colouring. Doses should be weak in the early stages, the strength being increased gradually as growth proceeds; strong applications suddenly applied are most dangerous. In general, feeding should cease when flower-buds show signs of colour. A good principle to adopt when feeding is 'little and often'.

Pests and Diseases. Hardy perennials are singularly free from pests and diseases. Plants making fleshy growth are liable to slug damage, and the best course to take is to protect the crowns with a dressing of coarse sand. As an alternative, weathered coal ashes may be utilized, but these are not recommended on light soils. Where infestation is heavy, this protection may be supplemented by the use of proprietary anti-slug preparations. Some plants of the daisy family are liable to attack from greenfly, and a nicotine or derris wash will deal with these effectively.

Few diseases cause serious trouble amongst hardy plants. Some subjects may be attacked by mildew, and dusting with green sulphur at an early stage will minimize the trouble; spraying with lime sulphur is also effective. Generally speaking, with clean culture hardy plants will not have to face many disease attacks.

SELECTING AND STAGING FOR EXHIBITION

The eligibility of certain subjects to be included in hardy flower plant classes is often the subject of dispute, and on schedule makers falls a heavy responsibility in giving clarity to their classifications. Some expressions found in schedules, for example, 'herbaceous' and 'hardy perennials', lead to difficulties unless amplified. Herbaceous plants have perennial root-stocks with flower-stems which die down annually, therefore a hardy border carnation could not be included in a class for 'herbaceous' plants although eligible for exhibition in 'hardy flower' classes.

It must be noted that some herbaceous plants are not hardy. Shrubby plants are not herbaceous, but most kinds could be shown in a class for hardy perennials. The question of biennials, such as sweet williams, arises from time to time, and although these flowers are hardy, they are not perennial.

Arguments also arise over the inclusion of plants with bulbs, corms or tubers. It follows that the best description to be followed by the schedule makers is the simple one of 'hardy flowers'.

The schedule must make it clear that specimens in hardy flower classes must have been cut from plants growing in the open through the previous winter at least. In classes for more than one vase, the expression 'distinct' should not be used without the addition of the word 'kinds' or of the word 'varieties'. In this connexion delphiniums and heliopsis are 'kinds' of hardy flowers, and Lady Eleanor and Blue Gown are 'varieties' of delphiniums. The application of these suggestions will be found in the following classification of the Royal Horticultural Society for its amateur hardy flower classes.

> 'Six varieties of hardy flowers, one vase of each, excluding annuals, biennials, bulbous plants, shrubby plants, trees and plants which have been flowered under glass. Other things being equal, preference will be given to the exhibit representing the greater number of genera.'

It will be seen that six varieties of *Phlox decussata* could be staged, but in keen competition such an exhibit would lose points to an entry of six varieties selected from six genera. In a class of this kind there must be no colour variation in the individual vases. Where it is desired to permit such a colour variation, this must be expressly provided for in the schedule.

The bigger national exhibitions include classes in their schedule for displays of hardy flowers to fill a given space, but these classes can only be filled by those people with very large gardens or by trade firms. The amateur will usually only be interested in classes framed for a given number of vases. The problems of transport and labour make it difficult to fill classes of more than six vases, but with enthusiasm and determination, it should be possible for the small garden-owner to enter the smaller classes. In general, classes are for six, three or one vase.

A well-organized society publishes its schedule at an early date, and the keen exhibitor will make prompt plans after a careful study of the schedule. By avoiding last-minute decisions to exhibit, the planner will have a big advantage over the haphazard exhibitor. Many exhibitors have faced bitter disappointment by finding their cards marked 'Not according to schedule', and in nearly every case this arises from a perfunctory reading of the schedule. The conditions must receive the closest scrutiny, and advice be taken in cases of doubt. There may sometimes be temptation to introduce into a class some subject which is on the border-line, but this must be resisted. Take no chances.

Timing. At the outset the exhibitor must decide the number of kinds to be grown, after taking into consideration the date of the show. In the decision is involved the difficult problem of 'timing', which is only overcome by experience and observation. Some perennials, for instance, will be in bloom to cover a period of a month or more; others have a comparatively short flowering period. It is certain, however, that the exhibitor must play safe by providing a margin of plants from which to select. To fill six vases of distinct kinds, for instance, at least nine subjects should be grown, and for three vases. not less than five subjects. If the exhibitor has the space and opportunity, an even wider selection is advisable, especially to cover disappointments which may arise from adverse weather conditions.

Very few shows with classes for hardy flowers are held in May or June, and the main season is July, August and September. Where flowers are slow to develop, they may sometimes be pushed on by the application of weak liquid manure, but this must not be overdone. On the other hand, shading with muslin, hessian or sacking will assist in 'holding' blooms. Too-quick development can also be retarded by a copious watering the day before cutting, thus creating cool conditions.

In the selection of subjects, the exhibitor is recommended most strongly to avoid old and discarded varieties and to concentrate on modern ones. Much may be learnt by visiting shows, noting the methods of staging and the type of subject chosen by successful exhibitors, who will be found ready to give good advice.

Cutting, Packing and Transport. Although the time of cutting for a show will be influenced by the distance the blooms have to travel, it is important that most flowers should have some hours in water before packing. The actual cutting is best carried out in the late evening when the sun has passed from the flowers, or in the very early hours of the morning before the sun is fully up. As the stems are cut, strip all unnecessary leaves and place immediately in a deep receptacle of water. For this purpose, oil drums which have been thoroughly scoured out are ideal, as a good depth of water can be provided. Certain subjects, such as anchusas and oriental poppies, flag on cutting, and it is advisable to seal immediately after cutting by dipping the ends in boiling water, or the ends may be charred. The flowers should then stand in a cool shed or room.

With stormy weather in prospect, some subjects such as phlox can be picked two days before a show, and will be better than if left to be battered by storms. Flowers travel best if they can be cut and packed when dry. During periods of very dry weather, most plants will maintain their freshness better if the border has had a good soaking the day before cutting. When the flowers have been brought in after cutting, the opportunity should be taken of going over them to remove damaged leaves or petals; this will save much time when staging. Even when great care is taken, unavoidable damage sometimes occurs, and the exhibitor is advised to carry reserves to the show.

Packing and transport is a problem not always easy of solution, especially where it is desired to stage several vases. Material for single vases usually does not provide difficulty. The most effective method is to use boxes made of light material and sufficiently long to take the flowers selected. A box such as is used for packing oranges can be adapted successfully. The boxes are better shallow as too great a weight of flower heads will lead to crushing. Lay tissue-paper over a base of newspaper at the bottom of the box and wrap each bunch or spike in tissue-paper before laying it in the box. If more than one layer is packed, place a protective covering of paper between layers and a last covering before replacing the lid. To avoid movement in the box, wedge the ends of the stems with cross pieces of tightly rolled paper.

When packing flowers with heads of specimen size, phloxes for example, each stem should be covered with tissue-paper, and the head may be cushioned by bunched pieces of soft paper. See that each bunch of flowers has a supplementary twist of paper or damp moss round the base of the stems to conserve moisture.

Where there is difficulty in obtaining a box, the following method of wrapping has been successful for transporting flowers by rail, when carried personally by the exhibitor. Wrap each bunch in tissue-paper, giving individual stems protection if necessary. Then open out on the floor of the packing room a double sheet of stiff brown paper, and place on this sheet up to four bunches of flowers. Roll the whole to form a conical bundle, the narrow end being tightly rolled round the stems of the bunches. This will leave the top of the bundle sufficiently open to enclose the flower heads without crushing.

Secure fairly tight ties about the lower part of the package, and if further securing is necessary, this may be achieved by joining the top folds with pins. Hardy flowers packed in this way, lightly shaken out on unpacking, will be found in excellent condition. Whatever method of packing is adopted, it is important that the bunches within the box or package be secure, as any movement may lead to damage.

Staging. There is a great art in effective staging. Much will be learnt by experience, and great attention must be paid to detail. The exhibitor will do well to bear in mind the points for which a judge will look when carrying out his duty, and the following is an accepted scheme of pointing in exhibits of hardy flowers:

	Points	
Quality of blooms	3	
Freshness	2	Apply to each bunch.
Elegance of habit	2	
Rarity or difficulty of cultivation...	3	
Variety of form and colour ...	2	Apply to exhibit as a whole.
Arrangement, naming, etc. ...	2	

The exhibitor is urged to allow himself ample time, as hurried staging is never successful. Good secateurs and a pair of small scissors should be carried to the show. Immediately on reaching the show, unpack and place the flowers in water; the stewards will be found ready to assist by indicating where vases and water are available. Ascertain where the classes are to be staged, and then commence to arrange the individual bunches.

Each stem should have a small section cut off before placing it in water. Unless the number of stems to be included in a vase is specified, be guided by the size of vase supplied when deciding upon the quantity of bloom to be included. The size of vase to be used is usually stated in the schedule, but if there is no note, an inquiry should be made. Aim at a well-filled vase, but do not crowd; arrange the stems for lightness of effect to give an all-round view. The arrangement must avoid all appearance of flatness or stolidity. Many prizes have been lost by good flowers being bundled into vases without attempt at arrangement. Set up the vases to display the characteristics of the flower exhibited; naturally tall flowers should not be shortened unduly.

It is of the utmost importance that the exhibit gives the impression of absolute freshness, therefore reject any stems showing signs of damage or running to seed. Rather include blooms which have not quite reached their best than flowers past their peak. Eschew coarseness or staleness.

As each vase is completed, examine carefully and remove any damaged leaves or petals. If small scissors are used for this, the arrangement will not be disturbed. Should a class be restricted to a given number of stems, a careful check must be made when the vase is arranged.

In setting up a vase with light-stemmed flowers, it may be necessary to pack the vase to achieve an artistic arrangement; for this purpose discarded stems may be pushed into the vase, and another suggestion is to use a small bundle of fine rushes cut to the depth of the vase. In either case, use no more filling than is necessary to set up the flowers effectively. To anyone finding it difficult to stage on the morning of the show, it may be said that overnight staging is entirely satisfactory, and, in fact, flowers are often fresher at judging time when set up in this way. Sometimes individual stems show signs of flagging, and may often be revived by removing a short portion of stem, the cut being made under water; plunging stems in water up to the neck of the flower will also be helpful in some cases.

Choosing Subjects. It is important to choose subjects for exhibition with care and discrimination. Hardy flowers are of three main types, spiral or spiked, flat-headed, and those with heads of loose panicles. Examples of each group are delphiniums, heliopsis and phlox. To achieve a balanced effect in a set of six vases, it is preferable to have each type equally represented, although this is not, of course, essential. With colour, too, aim at as wide a range as possible.

Avoid too many in dark shades; the set of six should embody light colours in order to overcome any effect of heaviness. The bunches must be well balanced, and one thinly filled vase in an otherwise well-proportioned set may lose many points; if a set of six vases includes two spiral types, they should preferably be of approximately similar size, for example, delphinium and eremurus.

Equal care must be taken in making up three vases; competition is usually very keen, and each vase should be perfect of its kind. The set of three will be most effective if of contrasting colours and representative of the three main types of hardy flowers. In the event of one of the vases including a subject of the spiral type and the other two of lowlier effect, the tall vase is best at the back. Showmanship has its share in staging, and a weak bunch can sometimes be masked by judicious placing among the other vases.

In close competition many small points count, and one of these is the correct labelling of the vases; the necessity for this is often stressed in schedules and it will be appreciated that the naming of the items in an exhibit is of great interest to visitors. At the completion of the staging the competitor must place his exhibition card face down on the table.

CULTURAL HINTS

A few points of guidance on the culture of those hardy perennials most often used for exhibiting are now given. Subjects are grouped according to their suitability for early, mid-season or late shows.

FOR EARLY SHOWS

There are very few exhibitions held before the end of June, but where this opportunity occurs, the following are some of the excellent subjects available.

Aster. The varieties *A. sub-caeruleus* Wendy and *A. yunnanensis* Napsbury cut well when fully open and make attractive vases.

Bearded Iris. There are many lovely varieties and the exhibitor would be wise to grow modern kinds. The bearded irises stand well in water and should be cut for show when the lower flowers on the stem are open. These irises like well-drained soil, not too heavy, and dressings of lime will be needed according to the nature of the soil.

Delphinium. The variety Pink Sensation is very early flowering and

A travelling box for flowers (especially for spiky flowers such as delphiniums). It is made of light wood slats and hessian.

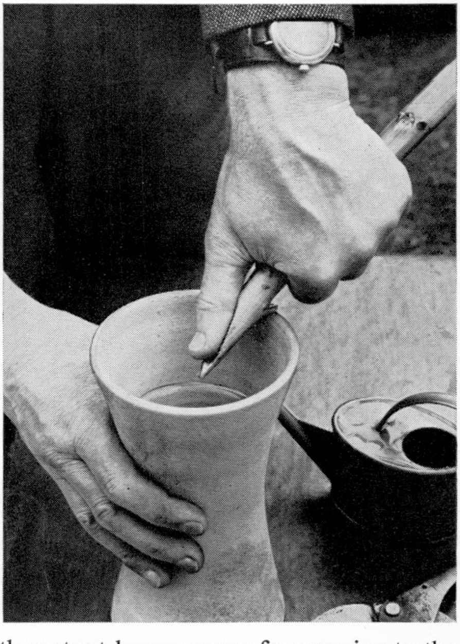

Left: Wrapping flowers in tissue-paper and then stout brown paper for carrying to the show. *Right:* Delphiniums are less likely to flag if the stem is filled with water.

A well-staged vase of heleniums. Surplus leaves and unopened or faded flowers have been removed without distorting the habit of the plant.

Exhibits of three vases of hardy flowers forming an attractive class.

an appealing colour at its season. For good results divide every two years.

Gaillardia. These often give early blooms. Two good varieties are Wirral Flame and Mrs. H. Longster. Gaillardias tend to exhaust themselves by too-free flowering and regular propagation by root cuttings is necessary.

Heuchera. A flower with graceful sprays, making up into dainty and delightful vases. Do not overlook the varieties Huntsman and Scarlet Beauty.

Lupin. Select varieties of the Russell strain. For good spikes, young vigorous plants from cuttings are best. Lupins sometimes droop after cutting; to prevent this the stems should be allowed to stand in a weak solution of starch water for some hours after cutting, and then transferred to clear water. Give the plants a good watering the day before cutting.

Peony. There are many varieties from which a choice may be made, and they provide a wide range of beautiful exhibition flowers. It is sometimes complained of peonies that they are not free flowering, but this is often the result of planting too deeply; the crowns of the plants should be set just below ground level. For specimen blooms, the plants must be disbudded, and careful staking is required; indeed, when well grown the stems need individual staking.

Trollius. These cut well and good blooms are obtained on an enriched soil which does not dry out unduly. A very good variety is Orange Globe.

Pyrethrum. These superb cut-flowers are grand for exhibition. Available in many varieties, the singles are the most attractive; Eileen May Robinson and Kelway's Glorious are most desirable.

Other good early subjects are *Lychnis*, *Viscaria splendens flore pleno*, *Betonica grandiflora superba* and the oriental poppies. The last-mentioned are inclined to drop when cut, and this may be avoided by charring the ends of the stems as they are cut.

THE SHOWS OF HIGH SUMMER

These exhibitions cover a wide field of attractive and most desirable subjects, and the selections which follow are well tried and reliable for the show bench.

Achillea filipendulina (*A. Eupatorium*). An attractive, long-stemmed plant with flat heads of rich yellow which is fine for show purposes. Good kinds are Gold Plate and Wallis's form. They cut well and make an effective vase.

Alstroemeria. These beautiful flowers are unsurpassed for show purposes. They take a little time to establish themselves, but from the second year after planting they flower freely. The variety Dover Orange is one of the finest plants of this colour. Where colour variation is permitted, a vase of Ligtu hybrids will command high points.

Anthemis. For clear yellow colouring, this flower is unsurpassed. Although the blooms close towards evening, they open again early in the day and will stage well. Loddon and Perry's variety are two of the best.

Campanula. Several kinds and varieties are available to exhibitors. Particularly striking for a July show is *C. lactiflora* in a good kind such as Prichard's variety; this type makes large loose heads of small flowers, which should be gone over before staging to remove faded blooms—grape scissors make an ideal tool. Other good campanulas are *C. grandis* Highcliffe variety and *C. persicifolia* Beechwood, the last-mentioned being a very vigorous variety of its type.

Coreopsis. This is a flower which is available for cutting over a period of several weeks, especially when seed heads are not allowed to form. The varieties *C. auriculata superba* and Badengold are the most striking for exhibition. Annual propagation by cuttings makes the finest plants.

Delphinium. The superiority of the delphinium as a border plant is unchallenged and, stimulated by the activities of the British Delphinium Society, it has become a grand flower for the exhibitor. Very beautiful effects may be created at the late June and early July shows with exhibits of delphiniums, either by the massed displays of the trade firms, or by the amateur's vase classes.

The advice on culture and the staging for show of hardy flowers already outlined in this chapter is applicable generally to delphiniums, but there is much supplementary guidance which may be given to the exhibitor of these beautiful flowers.

It is desirable to lay emphasis on the necessity for liming the soil for delphiniums as they do not like acid conditions; use hydrated lime for heavy land, and carbonate of lime for light. In order that the plants may receive detailed and close attention, set them in lines with two feet between the plants and the rows two feet six inches apart, giving, if possible, protection from westerly gales by affording the plants a backing of a hedge or fence.

Success can only be achieved by planting healthy, vigorous stock of modern varieties, and the best type of plant, without doubt, is the newly rooted cutting. Specialist firms will supply these young plants. The exhibitor may wish to increase existing stock from cuttings; for this purpose select growths when about three to four inches high, removing them with a sharp knife, cutting sufficiently low to take the growths away with a small heel from the root-stock. Short, stubby pieces are essential; at a later stage of growth the young stems become hollow and are then useless for propagation. Set the cuttings in a sandy medium in a cold frame, using either small pots or boxes, or inserting straight into prepared compost placed on the bottom of the frame. Water in and keep reasonably moist, avoiding over-watering. The cuttings will be ready in four to eight weeks' time, according to weather conditions; the young plants are then planted into the prepared bed, which had a dressing fourteen days earlier of hoof and horn meal, 1½ ounces, superphosphate of lime, 1½ ounces, and sulphate of potash ¾ ounce, each per square yard, lightly forked or raked in.

The young plants must be well watered in at the time of planting. and if dry weather ensues, further watering is essential until free growth is evident. The stem arising from the original cutting must not be allowed to develop, and later, as spikes are produced when the plants break into new growth from the base, these may be permitted to develop, but the flowering portion must be cut out as soon as colour begins to show. In the following summer these yearling plants will produce exhibition spikes. Start feeding at ten-day intervals when the plants are twelve to eighteen inches high, and cease when colour first shows on the spike.

Special attention must be paid to thinning and staking. Generally speaking, one spike only should be left on young plants, the exceptions being a few vigorous varieties which tend to produce coarse or distorted growth if restricted unduly; in such cases leave two stems. Certain kinds make a number of laterals, and these are best reduced to three on each spike. For effective support, use one stake to each stem at a height of about four feet out of the ground so that the flowering section of the spike is just clear of the stake. Supplement this at a later stage with a thin bamboo, known in the trade as a carnation tip, placed against the stem and threaded up through the florets until the tip is about six inches beyond the top of the spike. Tie in three or four places with soft twist. See that the ties are not too tight at the top of the spike to allow for the expanding stem.

These canes may be left in position when the spikes are cut for show, and this will give additional support when packing. Keep the ground moist by mulching and hoeing. Delphiniums must not lack moisture, and if dry conditions prevail, watering will be essential; this must be a thorough soaking on a basis of about four gallons per plant.

When cutting the spikes for show, remove with a slanting cut at about eight inches from the ground. Cut a small section from the stem when setting up at the show, again with a diagonal cut. In addition to methods of packing and transport already described, delphiniums can be carried in good condition by being laid in the bottom of a motor van, the floor of which has had a generous covering of paper; the spikes are laid side by side, separated with tissue-paper, and two layers may be transported this way. See that the packing is sufficiently close to prevent movement.

Here is a tip for preserving the freshness of delphiniums; when staging, hold the spike reversed and fill the hollow stem with water, using a jug or small watering-can. Place the thumb over the cavity at the end of the spike, then, keeping the thumb in position, turn the spike up and place it in the vase, removing the thumb when the spike is under water. The stem will thus remain full of water, and this will add appreciably to the time it will keep fresh.

Arrange single spikes upright in the vase, but where more than one spike is put up in the vase, they should be inserted at a slight angle outwards. To keep the spike in position, cut portions of discarded stems can be wedged into the vase. Make the best of the spikes available; select the finest for classes where competition is most keen. In classes for more than one spike, keep the poorest in the background.

Take the example of a spike which is not quite fresh in a vase of three spikes—this should be placed at the back of the vase. If an exhibitor is setting up next to a strong exhibit, the finest spikes available are best staged next to his opponent. In classes for, say, six spikes, two in a vase, have each pair preferably of similar type and height—if possible, too, keep each vase to the same depth of colour shading. Where three spikes are allotted to a vase, there is wider scope for arrangement, and contrasting shades are often very effective. For a good finish, insert a few clean, undamaged delphinium leaves round the mouth of each vase.

In judging delphiniums the following points are considered:—

The spike must have length, substance and symmetry, with florets so distributed that the finished effect will be that of a well-furnished but not overcrowded spike of pyramidal form.

Form of Floret. Whether single, semi-double or double, the pip shall be regular, fully open and of uniform character throughout. Sepals must be firm and of good substance.

Colour. Of whatever shade or combination should be clear and of some decisive character.

Condition. A spike should be as fully open as possible, but never at the expense of basal florets. Exposed seed pods or stripped stems and shedding florets will be deemed serious defects.

There is a wealth of varieties from which to choose, and the plantsman is recommended to consult with the firms specializing in delphiniums. Also the list of varieties published by the British Delphinium Society is most valuable for consultation. Bear in mind that the semi-double and double varieties will gain higher points than the singles. Where classes for the Belladonna type of delphinium are provided, these should receive consideration by the exhibitor; attractive varieties are available, and spikes of these dainty flowers make up into a good show vase.

Erigeron. Easily grown and cutting well, these are worth including in an exhibition collection. The varieties Mesa Grande, deep mauve, and Merstham Glory, violet blue, are recommended.

Eryngium. Of the several varieties from which a choice can be made by the exhibitor, *E. hybridium* Violetta and *E. tripartitum* are very good—their steely blues are valuable in a set of vases as a foil to flowers of vivid hue.

Hardy Border Carnations and Hardy Pinks. High-class subjects for a hardy flower class, whose treatment is dealt with in the chapter on carnations (page 35).

Helenium. There is no finer standby for exhibition than this grand race. Thinning of the growths in spring is all-important, with division of the plants every two years. Before setting in vases, the heads should have surplus leaves and unopened inflorescences removed, but this must be done judiciously so that the remaining growth still displays the true characteristics of the plant. Any individual blossoms seen to be fading should be removed with scissors. Two fine kinds are Madame Canivet and Moerheim Beauty.

Heliopsis. Much favoured by exhibitors for July shows, especially when grown disbudded for large blooms. Their culture is simple, but flagging will take place in dry spells, and watering, supplemented by a mulch, is then essential. The stems are somewhat hard and the bottom three inches should be bruised when staging. *H. scabra patula* and *H. scabra gigantea* are the two best.

Lilium. Where bulbous plants are allowed in hardy flower classes, the lilies will make up into commanding vases. The exhibitor can make a fine selection from the easier kinds such as *LL. candidum, testaceum, croceum, regale*, and *Hansonii*.

Lychnis chalcedonica. A good scarlet flower, which can provide a telling vase.

Penstemon. Of the hardy types of this big family, it is possible to recommend for show purposes the form known as *P. barbatus coccineus*, which freely produces graceful spikes with attractive tubular flowers in bright red.

Phlox. In *Phlox decussata* we have a superb exhibition perennial. A well-filled vase of heads of high quality will count high in a group of subjects. Regular feeding with liquid manure, and care that the roots are never allowed to dry out, not omitting thinning of weak stems, will bring heads of quality fit for any competition. In a good head the pips must not be ragged but firm and full, forming as complete a circle as possible; the truss should be full, but not crowded, the pips meeting but not overlapping. When staging, see that the heads are clear of faded pips; this may be done by gently shaking out the heads, supplementing this by hand-picking if necessary. There are so many excellent varieties that the exhibitor must be recommended to study the nursery lists.

Salvia. The type known as *S. superba* (formerly *S. virgata nemorosa*) is a popular border plant which can be very useful in a set of vases. Care is needed in cutting the stems to see they are fresh and not too far open. *S. haematodes* is a more recent introduction with attractive branching stems of a lovely lavender and this is excellent for show purposes.

Scabiosa caucasica. One of the very best of exhibition flowers. Culture is not difficult, provided spring planting is carried out and the plants are given generous dressings of lime. Two good varieties are Constancy and Clive Greaves. The stems are thin, and in staging it may be necessary to employ a little packing in the vases.

Solidago. Several varieties flowering at an early date are available, and can be relied upon for an effective vase. Two excellent kinds are Leraft and Lemore.

Other suggestions can be made to which the exhibitor may give confident consideration. These include *Bocconia cordata* Coral Plume, not an invasive variety; *Chrysanthemum maximum*, the double forms grown disbudded; *Echinops* Taplow Blue, to be picked carefully at the precise stage of freshness; *Eremurus Bungei*, an uncommon choice commanding high points; *Lythrum* Beacon; *Veronica longifolia subsessilis*, a particularly useful subject; and *Artemisia lactiflora*, another 'out of the ordinary' selection.

SHOWS OF LATE SUMMER AND AUTUMN

Many shows are held at this time, and the exhibitor has a wide choice among many beautiful subjects flowering towards the end of the season. Here are some of the kinds available.

Aconitum. Where this plant can be cultivated, on ground which is on the damp side, it can produce striking spikes fit for exhibition. Select Kelmscott variety or Barker's variety for something out of the ordinary.

Aster. Here we have tremendous scope among the varieties and species which are legion, and selection for exhibition is best made from *A. Amellus* and *A. novi belgii* varieties. The former type is easy to cultivate; note that planting should be carried out in the spring. Many beautiful varieties of the *A. novi belgii* section are available and excellent for exhibition. For this purpose and for garden decoration, they are best grown on the single stem principle. Each spring the clumps are taken up and divided into single growths which are replanted at intervals of at least eighteen inches. These grow on into strong plants of pyramidal form with branches flowering from ground level upwards, thus providing ideal sprays for the show vase.

In some gardens mildew is prevalent among michaelmas daisies, and a useful precaution is to dust with green sulphur at intervals of about ten days from early August onwards. Alternatively, the plants can be sprayed with lime sulphur.

For a selection of varieties, the exhibitor is recommended to make notes at shows, and a visit in the autumn to a good nursery is most helpful.

Echinacea. A plant of distinction, both in the garden and for exhibition. The echinacea does best in light, well-drained soil. The type plant is not attractive, and the variety The King should be planted.

Helianthus. Among these are superb exhibition flowers, some of the best being *H. multiflorus maximus* and Loddon Gold, both flowers of lovely form, and *H. sparsifolius* Monarch; all will furnish grand blooms when disbudded. After cutting place deeply in water and bruise or slit the ends of the hard stems for about three inches.

Kniphofia. Several varieties of this showy plant give late blooms, and of these Mt. Etna is very good.

Rudbeckia. Good cut flowers and grand for show. They appreciate generous culture. The dwarf *R. speciosa* is particularly attractive in rich yellow with dark disk. The varieties Herbstonne, a single, and the double form known as Golden Glow, are desirable kinds. When staging bruise the bottom three inches of each stem.

Solidago. A very fine form for a late show is the variety Golden Wings. This is easy to grow but benefits from thinning.

Thalictrum. The species *T. dipterocarpum* and its variety Hewitt's Double are exhibition flowers of great distinction. These plants like a position in the sun, but the ground must be well drained; an addition of peat or leaf-mould with a little hoof and horn meal added will be appreciated.

The exhibitor wishing to extend his range of late-flowering plants can select further from cimicifuga (for the damper places), liatris, *Dierama pulcherrima* (plant young plants from pots), *Physostegia virginiana* Vivid, and, where bulbous plants are permitted, *Lilium tigrinum splendens* and the Earlham varieties of montbretia are impressive.

Dividing a michaelmas daisy clump into single growths. These are planted 18 inches apart and make strong plants producing show sprays.

Erigeron crowns are divided into small clumps. Such newly planted clumps are being watered in.

The left-hand delphinium clump is being thinned to leave only the four strongest shoots.

Left: Staking a clump of delphiniums using three stakes. *Right:* Raffia or string tied round the stakes will hold the clumps in position.

Androsace helvetica, a real miniature with bright, stemless flowers.

Primula pubescens, Mrs. J. H. Wilson, is a superb alpine plant for the show bench, with luminous, lilac-mauve blooms with a white eye.

Left: Springtime in the alpine house, showing several good show pans. *Right:* A permanent open-fronted slat house with lights half-way for plunging alpines and rock shrubs in the summer.

CHAPTER TEN

Rock Plants

BY WILL INGWERSEN

THE FIRST aim of the would-be exhibitor of rock plants must be to bring them to the show table in as natural and healthy a condition as possible. The knowledgeable judge will look askance at an overfed, drawn and obviously unnatural plant. The essence of the charm of alpine plants is their aristocracy and air of breeding, and this is easily lost if they are forced in any way, or fed on a rich diet in an attempt to produce more and larger flowers. If it is in the nature of a species to grow to a height of twelve inches and bear flowers an inch in diameter, then that is the standard to aim at. The plant must obviously be in perfect health and vigour to stand a chance of success in competition with others, but it is most important to remember that among alpine and rock garden plants mere size is a minor qualification.

I was on the point of saying that the exhibiting of alpines is simple in comparison with the grooming and preparatory work which is involved in bringing florists' flowers to the point of ultra-perfection in which we behold them at flower shows, but on second thoughts I am not at all sure that this would be correct. To achieve success at shows with these children of the hills, many of them temperamental to a degree and with widely differing tastes and preferences, one must possess a considerable measure of skill in their cultivation. Such skill can only be attained after long acquaintance with the plants and a close study of their individual requirements. I think it is fair to say that one can standardize the methods of cultivation needed to grow exhibition chrysanthemums, dahlias, sweet peas or delphiniums far more easily than one can those needed to induce alpines to arrive at the show in their best condition.

TIMING FOR EXHIBITION

One of the greatest difficulties with which the exhibitor has to contend is that show dates are fixed far in advance. I know of nothing more difficult than to ensure that certain plants are in flower and at the peak of perfection on a certain date. Alpine plants are strongly averse to any form of retarding or forcing, and, once they have formed their buds and set foot on the road to producing their blossoms, they go ahead, unmoved by any attempts on the part of their agitated cultivator to coincide their time of flowering with the date on his show schedule. I should qualify this by saying that recent experiments have proved to me that some few alpines can be retarded slightly by refrigeration, but it is an extremely chancy business which may even result in the death of the plant, and is therefore a method only to be resorted to under circumstances of extreme urgency, and not at all if the plant is a valuable specimen. Needing some plants of a new and brilliantly coloured variety of *Phlox subulata* to be in flower for a certain show, and it being obvious that they would have passed out of flower at least a fortnight too early, I placed one hundred and fifty of them in cool store at a temperature of 30° F. The plants were in full flower with some buds still to be developed when they went in. They remained in store almost two weeks and were then taken out and gradually thawed. My greatest fear had been that the colour of the flowers would have been affected, but this was not so. The plants collapsed for a day and then the greater part of them recovered, and I was able to use about seventy-five of them for the show, and these were in perfect condition. I am certain that if greater care had been taken in the thawing out, all the plants would have been fit for exhibition. Plants which have been held for some time at just below freezing point should be gradually brought into a higher temperature with the change spread over several days. This could be a complicated process and one not likely to appeal to the average amateur exhibitor.

Attempts to force alpines can only result in drawn plants bearing little resemblance to the normal habit of the variety. Any judge who knows his business would disqualify such plants in favour of those which had been grown under natural conditions and were of typical and characteristic appearance. A visit to any early spring show where alpines are exhibited will provide evidence of this in the exhibits of traders who have forced their alpines in heat in order to show them early in the season.

One will obviously obtain a copy of the schedule of the show or shows at which it is desired to compete as soon as these are available, and after careful study of the classes one will decide in which of these to compete. Many schedules permit the lifting of alpine plants from the open ground and the placing of them in pots or pans, but if the plants can be grown in these containers throughout, it will be found more satisfactory. It is not easy to make a lifted plant look as though it has been growing in a pan. It is apt to collapse partially owing to root disturbance and will not compete on equal terms with a plant of a similar species which has become well established in its container.

If preparations are made in good time, often months prior to the date of the show, a good deal can be done in the way of timing. The plant can be kept in a cool place with little inducement to commence its growth until a reasonable period before it is required. If it is then brought into slightly more clement conditions, such as an alpine house or a cold frame (but *never* into a heated house) one can keep a certain check on its behaviour and it can be removed to its previous surroundings if it appears to be advancing too fast. From these and my previous observations it will be seen that it is easier to check a plant than to force it on, and bearing this in mind, one can to a limited extent control the time of flowering, but only within fairly rigid natural limits. I cannot stress too strongly the importance of making one's plans far in advance of the date of the show. It is very obvious, when examining the groups at any show of alpine plants, that many specimens have been brought along on the spur of the moment and have been shamed by invidious comparison with better-grown entries.

To compete with any hope of success it is vitally necessary to know what the plant exhibited is capable of. Armed with this knowledge, one has a standard at which to aim and some sort of yardstick by which to measure the progress of the plants being prepared. If possible, always prepare several more plants of the kind that is to be shown than are required by the schedule. No plants are more individualistic than alpines, and it is unlikely that if just three plants are prepared they will all be at the top of their form at the same moment. Similarly, where the schedule allows for a choice of variety within one class, it is wise to have sufficient plants ready to allow a selection of those best fitted to be shown, and a last-minute choice can be made from these.

CHOOSING AND PREPARING SHOW SUBJECTS

When choosing the actual plants which are to be exhibited, it is a good plan to picture to oneself what that plant would look like in its natural habitat or, in the case of a garden variety or hybrid, how it would appear if growing under ideal conditions. The plants to take to the show are those which most nearly conform to this image. It may chance that one particular plant has larger flowers or more flowers than some of the others, but if it is not completely in character, is possibly slightly drawn, or possesses some defect, then it is far better to take the more characteristic and typical specimen. It is entirely wrong to imagine that the judges are on the look-out for the largest plant, or the most immense flowers, or the plant bearing the greatest number of flowers. Other things being equal, these points would naturally bear weight, but the judges like best to see a healthy, well-grown, not overfed plant and one that is typical of the species or genus which it represents.

It is not always easy to decide whether to plump for rarity or beauty, if both cannot be present. Much will depend upon the type of show and the class in which one is competing. There are often special classes for rare plants and others for more common and easily grown plants. Here the choice is not difficult. In cases of uncertainty, rarity should not unduly weight the scales. A rare and difficult plant will frequently stand a poor chance in competition with a common one which is in perfect health and at the peak of perfection. It is also well to remember that in most alpine plant competitions, if judges are faced with a difficult decision and have to resort to close pointing, a species will usually carry the day over a garden hybrid or variety.

In a contest where the competition is likely to be keen, close attention should be paid to the smallest details. Judges who are faced with two plants of almost equal merit frequently have to take note of the tiniest points of superiority. The pot or pan should be scrupulously clean. It should conform to the sizes specified in the schedule. If stone chippings are used to cover the surface of the soil, they should be washed and dried before being applied and lightly sprinkled with water just before judging commences, the object being to bring the plant before the judges looking fresh and well-groomed. No small chippings should be showing amongst the leaves or flowers of the plant, and if the surface of the soil is left exposed, it should be weedless and lightly stirred and watered just before judging.

Certain plants would obviously not relish either a bare soil surface or a surface of stone chippings under natural conditions. In this case the soil should be lightly covered with thin sheet moss. It would be most unsuitable for a plant which delights in a cool, shaded position and peaty, acid soil, to be given a scree-like soil surface, and many judges would find this a point not to be overlooked in their deliberations.

Particular attention should also be paid to correct and neat labelling. Use a small label, on which should appear the name, natural order and country of origin of the plant. If it is a hybrid, the parents should be given. If the plant possesses a synonym under which it is frequently grown, both this and the true name should appear on the labels, together with the authorities for each, if known. An example of an informative label is as follows:

Primulaceae. Karawanken Alps.
Primula × Deschmannii
(PP. minima × Wulfeniana)

Some of these details may be thought fiddling and unnecessary, but they may well make all the difference between a first and a second prize. It is essential to be as certain as possible that the plant or plants one is showing are correctly labelled. In the event of any doubt, have the name checked by an expert before the plants are judged, and if there remains uncertainty, either indicate the fact clearly and request the judges' assistance in applying the correct name or withdraw the entry. I have seen many excellent plants disqualified and other entries placed first with only the brief comment on the failure's card, 'incorrectly named'. It does quite often happen that judges are faced with plants of such precisely similar merit that they are forced to seek defects of any kind which will assist them in their decisions.

Competitors are occasionally unable to appreciate the reasons why their entries have failed to win a prize. I know of few judges who would be unwilling, if tactfully approached, to give the reasons for their decisions. Such information can be immensely helpful to the beginner and he should not hesitate to seek it, if he can do so in the right spirit and without any feeling of injury.

It frequently happens that there is a class in a show schedule for a table rock garden, to be constructed within certain specified limits of size. Considerable ingenuity and skill can be exercised in the making of such an exhibit. Unless one has had experience, it is as well to spend a little time at home beforehand with a few selected stones and some soil and attain some knowledge of the best way in which to arrange the stones and to form a miniature landscape. The layout should be as natural as possible and, unless the schedule actually calls for a Japanese garden or something other than a rock-garden, the employment of figures, animals or miniature houses and bridges should be avoided. Try to create a natural piece of rock-work, leaving suitable planting places and arrange for one or two shapely small conifers or dwarf shrubs at key points. A sense of proportion must be retained and the little trees so placed that they are not overshadowed by the flower-stems of an adjacent rock plant. I have seen charming little junipers used in such a garden and their effect entirely spoiled by having the bright red flowers of a mossy saxifrage waving an inch or two above their heads!

Careful attention to finish is important, and the judicious use of small pieces of sheet moss and fine, washed stone chippings can achieve much in this connexion. It is also important, as far as is possible in such a limited area, to place the plants with due thought as to the suitability of the positions they occupy.

CHAPTER ELEVEN

Roses

BY BERTRAM PARK

THE AMATEUR gardener who loves roses has tasted but a sip of the joys of growing them if he has never cut a few blooms and put them up in competition at the local show : he cannot have the slightest idea how good his flowers are, how well grown they are, or how badly.

As I have often experienced when trying to identify roses sent up for that purpose to the offices of the National Rose Society, badly grown specimens may be completely unrecognizable. Yet how little extra care it takes to grow them well. Moderately well-cultivated plants giving presentable blooms are of the least exacting in the garden, while just that little extra knowledge, that little extra attention from a keen gardener will enable him to produce flowers fit to put up in any show.

There is no need for the 'small' man to be afraid of showing in the company of the biggest growers. There is some kind of handicapping in the schedules of nearly all shows, while at the big shows of the National Rose Society there are classes for amateur gardeners who grow and show their own roses without paid assistance. Moreover, there are sections with classes subdivided for growers of fewer than 100 plants, growers with fewer than 250 plants, 500 plants and 1,000 plants. Also there are classes for those who have never exhibited before and for those who have never won a first prize before. There is comparatively little difference in the prizes between those for the smallest classes and the biggest classes, so that every grower, big and small, has an equal chance to win good prizes. Is it not worth while then to 'have a go'? Start at the beginner classes, gain experience by watching others and then work up to the higher classes.

Showing roses is a wonderful hobby, and not the least attraction is the warm friendships you will make among the other exhibitors. Everybody is friendly, drawn together by a common enthusiasm, everybody will be helpful. At one of the big shows I once left behind the packing material which I use for putting in the vases to keep the stems up straight. I wasted half an hour of precious time trying makeshifts, all useless, when my keenest competitor came to my rescue and gave me sufficient reeds to pack my vases with. The beauty of this was that in doing so he must have known that he was helping me to beat himself. It is friendships like this that one makes in the rose world!

PLANTING

To start at the beginning, I am going to assume that our prospective rose exhibitor has ordinary knowledge of good garden cultivation and will not go into details of how to trench the beds, except to say that they must be reserved exclusively for roses and the ground not littered with other plants which may require totally different methods of cultivation.

There is no need to dig the beds three and four feet deep, two good spits will suffice, but perfect drainage is essential. On heavy land over clay subsoil, it is wise to build up the sides of the beds six inches or so with boards or stones in order to secure the better drainage. The surface of the beds should be level; if the surface has a rounded contour, higher in the middle, the liquid manure to be applied in due season will run off down to the edges, and be wasted, never getting to the roots at all. The perfect drainage is essential because of the large quantities of manure to be applied; only a fraction is actually taken up by the roots and the remainder must be washed away by the rains. It must not stay there and saturate the soil for another year or the soil will soon become sour and sick.

Any soil can be made to grow roses well if properly dug and manured with dung or compost. Heavy land is improved by liberal quantities of lime mixed in when digging the bottom spit; this helps to keep the soil open, and light dressings should be given on the surface before the winter digging about once every three years. Light land requires less lime in order to conserve the humus. Sandy and gravelly soils should have ample compost dug in; they will take more manure and fertilizer without detriment, as the surplus more easily drains away than on heavy land. The preparation of the beds should be finished by September to allow at least a month for the soil to settle before planting is proceeded with.

Left: Clusters of buds being reduced to the one strongest. *Right:* An exhibition bloom tied with wool and protected by a conical shade.

Left: A wire support for the stem of a show bloom. *Right:* Close-up of exhibition bloom tied with wool.

Left: A specially constructed case for exhibiting six specimen blooms. *Right:* The same box filled with prize-winning roses.

If the plants are to be bought, it is worth while to be sure that they are of first quality and come from one of the nurserymen who specializes in growing roses and not from a horticultural sundriesman who merely retails them.

If they can be got in at the end of October, or at latest by the second week of November, so that the roots can make good growth before the cold weather sets in, it may be possible to get good exhibition blooms for the following summer. Plant moderately firmly with plenty of granulated peat round the roots, and about a handful of bonemeal mixed into the peat and the soil round the roots. The advice given on later manuring must, however, be considerably modified if show blooms are wanted the first season, and much lighter dressings given. It is very unwise to manure heavily first-year plants; it might quite possibly kill them. It is also very deleterious to the future welfare of the plants to cut from those newly planted the long stems necessary for show work. And one stem only should be cut, then no more cuttings should be made from that plant for the rest of the season. It is far better, however, not to expect to show from first-year plants, with the exception of course of 'maidens' which you may have budded yourself if you have advanced thus far in the craft. I am therefore presuming that the plants are in not less than their second year before you begin to show from them.

PRUNING

The next important operation to consider is pruning. A lot of unnecessary bunkum has been talked and written about this simple subject, and I am not one of those who preach that very hard pruning is essential for exhibition blooms. Moderately pruned plants will look far better in the garden and they will be healthier and give a better return in flowers after the show season is over. For actual show purposes, the same number of blooms should be grown on the plant, whether hard pruned or moderately pruned. In the former case the whole plant is restricted in size and its vigour forcibly repressed, both below ground and above, while the moderately pruned plant is encouraged to grow freely, with its concomitant of a better root system for taking up liquid manure.

When growing for the show, one shoot only is allowed to grow from the pruning cut, and until after midsummer all other shoots below it are rubbed out so that there is one shoot and one flower to each main stem. Do not interfere, however, with new growth coming from the base; that is your foundation for next year's blooms. The method is as follows: first cut out all weak and spindly growth and dead wood, then likewise any main stem that did not throw out a good shoot from the pruning cut of the previous year as this shows either that that stem is deteriorating or that it has been affected by frost. Now cut all other ripe shoots of last summer's growth to about half their length, and if they have branched, then cut away all except the lowest and reduce that to about one third of its length, provided it is not less than pencil thickness. If thinner, then cut lower accordingly. Hybrid polyanthas may be pruned more lightly still or to about half the length of last year's growth, both main and side shoots. A good stout side shoot (of not less than pencil thickness) will throw a new shoot with quite a good truss of bloom. The above is all on the assumption that there is no frost damage, which is shown by discoloration of the pith in the centre of the shoot. It may be brown or yellow, and if there is the least evidence of discoloration then the cut must be made lower down to clean, green-white pith.

For years I have always said that there was only one tool to prune a rose with, namely a good, sharp pruning knife, but for many it is a difficult tool to use skilfully, and good, sharp secateurs may be used if they will make a cut without bruising the stem.

The cut is made to an eye which is pointing in the direction in which it is desired the new shoot shall grow. The stem is cut through with a slant, commencing level with the eye on the opposite side of the stem and emerging about a quarter of an inch exactly above the eye. Cut like this, the pressure of the sap flows straight on up the new growth and the cut quickly heals over.

Having dealt with the method of pruning, the question of when to prune is now of importance. If there is a large number of trees available, the pruning date is of less importance, as there will always be some quicker- or slower-growing than the average, but if you only have a limited number of trees, every one must pull its weight and be made to have its blooms at their best at a given time. Every variety has its own average time from the date of pruning to perfect bloom, and that time can only be gauged in your own garden and under your own conditions of cultivation by taking careful notes every year.

As a *guide*, I will give the time my own plants take in *my* garden in Middlesex under *my* conditions of cultivation.

	Wks.	Dys.
Candeur Lyonnaise ...	14	3
Dame Edith Helen ...	12	1
Directeur Guerin ...	12	—
Dr. F. G. Chandler ...	13	1
Glory of Rome ...	15	—
Mrs. Henry Bowles ...	12	6
Peace	13	—
Percy Izzard	14	—
Phyllis Gold	13	1
Pres. Chas. Hain ...	12	3
Sam McGredy ...	12	—
The Doctor	11	2
Christoph Weigand ...	12	5
Ena Harkness ...	11	6
Geh. Duisberg ...	11	3
Ethel Somerset ...	11	4

	Wks.	Dys.
Golden Melody ...	13	1
Lady Sylvia	11	4
Lal	11	2
Mabel Francis ...	12	1
Mrs. L. B. Coddington	10	5
McGredy's Pink ...	13	1
Pres. Herbert Hoover	12	4
Polly	12	6
Signora	11	4
Sir Henry Segrave ...	11	6
Stirling	11	6
Dainty Maid	11	2
De Ruiter's Herald ...	12	—
Frensham	14	5
Karen Poulsen ...	11	3
Van Nes	13	3

Thus, supposing the show date is July 1, calculate back for Candeur Lyonnaise fourteen weeks and three days, and that is the date it should be pruned. The chances of May frosts or other emergencies cannot be calculated for, but the above is the principle on which I work after observations over a number of years, and it usually works out right on the average.

FEEDING

One of the earlier writers said that the 'garden should be for the rose, not the rose for the garden'. I entirely disagree. Although I have always been a keen exhibitor, I have always tried to make my garden as a whole picture, and I do not think it right to spoil it just for the sake of exhibiting, nor is it necessary to do so in the slightest. The subject of manuring is closely bound up with this policy. It is quite possible to mix up a liquid chemical fertilizer, half an ounce nitrate of ammonia and half an ounce phosphate of potash to a two-gallon can of water, and with this to water the plants well at weekly intervals from May to July. It is a short-term policy of producing good exhibition blooms for a time, but in the long run it would ruin the garden.

I used this method for some of my beds in a previous garden, and in five years the soil was sick and exhausted. There was nothing to be done about it except to replace the soil eighteen inches deep with new virgin meadow top-spit.

The policy of manuring must be based on a firm foundation of organics, dung and/or compost. With that, chemicals may be added as required, but in a properly balanced formula. The first organic manuring is in February or March, when bonemeal or meat and bone meal may be scattered over the beds at the rate of a handful to each plant. A fine powder is quickly available to the plants, but it is also long-lasting—for the whole year or more. White steamed bonemeal is almost useless, as most of the nitrogen has been taken out of it. It should be a dirty yellowish colour, and if it has a nice, rich smell, so much the better!

After pruning, the surface of the beds is lightly forked over, the bonemeal turned in and the beds tidied up. Then comes the solid foundation of all good gardening, or at least good rose gardening—two or three inches deep of good farmyard or stable manure, diluted with a proportion of well-made material from the garden compost heap. The whole of the surface of the beds is covered with this, and if weeding is subsequently done with a 'Sproughton' or dutch hoe, the surface need be very little disturbed the whole summer. It is lightly forked into the soil the following winter.

I can hear someone saying that it is quite impossible to get farmyard or stable manure. It is admittedly difficult in these times, and if you cannot get it—well, you cannot, and that is that. Then the compost must be used alone, or with the addition of granulated peat, if necessary, to make it up. This compost will be deficient in available nitrogen, but that can be provided by the dried blood to be mixed into the liquid manure now to be prepared.

In my own garden I have a fairly large number of plants, and the following mixture may seem a large quantity to some, but it can be made up in the same proportions to any quantity required. I have two corrugated iron tanks holding about thirty-five gallons each, and these are well painted on the inside to prevent rusting by the chemicals. Tank No. 1 is about one-third filled with dung, horse, cow or sheep, and filled up to the top with water. It may not be possible to get sufficient dung to put on the beds, but at least sufficient can be obtained to make up this liquid manure tank.

Into the other tank, No. 2, goes six pounds potassium nitrate, three pounds ammonium sulphate, sixteen pounds superphosphate, ten pounds potassium sulphate, two pounds magnesium sulphate (Epsom salts), and one pound ferrous sulphate (sulphate of iron).

The reason for the two sources of nitrogen is that the first is very quickly leached out but is more quickly available to the plants; the second is longer retained in the soil. If your soil is very alkaline, i.e. chalky over a chalk subsoil, the last two ingredients should be doubled in quantity. The tank is filled up with rain or soft water and stirred at intervals until the chemicals are dissolved. It may take two or three days.

These two tanks now contain 'stock' solutions, to be diluted when required into another thirty-gallon tank on wheels which can be pulled about and from which to water the beds. For use, I take nine gallons (after well stirring up) from the No. 1 tank. For this purpose I have a pail with half the top covered over with half-inch galvanized wire net, which strains the solid from the liquid. Then I add three gallons from the No. 2 tank (well stirred up) and fill up with another eighteen gallons of tap water (my tap water contains a high proportion of lime, which is beneficial). As a final addition I put in nine tablespoons of dried blood and stir the solution until this is dissolved. The dried blood must not be added to the 'stock' tanks, as if kept in solution for long it will putrefy.

The mixed liquid should not be given to dry soil. If there is a drought between April and July, the beds should be well watered so that the soil is moistened well down below the roots, and make sure that sufficient is given to get thus far down.

This mixed liquid is not all in solution, so that it must be stirred up every time before the watering-can is dipped into it. It is used, poured round and between the plants, to the amount of about one gallon to every four plants.

Now this is pretty strong feeding even for established plants, and if you like to risk it on autumn-planted first-year plants—well, you have been warned! But if you do, then dilute it still more with about eight times more water.

I have occasionally used a sprinkler for watering the beds, but I think a hose pipe is better. If the foliage is kept dry it is less likely to become infected by rust or black spot if those diseases are in the neighbourhood or have been in the garden before.

This liquid manure I give once a week from mid-May to mid-June, then I use water only until the summer shows. If there are any shows about the end of July, the liquid manure can be given once more about July 10, but after that there should be no more manuring for the rest of the year. Should forcing manuring of this kind be continued longer, the plants will be throwing up soft, sappy, watery shoots right into the autumn which would never ripen before the winter and would certainly be killed by the first frost, and almost certainly the health of the plants would be affected for the following year.

PEST CONTROL

After working hard and getting your plants into the most promising condition possible, it is most exasperating to find, on going the rounds one morning, that one of the most promising buds has been eaten into in the night by a winter moth larva or a red rose maggot. From the first week in May until the sepals turn down and show the full colour of the bud, it is necessary, therefore, to make a routine spraying against such pests.

There are many insecticides which may be used, but I now use one only which answers every purpose required. This is a DDT-pyrethrum mixture supplied in solution in white oil. It is sprayed over and through the plants by means of an 'atomizer'. This delivers the liquid in the form of a fine mist which penetrates right into the foliage. A calm atmosphere is essential, and an early morning on a fine day is best. In warm, fine, dry weather it may be used in late afternoon, but it is desirable that the oil should evaporate as quickly as possible and before night time. This insecticide gives an almost immediate kill on contact with every kind of insect or pest of other description, and the DDT content is deposited, although invisible, on the plant and catches any pest which may escape the direct action but crawls about afterwards.

It is not wise to spray opening buds, and it is just at this time that one of the most predatory of pests may get busy. This pest is the thrips, a minute fly easily overlooked by the naked eye, which can completely ruin a bloom. The only *certain* preventive from the time the calyx breaks is to go round with a camel-hair mop and actually powder each opening bloom lightly with DDT powder. Yes, you have to go to quite a little trouble to produce those prize blooms for the show—but is it not worth it?

VARIETIES

Choice of the best varieties for showing is difficult from a catalogue description, so I have drawn up limited selections of varieties best to be relied on. The following are those that will give large specimen blooms:

Candeur Lyonnaise (white), Dame Edith Helen (pink), Directeur Guerin (buff yellow), *Dr. F. G. Chandler (deep scarlet), Glory of Rome (light crimson), *Mrs. Henry Bowles (pink), Peace (light yellow tipped with pink), Percy Izzard (buff yellow), Phyllis Gold (yellow), Pres. Chas. Hain (light yellow), Sam McGredy (light buff yellow), The Doctor (pink).

The following is a list of eighteen decoratives which I consider to be among the most reliable for show work:

Christoph Weigand (pale pink), Charles Gregory (brilliant scarlet and orange), *Dr. F. G. Chandler (deep scarlet), Ena Harkness (scarlet), G. Duisberg (yellow), Ethel Somerset (pink), Golden Melody (buff yellow), Lady Sylvia (pink), Lal (pink), *Mabel Francis (pink), *Mrs. Henry Bowles (pink), Mrs. L. Coddington (pink), McGredy's Pink (pink), Pres. Herbert Hoover (pale orange and red), Polly (pale flesh), Signora (rich yellow and red), Sir Henry Segrave (pale yellow), Stirling (cerise pink).

Among the wealth of new varieties now appearing the following may be specially recommended: Karl Herbst (red), Eden Rose (pink), Grandmère Jenny (pale yellow, edged cerise), Monique (a very fine decorative pink), Yves Latieule (yellow), Symphonie (shading deep pink), Michelle Meilland (pale pink), Tallyho (crimson), Charlotte Armstrong (rich pink), Rubaiyat (bright crimson), Sutter's Gold (yellow). There are many more which should be watched for, and may be relied on if they have received the National Rose Society's Trial Ground Certificate.

Some in this last list are suitable for either section, and those marked *, although officially classified as decoratives, will equally well give large specimen blooms. Any decorative may be shown in the specimen bloom classes, but those in the first list, excepting those marked *, are barred from the decorative classes. The purpose of this is to prevent mere size from overweighting and dwarfing the smaller varieties in the decorative classes.

The following are among the most reliable varieties for showing in the hybrid polyantha classes: Betty Prior (bicolor pink), Dainty Maid (pink), De Ruiter's Herald (scarlet and orange), Frensham (crimson), Van Nes (light crimson).

Among the newer hybrid polyanthas, or floribundas as they are now called, Commonwealth (bright crimson), Wilhelm Teetzman (dark scarlet), Tantau's Triumph (orange-scarlet), Fashion (salmon-pink), are to be recommended.

EXHIBITING

Shades and Protectors. Most modern roses have stouter petals and are much more resistant to wet and bad weather conditions than many of the older varieties, nevertheless it is necessary to have bloom protectors ready. There are two kinds, one made of thick oiled paper and the other of white cotton, the latter in two sizes. They are cone-shaped and provided with a stout wire spring which clips on to a half-inch-diameter wooden stick about four feet high.

Early in June it is time to commence marking the likely buds and fixing the sticks in position. The sticks at this stage are serving only to mark the 'possibles'. For instance, a given class in the schedule requires three vases of decoratives of six stems each, and for each vase of six stems at least ten possibles are marked. From time to time one bud may be looking better than another, so a stick may be shifted to mark the new selection.

Disbudding is attended to as soon as the side buds can be snapped off with the fingernail without risk of injuring the centre bud. Only one bud is left to grow and develop on each stem. Polyanthas are left to grow in clusters, of course, and they do not require the protectors as the petals are tougher than the average hybrid tea. The 'large specimens' are not exhibited in bunches but as individual blooms and they are marked similarly.

Show Boxes. At the National Rose Society's shows, these 'large specimens' are required to be shown in standard-size boxes, fitted with standard water tubes, provided by the exhibitor. Vases and bowls are provided by the Society and are obtainable in the show hall.

For a class of six specimens, at least ten or twelve possibles should be marked, and some kind of box must also be provided to take a number of spares to the show hall.

A fortnight before show date the protectors are placed in position but high up above the buds, at least twelve inches above them. Only if wet weather prevails should they be lowered, and then not right on to the buds but sufficiently clear of them that if the stem is bent or blown about the buds will not touch the rims of the shade; this enables air to circulate freely round the opening and swelling buds. If the protector is wet and right over the flower, it creates a damp atmosphere which is more harmful than if there were no shade there at all.

Ties. Ties for the blooms are now prepared. Before 1939 there was obtainable a very thick 'Berlin wool', which was ideal for the purpose; it was very soft and stretched with the swelling blooms and never got too tight. This is no longer obtainable, but after much searching I have found a good substitute in an artificial silk rug 'wool'; it is thick and soft, but does not stretch as well as the old

Berlin wool. After the blooms have been tied it is therefore advisable to watch the blooms daily to see that the tie is not strangling or marking the petals.

Four or five days before the show is the time to start putting on the ties. The piece of wool is placed right round the bloom and fixed with a double twist; this is the first stage of a reef knot but with an extra turn or twist with the first end. This holds quite firmly but can easily be loosened when required; the ties should be sufficiently tight to hold the petals firmly in place but not so tight as to risk marking the softest petal. The object is to prevent the petals from opening but to allow them to grow and lengthen without losing their form. Once the ties are on, neither they nor the blooms must be allowed to get wet.

Varieties may differ a lot as to the best stage at which the ties should be put on. Glory of Rome, for instance, a popular exhibition rose, has to be tied very early in its development, seven or eight days before the show. Without the tie, the flower will open into a confused bunch of petals without form or shape, but the tie will keep the petals together and make them grow to the pointed 'classical' shape which is essential. Pres. Chas. Hain can only be tied the day before the show, and then not unless the atmosphere is quite dry, for the petals are so delicate that the softest tie will mark them if left on for long. Many other varieties have individual characteristics which can only be learnt by observation and experience.

Cutting. The cutting of the blooms must be done in the very early morning or the late afternoon and evening before the show day. On a dull day cutting can commence about five o'clock, but on a hot, sunny day it is better to wait till later when the sun is off the beds. The decoratives should be cut with as long a stem as possible; the end of the stem should be slit for about two inches and then placed immediately into a deep vase or pail of water.

They should be carried thus to the shed or a convenient place for the final arrangements. After cutting it is unwise to carry them about without first putting them into the water, for the ends will quickly dry and then will not take up water so easily without trimming again, which means losing some length of stem.

The specimen blooms need be cut with only six inches of stem, and the foliage is immaterial, but with the decoratives the clean quality of the foliage is important. In the shed the first thing to do is to remove the tie and examine the bloom; if it is in right condition, the outside petals will open a little and it will now be impossible to tie them back again, so without shaking or loosening the inner petals, the tie is slipped on inside the outer row of petals. It remains there until the final staging on the show bench.

The lowest one or two leaves are pulled off the stem and the thorns removed, either by snapping them off with the fingers (gloved!), or if they will not easily snap off, then they must be cut off with the pruning scissors. It is necessary to remove the thorns because otherwise they will always be catching on to something and may tear and seriously damage the foliage on neighbouring stems.

Wiring. It is advisable, but not always necessary, to wire the stems. It is advisable because when arranging them in a vase or bowl the stems must be neatly and evenly spread out. The wired stem can be easily bent down to a required position and will stay there. The wires are of soft iron, such as are used by florists, of about twelve or fifteen inches in length. They are looped round the neck just below the calyx and twisted round and down the full length of the stem. The specimen blooms have special spring wires to fit into the water tubes. When trimmed and wired, the best of the specimens are placed into the tubes in the exhibition box, with sufficient spares in another box, and the lids are lowered but not closed right down.

If it is possible to do so, the decoratives should be carried to the show in water, but if this is not possible, then they should be left overnight in the deep vase or pail standing in a cool draught-free place; leave them to drink up as much water as they will. The following morning they can then be packed in shallow boxes of wood or cardboard between layers of soft tissue-paper.

Although the exhibition vases are provided, the roses cannot be just placed in them anyhow; some packing material must be used to support the stems. The best for the purpose is either cut lengths of reeds or *Lonicera nitida*, and personally, I prefer the latter. In fact, I grow a hedge specially for the purpose. Fill up the vases with this, and then when the stems are pushed in they will be firmly held exactly where they are wanted.

It is essential to be up early on the morning of the show to allow ample time for staging without being hurried or rushed. At the show hall, find out where your classes are situated and put out everything ready. Obtain the bowls or vases, fill them with water and pack the vases with the reeds or lonicera; the bowls are provided with double grids to hold the stems.

The decoratives and hybrid polyanthas should be staged first, for being smaller- and thinner-petalled than the specimen blooms, they are less likely to lose their form between the staging and the time when they will have to catch the judge's eye.

If the decoratives have been brought to the show packed in boxes, the ends of the stems should be cut again to enable them readily to take up more water. The stems should not be pushed down in the vase more than just as far as is necessary to reach the water; the effect of long stems is pleasing. They should be carefully spaced out with the highest in the centre. The wires will hold the stems in place, bent down and outwards where required to balance the bunch. The arrangement must look equally well when viewed from any side, and must not only face the front. Remember, this is a decoration and the quality of the blooms is not the only consideration as it would be with the specimen blooms.

Dressing. We must now consider the preparation of the special box blooms. Take each one separately, remove the tie and open out the outermost row of petals—some exhibitors use a camel-hair mop brush, I use my fingers—then work on the second row of petals similarly. This process is called 'dressing' the blooms, and skilful 'dressing' can make all the difference in close competition; it is quite an art; watch some of the more experienced competitors. The petals should be opened so that they form a complete symmetrical circle, with the edges of the petals carefully reflexed outwards. A damaged petal will lose points, and sometimes another petal can be brought down to cover up the damage (a judge will not actually touch a bloom when pointing it for award).

A very badly damaged outer petal can sometimes be entirely removed, but this is liable to spoil the regular shape, and it is only safe to do so when another petal can be firmly pressed down to take its place. It is a risky proceeding and should only be done as a last resort; if the gap should show, it will certainly lose more points than the evidence of slight damage.

The bloom being satisfactorily 'dressed', the tie should be carefully slipped back over the inner petals to keep them in place and prevent them from opening; the tie should remain in place until the last few minutes before judging time. Make sure, however, that they are removed in due time, otherwise the exhibit may be disqualified. Finally, obtain the cards and place them face downwards in front of your stand, after which there is nothing more to be done but to wait patiently for the verdict.

Well, good luck and good showing!

CHAPTER TWELVE

Shrubs and Trees

BY FRANCIS W. HANGER, A.H.R.H.S.

FLOWERING SHRUBS and trees are being grown more extensively in gardens of today, giving natural-looking results which need the minimum of attention. Economic conditions have forced this type of gardening upon us, creating interest in the more labour-saving garden plants. This interest comes at a time when the wealth of trees and shrubs was never greater, owing mostly to introductions during this century from the Himalayas, China, Japan and other countries. This type of gardening has its compensations, for if well planted, these plants quickly become established, growing larger and larger each year, giving bigger and bigger displays of flowers annually.

The more important horticultural societies are helping to popularize this new form of gardening by providing classes at their shows for cut sprays of hardy flowering trees and shrubs, arranged in vases.

During the spring pageantry there is ample opportunity to display beautiful arrangements of early-flowering varieties. In the south-west and more favoured districts, the field of choice is very rich. The lovely lilac blue *Paulownia imperialis*, *Magnolia macrophylla* with its immense leaves and flowers quite a foot in diameter and *Camellia reticulata* with rose-pink blossoms up to six inches across, are the monarchs of the show bench.

But hundreds of other trees and shrubs stake their claims; *Magnolia Campbellii* and *M. mollicomata* produce large rich pink blooms during early and late April respectively, to be followed by *M. sinensis* and *M. Sieboldii* both having wax-white petals surrounding their crimson stamens. The evergreen *Camellia japonica* hybrids, the rhododendron species and the fiery red *Embothrium lanceolatum* can rightly claim to be the aristocrats of the hardy flowering tree and shrub world, which win the first prizes in their seasons at the best shows.

As the season advances ceanothus, cornus, philadelphus, lonicera, spiraea, berberis, buddleia, hypericum, catalpa, caryopteris, hoheria, halesia, tecoma, hydrangea and scores of other genera provide material in abundance for exhibiting during the summer months. By the time the last of these has flowered glorious autumn colourings of foliage, fruits and berries will have begun, to continue well into December, and be joined with sprays of *Camellia Sasanqua*, *Jasminum nudiflorum*, *Viburnum fragrans*, and the wych-hazel *Hamamelis mollis*.

SELECTION AND PREPARATION FOR THE SHOW

After obtaining the schedule in advance, study it thoroughly and make yourself familiar with the various sections and its classes—especially those you intend to enter. The most exquisite arrangement or the choicest of rare shrubs if not entered according to the schedule must be disqualified at judging time and probably cause much disappointment.

With hardy shrubs it is advisable not to cut your sprays too far in advance of the show. True, in some cases when the weather is unkind and cold in the open, a little forcing in a warm greenhouse with plenty of syringing with lukewarm water may be necessary to hasten the development of the more backward buds in time for the show. However, generally speaking, this practice with hard-wooded sprays of trees and shrubs is not to be recommended, as the flowers on such branches usually lose colour and often flag at the wrong moment. If this must be done to enable a plant to be entered in a certain class, do not use a stove house to open your blossoms but rather a more temperate house, with plenty of moisture.

Should the exhibitor live a long distance from the show, the best time to cut the flowers is early—very early, before the sun is powerful—in the morning before the show. This enables the exhibitor to place the sprays deep in water for several hours before travelling to the show. On arrival at the show the flowers must immediately have their stems recut and again, if possible, be placed deep in buckets of water for as long a period as possible before being arranged in vases and set out in their respective classes. With the selection of cutting material it is wise to remember that freshness gains points, and a few buds unopened or about to open denotes freshness and this is to the exhibitor's advantage.

When exhibiting cut portions of trees and shrubs, care must be taken to enable the hard wood to absorb the water. Always cut the stems at an angle—a flat or horizontal cut may rest on the bottom of the vase and so prevent the absorption of moisture. As an additional aid, the stems should be split quite a few inches from the base upwards. Some exhibitors smash the stems with a hammer, but this method is more successful with soft herbaceous plants.

The transporting of large consignments of cut shrubs to a show from long distances can be a difficult matter, especially if the material must travel by train and boxes must be used. In this case special care is needed to enable it to appear before the judges in the best possible condition. Cut branches of trees and shrubs do not lend themselves easily to boxing in the same manner as the straight single stems of carnations, chrysanthemums and other herbaceous plants.

Large sprays should be tied or drawn together before packing and laid in ample-sized boxes in such a manner as to prevent movement of any kind. Smaller branches can be drawn or placed between or among the large ones, conserving room. It is a mistake to use tissue-paper excessively as damage may result. The boxes should be lined with paper, after which little paper is necessary. A stiff hazel stick fixed firmly crossways in the centre of the completed package is usually sufficient to anchor all firmly.

Always use cord or strong string and tie firmly all boxes transported by rail, as nothing is more disastrous than the opening of packed exhibits by the breaking or untying of ropes on railway platforms.

I have done much successful exhibiting of cut trees and shrubs, especially rhododendrons with their huge trusses of delicate flowers, and whenever possible I preferred tying the various shrubs in bunches, placing them in water and taking them the whole journey by car or lorry, using no paper at all. Water drainage pipes, with the large end filled with cement and cut off at the desired length make excellent heavy-bottomed vases for the work. The vases should stand as closely together as possible to prevent swaying *en route*, and if necessary they may be tied to avoid tumbling over.

The importance of all exhibits being perfectly fresh has already been mentioned, and this must be borne in mind when the final selection of subjects to exhibit is being made. Rarity is another excellent point-obtainer, provided the rarity is not insignificant; a rare and beautiful shrub is the ideal. It is obvious that some of our common flowering shrubs have been made common because of their indisputable beauty which has made them desirable to all garden lovers.

Again, when selecting for exhibiting, keep a sharp look-out for the better form of the type. This occurs in a large number of plants and the exhibitor who stages the improved form should win. All judges look for good cultivation; this applies to trees and shrubs as much as to vegetables, therefore see to it that your shrubs have all the necessary preparation when planting and are also fed when necessary. To be a successful exhibitor one must be prepared for plenty of hard work, giving careful attention to all details.

When at all possible, extra vases of shrubs for exhibition should be cut and taken to the show. This will allow for accidents and also enable the clever competitor in some classes to score, by preventing the judges from making comparisons between identical exhibits.

All successful exhibitors are good judges; they should be, to be able to select the prize-winning exhibits. The clever person who has taken the trouble to take the extra vases of different kinds of trees and shrubs to the show will be in the position to ring the changes with his exhibits, and when some exhibitor has identical varieties in better form, will replace his own inferior vase with a different kind or variety.

In classes requiring several vases of trees or shrubs highest points are allotted to examples of different genera, therefore it is wise to show only one vase from each genus.

AUTUMN EXHIBITS OF BERRIES AND COLOURED FOLIAGE

All the foregoing remarks for flowering trees and shrubs apply equally strongly to exhibits of cut trees or shrubs in fruit or berry, or to exhibits of autumn coloured foliage. With the latter, experience and disappointments have proved that many autumn colouring trees and shrubs, which appear beautifully lovely when in the open with the sun on them, are most disappointing in a dull hall or room without the sun or with artificial lighting. A good example is *Quercus coccinea*, a perfectly lovely tree in the autumn sunshine, but cut and placed in a dull hall the leaves look merely sombre. Dead leaves are not autumn colouring and although they appear exquisite in the sunlight on the ground under the trees, such lifeless leaves are unattractive indoors.

Real autumn colouring of the foliage has life, and usually appears for a period immediately before the dead, drooping stage. When selecting such vases of foliage for exhibiting, try and choose varieties with a mixture of gold, orange, or yellow mingled with the scarlet or red of the leaf. An excellent example is *Fothergilla monticola*, or *Acer vitifolium*. In a collection of several vases of such exhibits, true yellow foliage is always admired, and it has the advantage of lighting up the remaining foliage in the exhibit. Where *Carya alba* (syn. *C. tomentosa*) is grown, this hickory will prove to be the best of yellow-colouring trees.

Classes for vases of shrubs with decorative fruits are becoming more popular and most interesting. Here strict attention must be paid to the colour of the berries. Red naturally predominates, yet there are plenty of yellows, whites, blacks and even blue fruits and berries. If at all possible and unless of exceptional rarity and beauty, black berries or fruits should be left out of small classes as their colour naturally makes them dull.

The beautiful porcelain-blue gaultherias or the sky-blue *Symplocos paniculata* arranged immediately in front of the yellow *Celastrus orbiculatus*, or the heavy-berried *Pyracantha Rogersiana* var. *flava* or *P. Rogersiana*, var. *aurantiaca*, always scores, as do good white-berried shrubs, staged near the glistening red fruits of *Viburnum betulifolium*, or other red-berried subjects.

STAGING

It is the practice of most horticultural societies to provide identical vases for exhibitors competing in classes for collections of cut shrubs, as this provides for equality. Before commencing to arrange the separate vases, a close inspection of the space allotted to the display should be carried out. This is of great importance, as the amount of space provided governs the size of the display in each vase.

When special small-necked vases are provided, as for single-truss classes of rhododendrons, care is needed when staging not to use too much moss to keep the truss in that perfectly upright position. Should excess moss be used the little water available will not be sufficient to keep the blooms fresh. Wilted plant material in a flower show cannot be tolerated, and nothing is more disappointing to the public than to view a prize-winning exhibit that is flagging badly by the time they see it.

Foliage plays a very important and essential part in the appearance of exhibits and due care must be paid to the removal of any damaged leaves; at the same time, remove very young soft leaves and shoots, as these are delicate and bruise and wilt easily. As far as possible, choose tall, graceful sprays with good healthy foliage, and should the

Left: Embothrium lanceolatum with flaming scarlet flowers in May. This has long been the goal of tree and shrub enthusiasts. *Right: Berberis lologensis* has attractive orange-yellow flowers, shaded apricot, in April.

Left: Pieris taiwanensis bears pure-white lily of the valley-like flowers in April. *Right: Halesia carolina* has white snowdrop-like flowers in May and June.

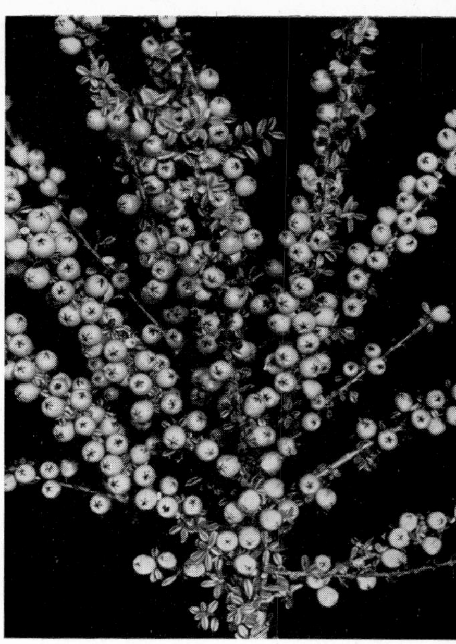

Left: Rosa rubrifolia—the deep red fruits are superb in an autumn berries class. *Right: Cotoneaster conspicua* is always a winner when its branches are covered with bright orange-red berries.

Left: Celastrus articulatus, which has capsule-like fruits that, when open, display scarlet-coated seeds. *Right: Pernettya mucronata* and its hybrids with white, crimson, purple and mauve berries, are always favourites in October.

plant possess large heavy-looking leaves do not hesitate to remove sufficient to avoid an appearance of heaviness.

Some shrubs when in flower, such as *Zenobia pulverulenta*, are best staged denuded of all foliage. In this way the arrangement of the waxy-white flowers is facilitated and unspoilt by the rather weather-beaten leaves of the previous year's growth. With such shrubs a few extra selected growth branches placed behind the blooms will suffice. With all vases of flowers, try to make a density of flower by adding shorter portions at the focal point; this should be in the centre of the arrangement towards the base.

The space allotted to this chapter is practically exhausted, yet a few words must be written concerning the arrangement of mixed flowers, and fruit, berries, and coloured foliage. In this, probably the choice of container is the most important factor. Do not use too dainty or inadequate a bowl or vase; use one of suitable size and weight for your particular arrangement. When planning an arrangement, always remember it must possess public appeal. To achieve this you must create a picture that will appeal to the judges by either its originality, beauty of design, colour harmony, or its ingenuity.

CHAPTER THIRTEEN

Sweet Peas

BY D. GOURLAY THOMAS

THE SECRET of success in exhibiting sweet peas is ultimately a matter of personality. Two men may have equal opportunities but one wins the coveted prize because of his attention to details which the other brushed aside as unimportant. In the keen competition of to-day, nothing can be overlooked, trifling though it may seem, which helps towards producing the perfect exhibits. If genius is the infinite capacity for taking pains, then prize-winning in a worthy sweet pea competition is the reward of resolute attention to details.

CULTIVATION

One must begin with the seed itself. There are seeds and seeds as there are stocks and stocks. One leading seedsman I know even numbers his stocks so that careful comparison may be made between one lot and another, and anything inferior is ruthlessly discarded. Do not make any mistake. We cannot grow good flowers from bad seeds. And when it is a matter of national competition, to which the acknowledged experts bring their products, even good seed is not good enough; we must get the *best*, true to variety, colour and type, and full of vitality. So the first thing is to get seeds from a reliable firm. There are many who specialize in sweet peas and I can bear witness to the scrupulous care which they exercise in discharging their obligations in this direction. Not lightly would they surrender the trusted position which they have won by years of honest dealing. Their name is the guarantee of their merchandise.

Now the next things concern the preparations, first of the potting stage and then of the flowering quarters. Aim at surgical cleanness and thoroughness in every detail. Scrub the pots. Get them as clean as an honest scrubbing can make them.

And then as to your compost; put a conscience into that too. Clean loam, clean sand, clean leaf-mould. The very thought is an inspiration in itself and gives a thrill to the preparation. I cannot agree with those who argue that the compost does not matter when it is a matter of future exhibition. Everything matters. It may be true that we can make up for a bad start, but we can do still better with a good start. Well begun is not only good fun but a good, firm stride towards the prize to be won.

Artificial fertilizers in the compost are unnecessary and, in my experience, more harmful than helpful. Avoid them. The only addition to the above—clean loam, clean sand, clean leaf-mould—which I recommend is a little fine bonemeal. A compost of three parts loam to one of sand, one of leaf-mould, with a handful of bonemeal to about a bushel of the compost, is ideal. Mix these thoroughly at least three weeks before using.

It may be necessary to chip some hard-skinned seeds to ensure an even germination. Such varieties are Romance, Gwendolen, Reconnaissance, Captivation, Tell Tale, Rubicund, Crimson Emblem. A mere chip on the opposite side to the 'eye' is sufficient. Its object is to give the moisture in the compost a chance to penetrate and awaken the seed to growth. Lavenders, wrinkled and round seeds should never be chipped. A number of modern varieties, probably with the blood of 'The Fawn' in them, such as Bonnie Ruffles, Pacific, Silver Jubilee, Radar, Golden Star, Margaret O'Brien, etc., need more careful treatment. In America, a preparation known as 'Spergon' is used to protect them from decay. In any case, a little peat added to the compost will be found to be sufficient, provided that the seeds are germinated swiftly in a warm temperature of 55° to 60° F.

The next step is a hardy upbringing. We must decide first of all when to sow the seed—autumn or January. For the early shows, without doubt, the autumn. For very late shows, the spring, or rather January. I think most exhibitors would agree with me that the full perfection of colouring is only seen in autumn-sown sweet peas. Besides, they bloom at least three to five weeks earlier and give stronger stems and bigger flowers, especially for the early shows.

Whether the plants are autumn or January sown, it is absolutely essential that they should be brought on as hardy as possible. Coddling of any sort is disastrous. The cold will not hurt them, neither will strong winds in the early stages. The only adverse elements to be avoided are hard frosts and the pitilessly icy rains of winter. Expose them to the light and air. Aim at sturdy, short-jointed stock. If the colour of the leaves is a dark green with a purplish tinge to it, shout for joy. This is the sign of a good beginning.

During the winter months it will be wise to keep the plants on the dry side. I do not mean bone-dry, but in a condition nearer dry than moist. During one severe winter, plants that were dry succumbed; those that were somewhere half-way between moist and dry survived, and as soon as happier conditions prevailed not only recovered from the temporary setback but grew away well.

As soon as the lighter days come, then give the plants a good spraying with soft rain water to freshen them up. A few crystals of permanganate of potash in this will act as a deterrent against greenflies and keep the plants clean and healthy.

If no basal shoots have formed by the end of January, then the growing-tip of the plant should be pinched out to encourage these. It is no use training the original growth up the bamboo, for the reason that it will go 'blind' when the plant is about three feet six inches to four feet high. So the strongest of the basal shoots is chosen—one is generally enough in these days of keen competition, though some exhibitors pin their faith to two main growths in the more vigorous varieties like Mrs. C. Kay, Mrs. R. Bolton, Reconnaissance, etc., arguing that *two* main growths make for a more balanced plant, whereas one haulm only in such varieties inclines them to throw 'gappy' flowers. It is impossible to lay down any hard and fast rule on this point. One must be guided by common sense.

I cannot help recalling the dilemma of a local football enthusiast in this connexion, who had been continually shouting his instructions to his hero, 'Head it, Harry boy ', 'Shoot, Harry lad ', and so on, much to the crowd's annoyance. Presently, his hero, with the ball at his feet, was surrounded by five stalwart opponents. The crowd waited in breathless silence to hear what instructions would be forthcoming in so difficult a situation. It came all right: 'Use your own judgment, Harry boy ', said the unabashed instructor, and the crowd roared with laughter.

There are many occasions in sweet pea growing where we can only say to the grower: 'Use your own judgment, friend'. Experience, after all, is the best teacher.

No good grower will ever allow his plants to bend over in the pots for want of a twig or two. He knows too well how easily disease can enter a plant through a cracked or bruised stem, so he safeguards against such a possibility by inserting a few twigs to keep the plants upright. This is specially necessary in very windy areas.

Further, an occasional poke with a strong bit of wood to prevent the surface soil in the pot clogging, as long as one is careful not to damage the roots, is of real value and helps aeration.

In the early spring, keep a sharp look-out for greenfly and also slugs and snails. Without any doubt more harm is caused to the sweet pea by greenflies than by all its other enemies put together, so liquidate this pest without mercy. Any good insecticide, avoiding nicotine, will do all that is wanted, but a word of warning is necessary. Do not use too strong a solution, or you will kill the plants instead of saving them. Use less than the amount advised rather than more.

I know nothing better as a preventive against slugs and snails than a little powdered Meta and bran mixed together. Put a little of this in small heaps along the row and the result will amaze you, if you have not previously tried it. It is a most effective remedy. Birds sometimes peck at the growing tips of the young plants and do a lot of damage. They laugh at bird-scares, 'cats' eyes' and the like. Black thread strained across the tops of the plants is the best deterrent.

But it is time we were giving some attention to the flowering site. Where ought that to be? Well, keep away from the shade of walls or trees. Have the plants out in the open with the rows running from north to south, so that they have the sun upon them all day.

Better than the orthodox trenches is to dig the site right over to a depth of two feet. Two feet is ample, provided the bottom is thoroughly forked to make for good drainage. Incorporate farmyard manure, cabbage stumps, compost, in the bottom, and keep the soil as far as possible in the same order as when you started digging. That is to say, do not bring the bottom soil to the top. Keep the bottom soil at the bottom, the top at the top. Six, seven or even eight inches of manure is not too much in the bottom spit, provided it is thoroughly mixed with the soil and in a state of advanced decay. Farmyard manure at least a year old is excellent. For many this will be unobtainable. Then use home-made compost which is a first-class substitute.

This can be made of lawn-mowings, weeds, cabbage and lettuce leaves, beech and oak leaves, and anything else of that nature. Prepared in good time this can be a really valuable manure. Hops may also be used, though they are very expensive nowadays. Poultry droppings—if old—can be used in moderation. The nitrogen content in fresh poultry manure is rather high and a bit hot for sweet-pea roots. In any case, manures must be limited to the bottom spit. Wood ashes, bonemeal, and a sprinkling of superphosphate can be mixed well with the second spit, but keep the top nine inches or so quite clear of all manures—farmyard or artificial.

Dig the site, if at all possible, in the late autumn, so as to give the soil time to settle by the spring. Sweet peas do not thrive in a loose medium. A heavy dusting of lime over the whole site will help to sweeten the soil, and later release the salts for assimilation by the sweet-pea roots. Leave the surface in ridges, rough and open to the action of frost, rain, wind, snow and sun.

In late February or early March, in favourable weather, rake the rows into a fine tilth. If this can be repeated a day or two before transplanting, all the better. Some growers give the rows a light dusting of a sweet-pea fertilizer, such as Clay's, a fortnight or so before transplanting. They argue that it counteracts any check the plants may suffer in being moved from the pots into their flowering quarters.

All that I am anxious to make transparently clear at this point can be put briefly thus. *Never* try to transplant unless the plants have been well hardened off by exposure both night and day. It is folly, and sometimes fatal, to put unhardened plants straight from a frame, or a greenhouse, into the open ground. Secondly, disturb the roots as little as possible. Plant with the ball of soil intact round the roots. It is wise to give all the pots a good watering about a week before transplanting.

When is one to transplant? Some growers in favoured areas like Devon and Cornwall transplant the very young plants in January and protect them with cloches. These usually flower about mid-May and are at their best in June. Others without cloches wait for a fine spell in March and protect the plants with small twigs. It is not generally realized how great is the protection these twigs afford, from frost, wind, and slugs. The very fact that the plants are off the ground is itself an asset. Once planted, give the seedlings about a fortnight to settle down and make headway. When this begins, then comes the time for almost daily attention.

I am assuming, of course, that all the bamboo canes and structures are in their place. The canes ought to be at least ten inches apart. I have called attention in another place* to the possibility of putting the bamboos, as one does with bean-sticks, in a double row, crossing them about six to eight inches from the top—that is, with eight-foot bamboos. A bamboo put in vertically every seven or eight feet gives added strength to the structure. Whether this, or some other method

*See *Sweet Peas for Garden and Exhibition*, D. Gourlay Thomas. (W. H. and L. Collingridge.)

of support such as wire or fish netting, is used, the plants will now demand daily care.

As soon as the flowering growth is determined, this is trained up the bamboo and all other growths cut away. Remember that this is an intensive, and in a sense artificial, way of growing sweet peas and their balance can soon be, and is often, upset by fluctuations in the weather, a too generous watering, or too early use of fertilizers. Keep clear of these, especially in the early stages. No fertilizers are wanted until the end of June or beginning of July, and only then if there is a shortening of the flower-stem and the plants look as if they need a tonic.

The use of the watering-can may be avoided by a good mulch of very old manure between the plants. This will keep the root-run cool. Failing this, stick to the watering-can rather than use a hose-pipe. With the watering-can you are able to use soft rain-water warmed by the sun; a cold douche from the hose may lead to severe bud-dropping from which it may take weeks to recover.

For the rest, pinch out all side-shoots as one does with tomatoes; cut off all tendrils and all young shoots which may come up at the base. The aim now is to concentrate all the strength and energy of the plant into that one main haulm. Soon you will find it is much thicker across than the width of your thumb and the leaves will be quite as big as lettuce leaves. Flower-stems will shoot out straight and strong to a length of twenty to twenty-four inches, and give 'fours' and 'fives' generously, especially in varieties such as Mrs. C. Kay, Mrs. R. Bolton, Lilacea, Lady Godiva, Josie, Ottawa, and Challenger.

Some varieties will benefit from shading a few days before the show. They are apt to bleach slightly in the very hot sun unless they are lightly shaded by butter muslin, or tiffany, or any light canvas. But given this shading, these difficult ones are to my mind the loveliest of all the varieties—Balmoral, very rich orange; Lochearn, Melody, Patricia Unwin—all golden salmon; Golden Star, golden cerise; Gold Crest and Dawn, rich salmon; Cynthia Davis, orange cerise.

PREPARING FOR THE SHOW

The question of show preparation is the trickiest of all. Some growers have grown first-class sweet peas only to lose the prize by their lack of experience in arranging their vases. So my first bit of advice is to order half-a-dozen vases from the Secretary of the National Sweet Pea Society, and practise this most important art at home. I will later describe the arrangement of the flowers in the vases.

The first thing to decide is when to cut. It depends very largely how far the show is from your home and, of course, the state of the weather. If the show is any great distance away, then whatever else you take into your calculations, you must make certain that your flowers get at least four hours drink before you pack them. Furthermore, you must cut them when they are dry. As soon as the dew is off them in the morning is a very good time. And cut each stem when the top bloom is half open or just less than that. It will open when the stem has been in water for a few hours.

Because you want flowers with the top flower only just opening, and because they can be tantalizingly few just at the time you need them for a show, it is necessary to grow at least twice the number of plants you need for a vase. If the essential number is fifteen stems in a vase, then you will need to grow thirty plants at least to make sure of a good show. Most growers make it thirty-six, and some—the pessimists!—make it even higher.

And the weather factor is a most vital factor in our consideration. One winner in a national show gained a first prize because he cut prior to a storm, although it was on the early side as far as the show was concerned; another would-be exhibitor had to withdraw his entry—a hailstorm had turned his sweet pea site into a place of desolation. Better cut too soon than risk a storm.

On the other hand, if the weather is favourable, make allowance for the four hours in water, time for travelling to the show and time to fix up the vases in time for the judging. Be prepared for an all-night 'do' if necessary. It will not seem nearly as long as it sounds, especially when a friendly rival will come round to have a word with you, another to have a pipe, and yet another to offer you some cherries or to borrow your watering-can! It really *is* great fun, even if you feel the next day as if the top of your head is not where it ought to be, and when your wife addresses you you are not quite sure whether *you* are incoherent or she is! It's all in the game.

Now about the varieties and the packing. Pick out your varieties carefully at home and put them in bundles of twenty. Do not trust to the light of the tent or the hall where you will have to stage your varieties. And make no mistake, if you see no difference between Melody and Patricia Unwin, or Cream Gigantic and Cream Frills, or Mrs. C. Kay and King Lavender, or Leader and Quebec—the judges will! Choose out your varieties carefully in the calm of your home; don't leave it to the more excited atmosphere of the exhibition hall.

Left: A sturdy shoot which is the obvious choice for tying in. *Right:* A twin shoot which must be tied in when there is no sturdy basal shoot.

Left: Tying in the selected shoot after the others have been cut off. *Right:* Side-shoots (as indicated by the arrow) and tendrils must be removed.

Left: The main stem has gone blind and will therefore be replaced by the sturdy basal shoot. *Right:* A side shoot will replace the damaged main stem.

Left: Bud drop of the first flower bud due to cold. Later buds healthy. *Right:* Close-up of a healthy head.

Left: Working among a good even stand of plants at the first flower-bud stage. *Right:* Tying to allow all the flowers to face the pathway.

Left: Layering round the end of a row. The stems are taken three canes forward. *Right:* Showing three stems rounding the end of the row.

Left: Trimming hedge clippings level with the vase top. These support the stems. *Right:* A well-staged vase of Mabel Gower arranged fan-wise.

The prize-winning exhibit of twelve varieties for the *Daily Mail* Challenge Cup.

A box about thirty-six inches long and twenty-four inches wide and six inches deep, made of strong plywood, is an ideal thing for taking the bunches to the show. Put a sheet of tissue-paper at the bottom of the box, place the bundles of twenty side by side and hold them securely by fastening a thin piece of stick firmly across the stems from side to side of the box. Several bunches can be carried in this way and the art is soon learned.

Remember to take with you to the show, reeds for the vases, a pair of sharp nail scissors, a clean sheet or two of white paper, and a rag to wipe the stems of the flowers when you take them out of the water-cans and place them on the white papers for a final choice of the best 'fifteen' before fixing them in their respective vases. The rag is more important than at first appears, for unless the stems are dried before putting them on the paper, it will soon get wet and so be useless as a background to pick out the best specimens.

And the scissors? I am a bit diffident about mentioning this otherwise most useful article, and the more so where sweet peas are concerned, because I do not believe in fingering the petals, but am convinced that they should be shown in their pure beauty as they are cut from the plants. But that, of course, is the whole point at issue here. Because they cannot be shown as they are on the plants, because they have to travel sometimes hundreds of miles before they are exhibited, it is possible that one or two are bruised or spotted at the fringe of the petals, and you have nothing to fall back upon. Leave the bruise or the spot and you are bound to lose marks. A judicious use of the scissors is justified, I think, in such a case, provided it does not interfere too drastically with the contour of the bloom. It will need very delicate handling indeed, for it must in no way alter the essential shape of the flower.

The reeds are needed to put in the vases to hold the flower stems firmly in position. No exhibition vase can be arranged without some such aid. And it is wise to bring your own. Wiser still to practise the art of arranging vases in the quiet of home or greenhouse for a few weeks before the show.

One of the finest exhibitors in the country, with a cigarette in his mouth, practises this art of flower arrangement, at the close of day when work is done, for many nights before a show. Unnecessary? So others have thought, but the results have justified this exhibitor rather than his critics. He has enough silver cups to start a jeweller's shop; they have not even enough to take one steadying drink after their discomfiture!

Believe me, the competition in sweet pea culture is so high at the present time that to miss one detail may suffice to miss the prize.

UNPACKING AND STAGING

But I have increased my pace a little and now need to go back to the place where we enter the exhibition hall, or tent, with our boxes. Make sure a thoughtless taxi-man does not dump these down too violently. It is amazing what energy some people can evoke for the wrong things!

First discover where the section in which you are going to display your main entries is situated, and at no great distance secure a place where you can arrange your vases. Then get the water-cans you need and before starting any arranging at all, put your stems into the water and let the flowers have a good drink. If the journey has been a long one, it may be over an hour before the flowers are fit to handle. The very look of them will soon tell you when it is time to begin arranging your vases. While you are waiting, fill the vases with water and fix in the reeds tightly, cutting them off level with the tops of the vases.

Now get ready for your first vase. Place your twenty to thirty stems side by side carefully on the sheet of paper and pick out your best fifteen. If you have any 'fives', immaculately fresh, keep them for the front of the vase. 'Fours' are essential in keen competition, but choose a fresh 'three' rather than a faded 'four', and if your top flower is not fully open, have no fear, in a few hours in a hot tent it will soon expand to perfection.

Put your decorative leaves in the vase first, one pair in the front looking like a big butterfly, and one at the back. Next fix six spikes at the back of the vase fantail-fashion, if anything leaning a little backwards but spread out like a fan, no flower overlapping another. Now place your second row of four or five spikes in similar fashion a little to the front of the back row and yet each spike showing up quite independently. In the front row, put in the remaining four or five special blooms. The whole vase when completed looks like 'my lady's fan', a thing of perfect balance and beauty.

An amateur may be forgiven for thinking that this is all very intricate, but a little practice will soon give him all the confidence he needs, and no one is more friendly in helping the beginner than the old hand. I have known some of them jeopardize their own chance of winning by helping a competitor simply because he had better flowers than themselves and deserved to win. I find myself responding to that kind of spirit at deeper levels than even the sheer beauty of the flowers evokes in me, probably because it is the spirit of which the flowers themselves are but a lovely reflection. In any case, watch the old hands at work. That is an education in itself and we soon learn.

What does a judge look for in first-class competition? These, I think, would be the deciding qualities—the size of the blooms, their number on a stem, and their placement, together with the length and thickness of the stems; the colour, quality and freshness of the blooms; their arrangement in the vases and their staging in such a way, by contrast or by harmony, as to reveal their finest quality.

The four or five blooms on a stem ought to be evenly placed. 'Gappy' blooms are evidence of erratic culture. Strong stimulants may cause this, either artificial fertilizers or doses of liquid manure, or even a faulty trench, or sometimes a period of heavy rain which carries the fertilizers down in wholesale fashion. It is partly for this reason that I deprecate the use of 'artificials' until late in the season.

It ought to be realized that some varieties are bigger than others, and that some throw 'fives' with prodigal generosity. These varieties make for massive vases, and are generally included in the leading dozens. The others are chosen mostly for their indescribably beautiful colours or for their even response to good culture.

Among these big varieties are Vanguard, Leader, Quebec, Romance, Josie, Gigantic, Cream Gigantic, Aristocrat, Eglantine, Clare Booth Luce, Gracie, Gwendolen, Rubicund, Gaiety.

Among those giving 'fives' freely are Mrs. C. Kay, Mrs. R. Bolton, Lilacea, Loyalty, Royal Mauve, Rosina.

And for sheer joy of colouring here are some lovely varieties: Princess Elizabeth, Cynthia Davis, Lochearn, Melody, Margaret O'Brien, Air Warden, Cheers, Lady Godiva, Cream Delight, Coral Beauty, Echo, Salmon Frills, Autumn Gold.

Now a further thought must be given, not simply to the arrangement of a vase, but to the arrangement of *all* the vases, so that they enhance one another's colour-values. Unfortunately, some colours are almost automatically excluded for this very reason. Some of the purples and the maroons, for instance, have a deadening effect on what is meant to be a bright corner, and others in the carmine class are such 'screams' that they would be better in a circus than a beauty competition! And the 'blues' for some reason are not good company; the lavenders are better.

Attention, too, must be paid to your neighbour's staging. Make sure that his vases which are next to yours do not 'scream' yours out of court. This may need a slight rearrangement, but it can generally be managed. In any case, give your exhibit a sense of richness and unity. Try to make the judge feel that you are exhibiting flowers of first-class quality and that they are of even merit whatever the variety, that you are as expert with the golden-salmons and the orange shades as with the creams and the lavenders. And, by the way, when you are exhibiting an outstandingly rich display, choose the creams and the cream picotees rather than the colder whites. Further, make sure that you include some at least of the salmon, salmon-orange, and orange shades, which, though harder to grow, are a sign of the keen enthusiast and greatly add to the colour-value of an exhibit.

For instance, I am certain that it was a vase of the lovely Melody which decided the issue in one of the most keenly fought exhibits I have ever known, where it was necessary to point not only vase by vase, but almost flower by flower. The entrancing loveliness of that perfect vase of Melody proved the final factor and deservedly so. In this class are such lovely varieties as Lochearn, Patricia Unwin, Princess Elizabeth, Golden Star, Cynthia Davis, Dawn, Royal Pink, Countess Baldwin, Princess Royal, Gold Crest, Balmoral, and Margaret O'Brien.

VARIETIES

What varieties, then, are we to choose for the best dozen? Here are notes of some which are on top of their form just now and likely to remain in the top rank for some years. Vanguard is probably the biggest of them all—a salmon-pink of even shading. Leader and Quebec are also big, much alike and yet distinct—these are also salmon-pink. Romance, a newcomer, is a pea of refined colouring, an appealing rose-pink on a cream background. Gwendolen is a well-known exhibition variety of similar colouring. Aristocrat and Eglantine are pink in colour on a white background, very frilly and huge. The latter is lighter in shade than Aristocrat. Clare Booth Luce, of American origin, is an unusual shade of rose-pink with many double standards. Gracie, a pale cream pink, I also put in this class of 'big' varieties, and Josie a mid-salmon-pink, on cream, because of their tendency to throw flowers with frilly, double standards, which make for weighty vases. Gigantic, Cream Gigantic, and Cream Frills also come in this class. Out of this lot an exhibitor could pick any three or four with safety. My choice would be Vanguard, Romance, Gracie, Josie, and Cream Frills. A newcomer that has great promise is Cream Delight, a Gold Medal seedling in 1948.

Among lavenders, Mrs. C. Kay is at present the outstanding favourite on account of its vigorous nature and its generosity with 'fives' of quality and size. It has won cup after cup in the keenest national competition as the best vase in the show, the 1948 cup being won by a vase of fifteen spikes, every one of them 'fives'! Another excellent lavender of deeper shade is the reliable Mrs. R. P. Butchart, a Canadian variety, of most even colouring. It does not give as many 'fives' as Mrs. C. Kay, but the 'fours' are plentiful and of good size. A third lavender to which justice has not been done is Lavender King, a variety mid-way between Mrs. C. Kay and Mrs. R. P. Butchart in colouring, and a vigorous plant. Lilacea, lavender, and Lavender Queen, lilac-lavender, have yet to win their spurs.

In keen competition, I should stick to Mrs. C. Kay and Mrs. R. P. Butchart.

Now for picotees: Reconnaissance, a rose edge on cream, and Tell Tale, a fainter rose edge on white, are without serious rivals. The first when well grown is superb, the second gives one the impression of great daintiness. For an orange-cerise, Mollie has long held the throne. Two newcomers in this section are bidding for royal honours, both awarded gold medals in different trials. The first is Cynthia Davis, a most vigorous and lovely variety, and Margaret O'Brien, an American seedling of entrancing colouring. Personally, I shall grow both, for they are quite distinct in form and colouring, and these two in a 'twelve', plus a salmon-orange or an orange variety will give the exhibit a wonderfully rich appearance.

Royal Mauve is without a rival at the moment as far as popularity is concerned. It is a beauty. Elizabeth Taylor is of similar colouring and is said to be a little larger, but I have not yet grown them side by side. The latter was awarded a Gold Medal at the National Sweet Pea Society's Trials in 1948. Marion Moon, a new mauve, will probably surpass both.

For salmon-pinks we have Echo, Greta, Silver Jubilee, Radar, Pink Beauty, Lady Godiva, Mrs. P. Simons, Pink Lady, Loyalty, Lady Sylvia, all of them good, and, the loveliest of them all, Princess Elizabeth, also a Gold Medal seedling of 1948.

Now let us see what we have got towards an exhibition dozen: Vanguard, Romance, Gracie, Josie, Cream Frills or Cream Delight, Mrs. C. Kay, Mrs. P. Butchart, Reconnaissance, Cynthia Davis, Margaret O'Brien, Royal Mauve or Elizabeth Taylor, Echo, Princess Elizabeth.

How did we come to leave out Mrs. R. Bolton?—the best

all-round variety ever produced, says one of our keenest exhibitors, and he is right. Almond-pink is the poor description given to this fascinating variety, but it is much more than that. In hot sunshine when the full colour is in it, one can almost trace orange in it; in any case, there is 'fire' in it and it is an outstanding exhibition variety. So that gives us fourteen.

A few golden-salmons to choose from are Lochearn, Melody, Patricia Unwin, and Autumn Gold. John Krabbi, a newcomer, is most promising. There are also some excellent scarlets like Air Warden, Startler, and the new Magnificence. Toreador, a salmon-scarlet, perfectly sunproof, is gaining favour among some exhibitors. Thriller is well-known. As an orange, Balmoral is unsurpassed. In the whites, Gigantic, Mt. Everest, and White Heather are first-class. Carlotta, rose-carmine, is still first in its class and an excellent exhibition variety, though its place in a 'twelve' needs careful choosing. Among other exhibition varieties, most of them new in 1949, are Josie, a soft pink on a rich cream ground; Mrs. P. Simons, an extremely frilly flesh pink; Ottawa, pale salmon-pink; Fire King, startling scarlet-cerise; Lady Godiva, a lovely flesh-pink; Harmony, a cream-pink of distinction.

Any of these could be used with confidence in an exhibition 'twelve'. My choice of a winning 'dozen' and the order in which I would place them would be as follows: Vanguard (salmon-pink), Cream Delight, Royal Mauve, Romance (rose-pink), Mrs. C. Kay (lavender), Mrs. R. Bolton (almond-pink), Cynthia Davis (orange-cerise), Reconnaissance (cream picotee), Margaret O'Brien (orange-cerise), Lochearn (golden-salmon), Princess Elizabeth (fawn-pink), Air Warden (scarlet).

A second choice would be: Quebec or Leader (salmon-pink), Lavender Queen (lilac), Cream Frills, Startler or Magnificence (scarlet), Marion Moon (mauve), Autumn Gold (cerise-salmon), Balmoral (orange), Tell Tale (picotee), Gracie (pale cream-pink), Melody (golden-salmon), Josie (soft pink on cream), Mrs. R. P. Butchart (lavender).

Once you have staged your exhibit, your work is not quite over. Remember that in a hot tent, the water in the vases is soon lapped up, and will need replenishing. It may be some time before the judges come to your exhibit, so make sure every vase has sufficient water before leaving the tent.

Further, put a small card (these are usually supplied in the bigger shows) bearing the names of the variety at the base of each vase.

See that the name is written, or printed, neatly. Take a last look at your exhibit before leaving the hall. Make any adjustments you consider necessary. Then wait as patiently as you can for the judges' decision. If you have won, your delight will be delightful if it is coupled with modesty (do you remember the gardener who won the first prize for his roses in 'Mrs. Miniver'?); if you have lost . . . well, losing today is only a spur towards winning tomorrow. And in any case, good luck!

CHAPTER FOURTEEN

Decorative Classes

BY VIOLET STEVENSON

THERE MUST BE many people who, having visited a flower show and inspected the entries in the decorative classes, have said, 'Why, I can do better than this.' If you are one of these people, then come along to the next show held in your district and help to swell the ranks of exhibitors. You will be helping the show and giving yourself a great deal of pleasure and entertainment.

The decorative classes are still one of the most popular sections of almost every flower show from the spectators' point of view, while from the competitors' angle, in many parts of the country, interest seems to have steadily dwindled. Why is this? My own opinion is, speaking generally, that the type of floral arrangement which we see at the show is too far removed from that which the modern woman uses in her home. Also, it is quite likely that there are many people who are under a misapprehension and feel that arrangements at flower shows must conform to certain archaic rules; that it is only exhibition flowers which should be used, and that they should be arranged along with masses of asparagus fern, ornamental grasses or, worse still, bulrushes. As they dislike this style of arrangement they do not take part in the show.

Unfortunately, many flower-show judges do still prefer the old-fashioned type of flower arrangement. But you must not judge them too severely. Many of them are grand old gardeners who were taught to arrange flowers that way when they were young and when those styles were fashionable. To them it is still the only correct way.

First, then, forget all preconceived ideas and arrange your show flowers as if you were in your own home. Let your arrangement of them express your own individuality. Let it be beautiful and, if you can, let it be original.

You should study the flower show schedule carefully in order to discover which class appeals to you or is most suitable. And here is a word of warning. Do not enter too many classes to begin with. Although in some ways showing is a serious business, it should also be fun. After all, it is intended to be a recreation. There is no enjoyment to be found if you enter so many classes that for days beforehand you are haunted by the fear that you will not have enough flowers or foliage; or that it is going to be difficult to find containers for all the exhibits; or if, when the great day comes, you have to do all your work with one eye on the clock. Time catches up enough with us as it is without letting it spoil the flower show!

So first select one or two classes. Your choice should fall upon that class which caters for the kind of arrangement that you feel best able to execute. For example, perhaps you have a table on which you always place a bowl of flowers so that you have become adept at arranging a formal bowl which looks the same when viewed from all sides; or maybe you have a sideboard or a hall table on which you have a basket of flowers; or perhaps you arrange the flowers on the altar in your church, in which case you will be most proficient at arranging flowers so that they face one way. Let these factors help you to come to a decision.

This brings up an important point. Never use a strange, that is a new, container for the first time at a flower show. Use only those containers with which you are thoroughly familiar. If you can have one or two rehearsals at home you will find them a great help. Practise with odds and ends of twigs, leaves and flowers until you are quite sure that you know just how long the stems should be, so that they and the container form pleasing proportions. This will teach you whether it will be best to place the central flower or the side flowers in position first. It is important to learn to work with decision. A rehearsal will help to give you the confidence you need. An arrangement never looks well once you start pulling it to pieces. You should know where every stem is to go—and why it is placed there.

Having decided which class or classes you are to enter and having selected the container (never leave this until the day before the show) and the holder you intend to use, read through the schedule once again. Are you quite sure that the container complies with the rules laid down in the schedule? Some flower show committees are very strict about the measurements of the containers which may be used. If these rules are not observed you may find that your entry is disqualified. The next thing to decide is, do the flowers you intend using conform to the rules set out in the schedule? If it calls for perennials then make sure that you are not using annuals or biennials. Check with your show secretary if there is any doubt in your mind. See that your entry is sent off in good time.

Now having decided that nothing has been left undone or overlooked, how should the flowers be arranged? First make up your mind that there will never be universal agreement upon this subject of floral arrangement, any more than there will be agreement upon the mode of painting a picture. Each composition should be a work of art; each should stir the emotions and, as far as flowers are concerned, the more pleasantly they stir them the better. I think that it would be very wrong of me to say that certain things *must* be done. But even so, there are certain pointers that will help the exhibitor to avoid pitfalls and to prevent him or her from producing some of the ugly concoctions put up under the name of floral art.

First let us clear one little matter. Most schedules state that ornamental foliage, grasses and berries may be used, but the schedule does not state that they *must* be used. Too often an attractive arrangement of flowers is ruined because the exhibitor, often at the last moment, has hidden the line and form of the flowers with maidenhair fern or snowberries. Do not do this. Unless foliage, grasses and berries add beauty to the colour, shape or line of the arrangement they should be left out. They should never be added as an afterthought, but should be used with the other materials to make a definite pattern.

Why does this old-fashioned style of incorporating extraneous materials still persist? It is a legacy from the past. Flower decorations have been part of our flower shows for well over a century and it is inevitable that a certain amount of convention lingers on. The editress of a book, *Floral Decorations for Dwelling Houses*, written in 1875, advises her readers to 'shroud the flowers with maiden-hair fern' and suggests wrapping the handles of the baskets with ivy or Japanese honeysuckle.

New entrants to the flower show are apt to copy the styles that they have seen on display at previous shows. They are really copying arrangements which have been used for a century and more. Do not arrange flowers in a certain manner simply because you have always seen them arranged that way. Try to see them with new eyes. So much has changed even in our own lifetimes. It is inevitable that floral decoration should change also.

In our homes we no longer use ornate silver epergnes, intricately

An arrangement in a bowl can have an 'all-round effect' yet need not be strictly formal. Foliage should be used to add line and/or colour.

The basket handle should not be hidden but should form part of the design and the basket should be treated as any other container. Mixed flowers are best grouped.

Pointed leaves, buds and small flowers look best at the edges of a composition. Allow stems to curve naturally.

Extra foliage, grasses or berries should be added only if they bring extra colour, line or grace.

fashioned bamboo flower vases, or massive rose bowls. The containers in which we place our flowers (which, by the way, have changed somewhat too) now conform to the more subdued type of furnishing we use in our homes. Why then should we save the old-fashioned ones for the flower show? Would it not be better to eliminate them as obsolete?

One of the most prevalent faults of competitors in these classes is the choice of the wrong container. Do not search the cupboards for the most elaborately patterned vase you have or for your finest specimen of cut glass. You will not be entitled to a prize because you have the most expensive vase in the show, neither will the splendour of the container be a substitute for inferior flower arrangement.

The container is the medium through which the flowers receive the water to keep them fresh. That is its primary use. If we wish to display the flowers so that their beauty is thoroughly appreciated, we must see to it that the receptacle in which they are displayed does not detract from their beauty. If it is possible to use it so that it enhances the beauty of the flowers or the arrangement, then so much the better.

Most containers are too large (although there are some which are too small) and they tend to dominate the arrangement by virtue of their size. This has probably come about because it is believed that the flowers should receive plenty of water. So they should, but a big vase is not necessary to provide it. After the flowers have been gathered they should receive a long drink in deep water. They should be stood in a cool place. Once the cells are well charged with water the flowers may stand in shallower water. As a general rule, stems should have one-third of their length in water. Some need a little more, others may be placed in much less and still last well.

You are much more likely to achieve correct balance of design if you take care to see that the tallest-stemmed flower (measured from the rim of the container) is at least one and a half times as tall as the container. This is no hard-and-fast rule but if you set out with this standard in your mind, you are much more likely to be pleased with the resulting arrangement. In this way you will avoid squatness. Of course, stems may be much higher than the one and a half times.

It is not necessary that the whole of the container should show; indeed, it is often better if it does not. The lower flower-stems may be allowed to fall gracefully, so that much of the container is hidden. This is especially attractive when arrangements for table decorations are being designed, the important thing here being to keep the arrangement low.

Next to be considered is the colour of the container. This should be part of the colour scheme (and you should have some kind of colour scheme) or its colour should be so neutral that it merges into that of the arrangement. It is not wise to use a container which is highly patterned. In most cases, the plainer the surface the better. Its colour may be contrasting, complementary or the same as that of the flowers or materials used in the arrangement, or it may be green. If green is used, every effort to get the right shade of green should be made. One should not use a blue-green container with a flower that has yellow-green foliage.

The container should be in keeping with the materials used. A delicate china vase will look out of character with orange pot marigolds, whereas a sturdy pottery container would reflect their own robustness. Woody-stemmed materials really do not look well in cut glass. If clear glass is used, see that the portion of stem under water is not untidy.

The shape is important too. Many flower show committees have bought vases which they supply to exhibitors. This is done so that the exhibition should have a uniform appearance. Most of the vases are a similar pattern, green with a narrow 'waist'. Although this type of container is quite useful for specimen blooms, avoid using it for an arrangement. The narrow waist prevents the stems of the flowers from reaching the bottom of the container unless they are stood upright. If they are placed so that they lie in a horizontal position, the narrowness of the vase restricts arrangement, and the stems fall out of the vase. Avoid using containers with narrow mouths unless you are to use thin-stemmed, very branching materials, or unless you are a skilled arranger.

The skill of arranging flowers lies in placing them so that they form a pleasing pattern and fall into place as you wish them to. If you are to do this easily, it is most important that you use the correct type of flower holder. There are several patterns on the market, but I find that the best type of holder is made from a ball of large-mesh wire netting. Use this for every type of container, from those that are as small as an egg-cup to those that are very large. Cut a piece of wire netting twice as long as the container and a little wider. Fold it over and screw it into a ball. Push it into the bowl. For a taller container you need a piece twice its height and a little wider than its mouth. Double the wire netting over and force it into the container.

If you are using a very shallow bowl, or if you think that the wire netting is liable to slip against the glazed sides of the container (as it sometimes does), place a piece of green Plasticine at the base of the container (a lump in the centre is usually sufficient) and press the wire netting into it. Alternatively use a pin-holder.

There is not space to enable me to go into great detail regarding colour, so I will concentrate on the more general faults and difficulties arising out of floral colour and colour combinations. Usually there is enough green present in the general make-up of the flower to make it unnecessary to add more. For example, if yellow chrysanthemums, which have good green leaves, are placed in a mauve container, there will be a colour harmony of yellow, mauve and green in fairly even proportions. But you may want to arrange the flowers so that you have a colour scheme consisting of mauve and yellow only, in which case it will be necessary to remove some of the foliage from the flower-stems and/or add more mauve flowers; for example, michaelmas daisies, mauve berries such as pernettya or any foliage that has mauve markings in it.

You should not use colours in equal quantity. An even quantity of mauve and yellow is not half as interesting as one which has been balanced by using less of the dominant hue and more of the other. This is where and when the use of extraneous materials becomes essential. The same remarks apply to any other colour harmony. Red and white, for example, may look quite crude, but if a mass of white with a focal point of red is used, or vice versa, the arrangement begins to take on a little more character. If foliage which is tinged with pink or with a tint of red, and that with darker shades of red is incorporated with the flowers, then often a perfect harmony is the result.

It is, of course, quite possible to produce a good result with a monochromatic arrangement. For example, if you decide to use pink flowers, a bowl of pink roses with green leaves would provide a harmony of pink and green, but if you eliminated most of the green leaves and used instead those leaves that had pink tints or shades you would tend towards a monochromatic arrangement which might be very charming. If other flowers are used with the roses and if you wish still to have a monochromatic colour harmony, then these too should carry on the same colours.

The most obvious faults arise from lack of colour consciousness. A sugary pink pyrethrum should not be placed with orange poppies or crimson peonies unless one colour may be led or merged into the other by careful blending and by using shades and tints of all these hues. Do not try difficult colour schemes until you have become proficient at arranging the more simple colour harmonies.

Nature provides her own colour schemes and you would do well to use these as a guide. For instance we all know because we have seen them so often that bluebells and ragged robins 'go' well together. So do violets and primroses. All hues of sweet peas, ten-week stocks, Shirley poppies, candytuft and 'Sweetheart' chrysanthemums blend with each other. If you use other flowers with any of these, they should be of colours which you know will harmonize. You can, for example, with safety mix blue with orange, red with green, violet with yellow, or green, white and black.

Discord may occur if flowers that bloom during the same season are placed together without regard being paid to the fitness of the association. For example, vases of michaelmas daisies, bronze chrysanthemums and red dahlias, like trumpet daffodils, pheasant's eye narcissus and hawthorn sprigs, or roses and gypsophila are all equally unsatisfactory.

Chrysanthemums are one of the most difficult flowers for the novice to arrange. Straight-stemmed round blooms fall into a stiff geometrical pattern unless care is taken to see that the right type of container is used. Choose one that has a fairly, but not too, wide mouth. See that the flowers are long-stemmed. If you have short-stemmed flowers, choose a shorter vase or alternatively use them with taller additional materials which will provide the required height. Avoid a squat arrangement.

You will need to incorporate some curving lines or line to break the stiffness. Pleasant effects may be achieved by trying to reproduce the contours of the flowers in the container. Thus a round, egg-shaped or oval vase will sometimes permit a more effective result than one with straight sides. Save that type for the spray and branching types of flowers. This is where additional foliage comes in useful, for it will often give good line and shape to a stiff arrangement. See that the material you use has a strong character. Avoid using fussy fern and grasses. Chrysanthemums have sufficient personality to overwhelm the other materials unless their personality is equally strong. Materials may provide a contrast in form; spiky and pointed materials for example.

If you have placed the flowers carefully and if the arrangement is not overcrowded, it will not need lightening. Buds and half-opened flowers may be used to break the monotony of the rounded blooms. They need not necessarily be buds of the same variety.

PART TWO

Fruit

By F.J. Rose, V.M.H.

CHAPTER FIFTEEN

Selecting and Staging Fruits

THE CULTIVATION of fruit for exhibition is a pleasant and interesting occupation. The knowledge that the fruit he grows will be seen and analysed by the general public is an incentive which makes the grower strain to produce fruit of the highest quality. It often leads him to depart from the orthodox methods of cultivation, and, by experimenting, to find out how to obtain that little extra which is so necessary for the exhibition bench.

Quality is the great essential for exhibition work. In many instances it may be combined with size. In others the gardener may have to choose between specimens of mere size, and smaller fruits of better quality, colour and finish. The wise exhibitor will choose the latter. In all cases the fruit must be of uniform size, perfectly finished and staged to the best advantage.

The selected fruits must be unblemished and this will mean that the grower must wage a constant battle against pests and diseases.

In recent years many mechanical tools have been introduced to suit gardens of all sizes. One of the most useful is the power sprayer. Not only does it save much time, but the work done with it is thorough and efficient. The pressure at which the spray material is applied ensures that it effectively covers every part of the tree.

The question of timing to have the fruit in the best possible condition must also be considered. This important question is linked with varieties and the methods of storing available to the grower. These matters are dealt with later when the different kinds of fruit are reviewed under separate headings.

Some kinds of fruit may be placed in cold storage should they be required for exhibition. Apples, peaches, nectarines, pears and plums have been kept for several weeks and proved to be in good condition when placed before the judges. Selected fruit should be slightly under-ripe, and the temperature of the store room should be about 40° F.

The fruit should be packed ready for transport to the show before being placed in the cold chamber. It should then be taken out about forty-eight hours before being judged, and the packages opened. The fruit will then 'sweat' and must not be touched until it has dried off—usually in about twelve hours. It will then be in good condition for the exhibition bench.

In fruit classes the show schedules speak of 'dishes'. For instance, 'Class 24—Six dishes of dessert fruit'. The word 'dish' is used in a general sense and is understood to mean any receptacle in which the fruit may be staged.

NUMBER OF SPECIMENS REQUIRED FOR A DISH

1 Pineapple
1 Melon
2 or 3 bunches of Grapes, as specified in the schedule
6 Peaches
6 Nectarines
9 Figs
9 Apricots
9 Plums
6 Pears
6 Apples
6 Quinces
12 Bananas
6 Oranges
9 Dessert Tomatoes, or 6 bunches of the smaller varieties
20 Strawberries
50 Cherries
50 Raspberries
30 Gooseberries
30 Bunches of Red or White Currants
1 pound of Black Currants
30 Damsons, Prunes or Bullaces
1 pound of Nuts

When the fruit is staged on a plate, this should first be covered with cotton wool or wood-wool, and each plate then neatly covered with tissue-paper. Leaves also may be used; those of the vine or ampelopsis (Virginia Creeper) are suitable. For the autumn shows the natural colour in the leaves is an additional attraction. The centre fruit may be raised on a wad of wood-wool wrapped in tissue-paper and this will improve the presentation of the dish. One variety only should be placed on one dish, and it is important that all dishes should be named. (Occasionally the wording of a schedule may allow mixed dishes, but it is very seldom.) Every effort should be made to preserve the natural 'bloom' of the fruit. Polishing of any fruit, particularly apples and pears, will not help the exhibitor; it is condemned by the judges and will count against the exhibit.

Some classes call for an arrangement of mixed chrysanthemums or rather, the schedule does not stipulate that they must all be of one kind. If you mix the varieties, then you will be able to make many delightful colour harmonies by using every description of chrysanthemum such as the tiny pompon, Korean, spray, single and so on in one arrangement. Many of the smaller varieties are most useful for table arrangements.

The foregoing remarks apply to dahlias also, but, if anything, these are often a little more difficult to arrange owing to their habit of the bloom facing one way.

BOWLS

When the schedule states 'a bowl of flowers arranged for effect', it is usually intended that the flowers should be arranged in a bowl of conventional pattern, that is, that the bowl should resemble a ball sawn in half. In this bowl the flowers should be so arranged that they, too, form half a sphere. The outline is not expected to be perfectly true, but the bowl should present the same appearance when viewed from any angle. This is one of the simplest designs for a flower arrangement. The most common fault lies in the habit exhibitors have of choosing a bowl which is too small, quite a contrast from the vase classes where the fault lies in the other direction. The size of the bowl will depend upon the type of flowers used. For example a bowl of nigella would not need such a large bowl as incurving chrysanthemums and yet it is surprising to see how often the latter are shown displayed in too shallow a bowl.

Place the wire netting in the bowl and make sure that it is quite firm. If necessary put a lump of Plasticine in the bottom of the bowl and force the wire into it. Next gauge the proportions that the arrangement is to take by placing the central stem in position. As this is to be a formal arrangement, much of its success will depend upon perfect proportions and balance so that every effort must be made to ensure that this central stem is in the correct position. It should be placed in the direct centre of the container. It should be the tallest stem in the arrangement and its tip should come directly in a line with the centre of the container. If the stem curves, then manipulate it until it falls into the position described.

In a hemispherical pattern the side stems which will lie horizontally should be the same length or longer than the central stem. They should be placed in position after the central stem and be allowed to lie at right angles to this. Later other, often more curving, stems may be placed below them so that they add a little grace to the arrangement and help to remove any stiffness of effect. After these main stems have been placed, roughly sketch in the outline of the arrangement. Avoid making it stiff or too precise.

If one variety of flower is being used, vary the outline and form of the arrangement by using buds and half-opened flowers. If mixed flowers are used, place the most pointed flowers and those with spiky forms at the extremities and the larger flowers (and leaves) at the base.

If an oval-shaped arrangement such as is used for a table decoration is to be made, then use longer-stemmed flowers at the sides. Such an arrangement need not necessarily be in a bowl. A trough or square container will serve just as well.

VASES

In many cases schedules do not make allowances for more than one style of vase arrangement, and you should make quite certain whether you are required to arrange the flowers so that they may be viewed from all angles or from the front only. Where the former is to be the rule, use methods similar to those I have just described for a bowl, except for the fact that here it will not be necessary to form a half sphere. You may place the flowers so that they form a pyramidal, oval, fan-shaped or fountain-like arrangement. For a vase which is to be placed against a background, that is, which is made so that it has a flat back hidden from view, begin in the same manner. Place the central stem in position first and then build the design. It really is important to get off to a good start. Unless that centre stem is right, you will never get the design correctly balanced.

BASKETS

Baskets still feature in our shows, although they are no longer used so much in the home. There is really no need for you to stick to the old-fashioned style of basket. A modern shopping type can be made to look as attractive as any other if you take care over the arrangement. Then too there are the types of basket used for gardening such as the Sussex trug.

The style of assembly is similar to that used with vases, except that one must take the handle into account. The most important stem may be placed so that it cuts across the centre of the handle or so that it is at an angle to it. In fact the whole arrangement may be designed so that it is at an angle to the handle.

TABLE DECORATIONS

The custom of setting flowers on the table when we have guests for a meal is a legacy from the age when meals were sumptuous affairs. It has come down to us from an age when it was believed that some flowers, for example roses, had certain powers to enable the guests to overcome that most embarrassing malady, intoxication. They were heaped upon the table, wine cups were wreathed with them, while guests and attendants alike wore wreaths of them on their heads. Gradually other flowers were used besides the rose, and the particular use of the rose became insignificant.

It seems that flowers were not used in such magnificent display again until the Victorian era. Then a new fashion became established. Hostesses sought to outdo each other in elaborate table displays. The centres of the great banquet tables were decorated with flowers. Often a large bowl was placed in the centre and small vases set round it, perhaps in the four corners of the cloth that covered the centre.

About this time also, ladies and their gardeners displayed their skill at table decorations at the local flower show. They used a small table which represented part of the banquet table and showed how they would decorate that particular part of the table. In this case it was quite legitimate to smother the area between the vases with trailing fern, flower petals, etc. From this practice we have been left with the legacy of the table decorations of our twentieth-century shows. It is almost forgotten that the original table supplied represented only part of the large table—the space in the very centre, in fact. The show authorities provide the same small tables and the exhibitors continue to decorate them in the way of their forefathers.

Many flower show committees are now providing tables that are to be found in the average home. The decorations are changing accordingly.

If you enter in this class, forget all the table decorations you have formerly seen and set out to decorate the table as you would like to do it if you were giving a party. Leave room for the dishes, plates, and cutlery. Take care that none of the arrangements is so tall that you cannot see the people on the other side of the table. Start right by choosing the correct containers. These should be low. It will then be possible to place the stems so that they extend along the table. It is length and not height that is important here. The containers may be quite shallow, for if the flowers have been looked after properly from the time they were picked they will stand quite well.

An unusual table decoration is often attractive, but it must not be too garish. It is very distracting to have to sit before very strident colours. Flowers are there to furnish the table, but it is not good furnishing to overcrowd.

In many cases you will be allowed to provide your own tablecloth. Here again, do not be misled into thinking that it is the finest lace or damask cloth that will catch the judges' eye. Let your cloth and flowers be linked by colour if you can. Colour schemes other than all white ones will look well. Why not let the cloth be a tint of the flower colour you intend using? For example, a very, very pale pink with 'Sylvia' roses, or it may be a tint of a complementary or contrasting colour such as very, very pale mauve with soft primrose-yellow chrysanthemums, or a delicate blue with eschscholzias, or maybe a pleasing contrast of dark oak. If you use lace cloths, they could be placed on a background of any colour you desire but, of course, the colour should link up with the flowers.

As always, the container should fit into the scheme of things, and in the case of table decorations the container should not show very much. No one wants to sit looking into the china face of a bowl when there are flowers to be seen.

The manner in which the vases are placed on the table is an important and controversial point. Assuming that you have an average sized dining table to work on, you may feel that one bowl of flowers is sufficient. This is permissible. You do not have to cover the table. But if you do use one bowl only, see that it is attractive enough to warrant the title of 'table decoration'. Alternatively, you may feel that one bowl and two small ones is more to your purpose. If you place these down the centre of the table, you should indicate that two people (if the schedule calls for a table for four, and it often does) sit each side of the table, that is on each side of the flowers. Very plain mats may be used to indicate this. Alternatively, the flowers may be placed on a diagonal, leaving room on every side of the table for one guest. An 'S'-shaped design may also be carried out, and guests seated in the same manner.

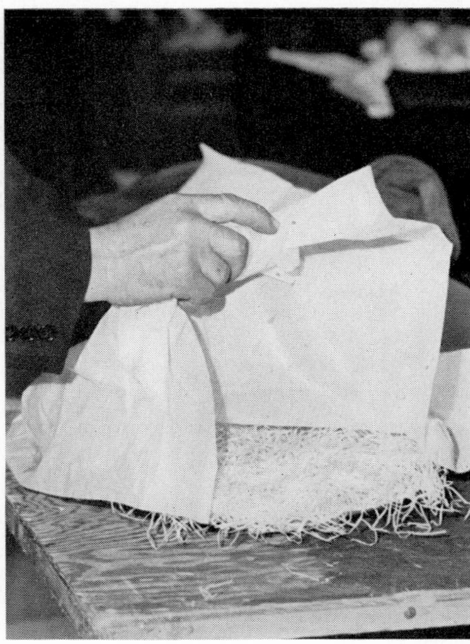

Left: Unpacking specimen fruits each wrapped in tissue-paper and protected with wood-wool. *Right:* Preparing a dish with a padding of wood-wool and a tissue-paper cover.

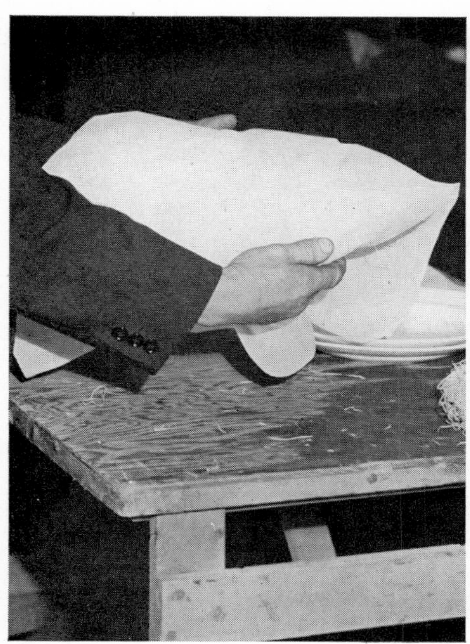

Left: Tucking the tissue-paper under the prepared dish. *Right:* Staging Emile d'Heyst pears. Note the centre pad to raise the fruit.

The prize-winning exhibit in a class for nine varieties of hardy fruit.

Plums packed in tissue-paper over cotton wool. Marks are lost in close competition if the specimens have lost their 'bloom.'

In showing collections of fruit efforts should be made to make the exhibit attractive. Stands of different height may be used to raise some of the dishes. The best dishes—those the exhibitor wishes the judges to note especially—should be lifted so that they catch the critic's eye. Wire stands are sold by sundriesmen for this purpose. If wood or other material is used the colour of the stands should blend with the fruit. Light stained oak will suit very well.

The schedules of some provincial shows provide for a decorated table of fruit or a decorated collection of fruit. The decorations are judged separately. Great care should be taken in selecting flowers for this work. Yellow, orange and red are colours which blend with fruit. Pink, blue, mauve and purple should be avoided. A pretty and successful decoration seen at the Shrewsbury Show, held in August, consisted of *Lilium superbum*, *L. Henryi*, montbretias and nasturtiums, with a few white trumpet lilies and some lily of the valley. Light grasses were used with the flowers, and *Asparagus plumosus* draped from the vases to the table. The floral decorations should not be allowed to detract from the fruit. Tall vases placed down the centre of the table or against a wall will serve as a background. Small vases only should be used among the dishes and so placed that rather than detract from, they will enhance the value of the fruit. Tiny ferns in thumb pots may be helpful. Coloured crotons and dracaenas are sometimes used but are not recommended.

R.H.S. TABLE OF POINTS

Grapes			
Muscat of Alexandria ...	12	Figs	7
Canon Hall	12	Apricots	7
Muscat Hambro	11	Pears	6
Madresfield Court ...	11	Apples	6
Mrs. Pearson	11	Dessert Plums	6
Mrs. Pince	11	Strawberries	6
Prince of Wales	11	Cherries	6
All other Grapes ...	10	Raspberries	5
Peaches	8	Gooseberries	4
Nectarines	8	Other Fruits and Nuts; with	
Melons	8	Tomatoes if admitted ...	3

(Pineapples, bananas and oranges are not grown now in this country and are therefore omitted from the above list.)

When exhibiting in competitive collections of fruit, it must be borne in mind that the maximum number of points which may be awarded per dish will vary according to the kind of fruit. The table is taken from the Royal Horticultural Society's *Rules for Judges*, and is the standard taken by most societies.

It must therefore follow that the exhibitor should choose as many dishes as possible from those kinds of fruit which carry the highest number of points. As an example, should the schedule read 'A collection of twelve dishes of ripe dessert fruit; twelve distinct varieties, not less than nine kinds, and not more than two varieties of a kind, one dish only of both black and white grapes allowed'—the maximum number of points could be obtained by exhibiting the following dishes:

Grapes—Muscat of Alexandria	12
Grapes—Madresfield Court	11
1 dish Peaches—Peregrine	8
1 dish Peaches—Violette Hâtive	8
1 dish Nectarines—Pineapple	8
1 dish Nectarines—Humboldt	8
1 Melon—Superlative	8
1 Melon—Hero of Lockinge	8
1 dish Figs	7
1 dish Apricots	7
1 dish Apples	6
1 dish Pears	6
Total number of possible points	97

Nine distinct kinds have been included, as for purposes of exhibition, black and white grapes are allowed as distinct kinds of fruit.

In competitive classes the number of fruits to be shown is specified and plates are provided. In large exhibits when competitors are asked to fill a given area, or in non-competitive exhibits, the size of the receptacles for displaying the fruit will depend on the space to be filled. Small plates of fruit are not attractive in a large exhibit and should be avoided. In a comprehensive display the fruit may be shown in market packs and also neatly arranged in baskets or other suitable receptacles. The market pack is placed at the base and the displayed fruit raised on stands. Grapes, carefully packed in baskets or 'flats', should also have the best bunches shown on boards. Peaches

Excellent specimens of Howgate Wonder, though the net marks will lose points in close competition.

The large yellow fruits of the Leveller gooseberry make an attractive addition to a collection.

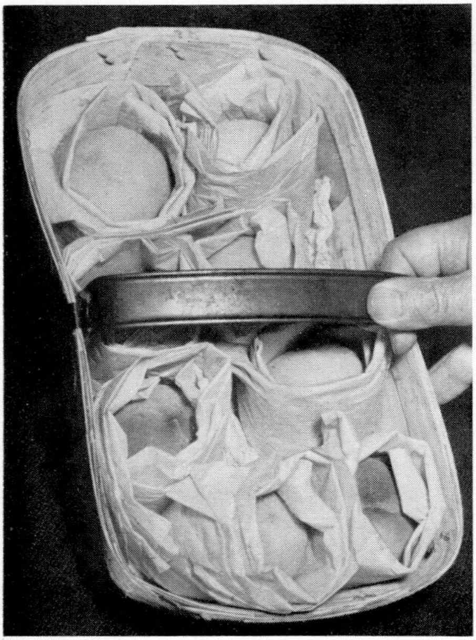

Left: Peaches can be carried to the show in a chip basket but should be wrapped individually to protect the bloom. *Right:* A specimen melon, King George.

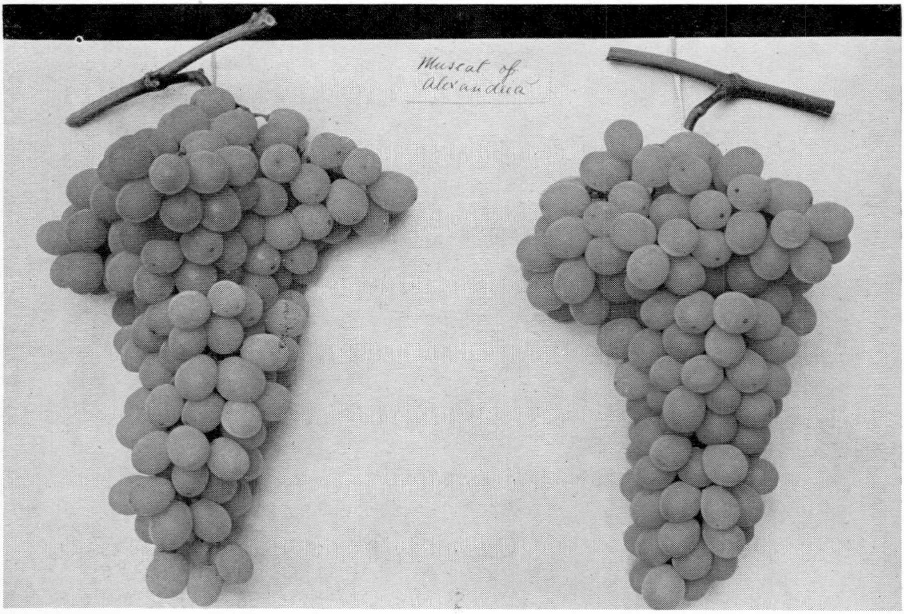

Muscat of Alexandria, the highest-pointed grape. Grapes are always shown attached to a white board.

and nectarines should be exhibited in boxes. These should be lined with white paper and the inset covered with white cotton wool before the fruits are placed in position. The boxes may hold twelve or fifteen according to the size of the fruits.

Apples and pears are shown in standard half-bushel or bushel boxes and also attractively piled up in baskets. For neat arrangement, a box is first turned upside down on a board and the bottom removed. The first layer, the one which will be seen, is first carefully arranged with fruit of even size and colour. The box is then completed, any vacant spaces being filled in with sawdust or cotton wool to keep the fruit rigid. The bottom is then screwed on and the box turned the right way up, care being taken to hold the loose board firmly in position while turning. The box of apples or pears will then have a neat and attractive appearance. Cherries and plums may be exhibited in a similar way. The boxes are smaller, usually to hold about twelve pounds of fruit. Apricots, blackberries and hybrid berries, figs, raspberries and strawberries may also be shown in boxes as well as displayed in baskets. The boxes must be shallow, to hold one layer only. All boxes should be neatly lined with white paper.

TREES IN POTS

Fruit of exhibition quality may be grown on trees in pots. Such trees are offered by fruit-tree nurserymen of apples, pears, plums and gages, peaches and nectarines. Many of the apples, pears and plums exhibited at the August shows are produced with the help of glass. The trees are worked on dwarfing stocks and are grown in large pots or wooden tubs. They are wintered out of doors and brought into the houses in February or early March. In gardens where there is a large amount of glass, pot trees present no difficulties. In smaller gardens, the exhibitor has to improvise in many ways. Very little artificial heat is used, for fruit trees will not stand hard forcing. The trees are potted or top-dressed each year; they will, in fact, produce first-class fruit for many years with an annual top-dressing only. Careful feeding is practised till ripening commences; manure water is used and periodic dressings of a concentrated organic and balanced manure. The fruit must be thinned at the discretion of the grower. When danger of frost is over, the pots may be stood out of doors in a position sheltered from the wind but exposed to the sun. The fruits will then attain that rich colour and finish so essential for the show bench.

PACKING AND TRANSPORT

Packing and transport to the shows are questions of importance to the exhibitor of fruit. The following notes refer to competitive small exhibits and to fruit which is to be displayed on plates or in shallow baskets. Much of the fruit in larger and non-competitive exhibits is packed ready for exhibition, the coverings only to be removed at the show.

Grapes are exhibited on boards, an appropriate size being fifteen inches by ten inches. Each board should have an adjustable leg at the back and be covered with pure white, rather stiff paper. A pale yellow covering is sometimes used for white grapes. The bunches are cut with secateurs and secured by string to a staple at the top of the board. The boards with the bunches secured are then placed in boxes, each board being tied to the side of the box. Boxes are usually made to hold four or six bunches.

Peaches and Nectarines are packed in special boxes. These are eighteen inches by twelve inches by four inches, and each has an inset over which is placed thick felt. Holes are cut in the felt in which the fruits are placed. Insets are made to hold twelve or fifteen fruits according to size. Strips of cotton wool or wood-wool wrapped in tissue-paper are placed between the peaches and a thin layer of the same material is placed above them. Packed in this way there is little fear of the fruit being bruised.

Melons are wrapped in tissue-paper and packed, a single layer only, in boxes or small hampers. Wood-wool should be packed round each fruit.

Plums. In packing plums, every effort must be made to retain their natural bloom. An excellent way to do this is to make cups of brown or stiff white paper and attach them to small bars across the top and just inside the box. The plums are cut off with scissors, the stem being held with one hand, and placed one in each cup. In this way the fruit will travel long distances without loss of 'bloom'. Another way is to place each fruit in a leaf. These are then placed, a single layer only, in shallow boxes.

Apples and Pears. These are wrapped in tissue-paper and packed in boxes with wood-wool between the fruits. The boxes should not be deep, allowing not more than two or three layers.

Apricots and Figs. Each fruit is wrapped separately in a leaf and packed in shallow boxes, one layer only.

Cherries, Currants, Gooseberries, Blackberries and hybrid berries are also packed in shallow boxes, and in all cases there should be sufficient packing below and a covering of leaves above to prevent the fruit from moving during transit.

Raspberries and Strawberries. If these fruits are of super quality, each fruit should be placed in a leaf and then packed in the same way as apricots and figs.

CHAPTER SIXTEEN

Fruits Described Alphabetically

APPLES

Maximum Points 6

APPLES ARE exhibited from August onwards. In classes for a single dish of apples, the number specified is usually six. In provincial and local shows it may be five, and in competitive collections of fruit the number may be seven. Fruits for the August shows are mainly grown in pots. Some early varieties picked from trees grown out of doors may be used during August, but such fruit cannot compare with well-known and high-class dessert varieties brought on gently under glass.

At most of the large provincial shows held during August, good specimens are shown of such high-class varieties as Cox's Orange Pippin, Ellison's Orange, Ribston Pippin, etc., and these will always score in competition with varieties like Beauty of Bath, Langley Pippin, or Worcester Pearmain.

From September, exhibition apples are selected from trees grown in the open. They may be grown on any of the usual types of tree seen in private gardens—cordon, pyramid, bush or standard. Bush trees on Type I or II rootstocks will produce excellent fruit for exhibition. The keen exhibitor selects his fruits some time before they are picked. Occasionally one may see them secured to the tree by green twist or raffia attached to the stem of the fruit. The selected fruits are carefully exposed to the sun, so essential for securing the necessary colour.

Opinions differ as to the correct size of dessert apples. The Royal Horticultural Society gives two and three-quarter inches diameter as the ideal size for many varieties, though this may be exceeded for others which are naturally larger. No hard-and-fast rule can be followed and the question is best settled by the exhibitor. Good specimens of moderate size, colour, and finish are essential. All fruits must be of uniform size—a very important point with the judges.

With culinary apples, fruits of large size are permitted, but mere size is not all that is required. Quality and finish are also looked for. Large, coarse fruits of poor quality cannot compare with those of smaller size but better colour and finish. Many varieties of culinary apple do not colour. When showing these varieties the fruit should be of good shape and have a clear, unblemished skin. The successful exhibitor will obtain size, quality, and colour by careful and thorough cultivation.

Summer pruning of apple trees may be practised. Many growers allow the shoots to grow till late July or August, when they are pruned back to four or five leaves. This may prove satisfactory for bush trees, and the additional light and air will improve the fruit.

For all trees of apples, sweet cherries, pears and plums, trained on walls and fences, the method employed by the writer with success is to pinch all shoots as soon as they are strong enough, at the third or fourth leaf, and to continue to do so to subsequent growths until ripening of the fruit commences.

A certain amount of colour can be introduced into apples by laying the selected fruits on damp moss, in trays or boxes, lightly spraying them over occasionally with soft water and placing them in the sun. This artificial colour is easily detected and does not find favour with the judges.

The question of the manuring of apple trees is linked with soil texture and conditions. The gardener would be wise to study the results of experiments carried out at the research stations. It is the practice of some growers to give a dressing of muriate of potash to all fruit trees during the winter months, and this is to be recommended. Other feeding may be according to crop. Trees and fruit will benefit by a dressing of a good, well-balanced compound manure when the fruit is set, and a mulch of farmyard manure will also help. Apples do not as a general rule require watering, but during very dry weather this may be necessary.

Scab is one of the most troublesome diseases of the apple, and fruit affected by this fungus should not be exhibited. Lime-sulphur is the fungicide generally recommended for scab control. Sprayings may be given at the pink-bud stage, at petal fall, and again three weeks later, at strengths recommended by the makers. It should be noted that a number of varieties of apple are sulphur shy; among these are Peasgood's Nonsuch, Rival, Charles Ross and others.

A spray used by the writer with apparent success is Tetramethyl thiuram disulphide plus nicotine and quassia. This is given at petal fall and twice or three times later at intervals of eighteen to twenty-one days. Fruit so treated has been clean and the trees have not suffered by its use. A winter spray of tar oil or DNC followed by the above treatment will give good results against both insect and fungoid pests.

Apples for exhibition should be picked when fully ripe, i.e., when the fruits part readily from the tree. They must be handled carefully and stored in a cool, dry shed of even temperature. The fruits will keep better if wrapped in oiled papers or in tissue-paper. They will 'sweat' when first picked and should not be wrapped till this period is over and the fruit dry.

VARIETIES

Eighteen popular dessert apples for exhibition

American Mother
Blenheim Orange (small fruits)
Claygate Pearmain (late)
Cox's Orange Pippin
Crimson Cox
Egremont Russet
Ellison's Orange
George Carpenter
Houblon
James Grieve
King of the Pippins
King's Acre Pippin
Laxton's Fortune
Laxton's Superb
Lord Lambourne
Ribston Pippin
Rival
St. Edmund's Russet

Eighteen popular culinary varieties for exhibition

Annie Elizabeth
Arthur Turner
Bismarck
Blenheim Orange (large fruits)
Bramley's Seedling
Crimson Bramley
Crawley Beauty
Crimson Peasgood's Nonsuch
Edward VII
Howgate Wonder
Lane's Prince Albert
Lord Derby
Mère de Ménage
Monarch
Newton Wonder
Peasgood's Nonsuch
S. T. Wright
Warner's King

APRICOTS

Maximum Points 7

The apricot is not grown to a large extent in this country, though good fruiting trees may be seen in many gardens. This is probably due to the fact that whole branches of the trees may suddenly die for no apparent reason. No definite cause for this has yet been advanced.

Classes for apricots only are seldom seen in prize schedules. They do, however, form a valuable 'dish' in a collection of fruit. In points (seven) they are worth less than peaches, nectarines and melons, but more than apples, pears and plums. Their rich colour adds to the attraction of the exhibit.

The best apricots are grown under glass, but good fruits may also be grown on walls out of doors. A south aspect is probably the best but they may also be grown on walls facing east and west. They may also be grown successfully in pots.

On walls, apricot trees are fan trained. The fruit is produced on wood of the previous season's growth and also on fruiting spurs. Careful pruning is practised to produce new wood to replace that which has been fruiting for two or three years. The fruit may need thinning and exposure to the light to ensure fruit of exhibition standard. On a south wall the sun may prove too strong and the fruits thus become spotted. The fruits for exhibition should therefore be lightly shaded when ripening.

Apricots will quickly deteriorate if allowed to remain on the tree till fully ripe. For exhibition purposes they should therefore be picked when slightly under-ripe. If carefully picked and packed, they will thus keep in good condition for several days. Apricots will ripen out of doors from mid-July to the end of August. The following is a selection of varieties in their order of ripening:

New Large Early, Hemskirk, Moorpark, and Peach.

CURRANTS—BLACK, RED AND WHITE

Maximum Points 3

Separate classes are provided by many societies for the various kinds of currant. They are also used in competitive collections of hardy fruit and in collections of mixed fruit.

BLACK CURRANTS

For exhibition work, black currants should be large and jet black in colour. They should be shown in bunches unless the schedule states that picked berries are allowed. A 'dish' of black currants consists usually of one pound, or a certain number of bunches is specified.

Black currants fruit on branches of the previous year's growth. A good moist position should be selected and the soil should be in good heart. The average economic life of the black currant is eight or nine years. Good, strong, healthy growths are essential for good fruit. These are obtained by hard pruning and judicious feeding. The trees should be cut down to within three or four buds of the base when first planted. Thereafter pruning should be carried out soon after the fruit has been harvested.

The great scourge of the black currant is the big bud mite, and trees so infected fail to produce fruit of exhibition standard. Strong, vigorously growing bushes appear somewhat resistant to the pest. Should the trouble appear, it may be kept in check by spraying with lime-sulphur in early spring just before the flowers open. The recommended strength of the lime-sulphur is one part to nineteen of water for most varieties. Some varieties are sulphur shy, particularly those of the Goliath group, and the strength for these should be one part lime-sulphur to forty-nine of water.

First-class fruit also cannot be grown on bushes suffering from 'reversion', a virus disease which is identified by the changed appearance of the leaves. There is a reduction of certain veins and of the marginal teeth. In its changed condition the leaf of the black currant resembles that of the nettle. Gardeners who suspect their bushes to be suffering from this disease and are not certain, should solicit the advice of their County Horticultural Adviser. All affected bushes should be grubbed out and burnt.

Black currants are gross feeders. A good, complete manure containing up to ten per cent potash may be given to the trees in spring before growth commences. When the fruit is set, a dressing of a nitrogenous manure will help to ensure large fruits. This may be in the form of dried blood, Nitro-chalk, or nitrate of potash. A mulching of farmyard manure should follow if possible.

There are many varieties of black currant; the following is a selection of the best:

Boskoop Giant—an old variety and one of the earliest to ripen.
Baldwin—a good variety of medium size. Will hang for some time.
Wellington XXX—one of the newer varieties.
Westwick Choice—very large, mid-season.
Daniel's September—a late variety, probably related to Baldwin.

RED AND WHITE CURRANTS

In competitive classes a 'dish' usually consists of three dozen bunches. These should be large and the berries of good colour, clean and clear.

These currants fruit on spurs formed on the older wood of established trees. In the initial stages, the bush should be pruned to restrict the branches so that sufficient air and light may reach the fruit. Some older branches may be periodically removed and new growths encouraged to grow from the base. In this way new life is imparted to the bush. The best bunches and the largest fruit will be found on the younger wood. Bunches six inches in length are not uncommon.

To obtain fruit of the highest quality for exhibition, summer pruning should be practised. This consists in cutting back the new growths in early summer to four or five leaves. During the winter they should be further shortened to about one inch. The leaders of the branches are not pruned in summer but should be cut back by about one third in the autumn.

Red and white currants can also be grown as cordons and are sometimes seen fan trained. They may be planted against walls, or trained to fencing wires across the garden. Any aspect will suit them. Red currants have been exhibited in November picked from cordons on a north wall. The young growing shoots of trees so trained should be pinched at about the third leaf and again as necessary. If fruit of special size and quality is required, the bunches may be thinned.

The most troublesome pest is the currant aphis. An attack is recognized by the blistered and often highly coloured leaves. In the summer spraying programme of a well-managed garden this aphis will be controlled, for spraying with an approved insecticide gives complete control.

Red and white currants respond to a good dressing of a compound manure before growth commences in the spring and another when the first fruits show signs of ripening. They do not require the nitrogenous manure recommended for black currants. Mulching with farmyard manure or compost is advised. Among other benefits it helps to keep the lower fruit clean by preventing the soil being splashed up on them during heavy rains.

Popular varieties are:

RED

Comet—an old variety, still one of the best, berries large.

Earliest of Fourlands—a good early variety of upright growth.

Fay's Prolific—another old variety with long bunches.

Laxton's No. 1 and Laxton's Perfection—these are among the newer varieties with probably the largest fruit of all.

Raby Castle—a good late variety.

WHITE

White Dutch and White Versailles.

BLACKBERRIES AND HYBRID BERRIES

Maximum Points 3

It is seldom that special classes are provided for these fruits. They are useful in collections of hardy fruit. In points value they are the lowest (three), and share this distinction with currants, nuts and culinary plums.

Fruits for exhibition should have the stem attached and be slightly under-ripe when gathered. They are best cut with scissors and placed immediately in the boxes or baskets for transport to the show. The fruit should be fresh, clean and of good size, according to the variety. A 'dish' usually consists of fifty fruits.

Blackberries and hybrid berries do not thrive well in light, sandy soil. They prefer it medium to slightly heavy. They should also be planted where there is some protection from the wind. Apart from this, they are of easy culture. The shoots of the current year's growth should be nursed and tied in while those of the previous year produce the fruit. The fruited wood is then cut out or pruned hard back, and the young growths tied in to produce the following year's crop.

Pests of these fruits are not numerous and are easily controlled. The most important is the raspberry beetle, the larvæ of which feed on the fruits, causing them to become hard and useless. This is controlled by dustings of derris powder or by spraying with derris or nicotine and quassia. The recommended time is about ten days after flowering has commenced and again about a fortnight later.

The following is a selection of the best-known varieties:

BLACKBERRIES
Bedford Giant—early.
Himalaya Berry—mid-season.
John Innes—late.
Merton Thornless—August-September.

HYBRID BERRIES
Boysenberry—very large.
Loganberry—the well-known hybrid of the raspberry and blackberry.
Lowberry—similar to loganberry, but black.

CHERRIES

Maximum Points 6

Cherries, with their rich colour and pleasant flavour, are among the most popular of our English fruits. Kent is probably the champion county for them, and innumerable motorists have appreciated those obtained from wayside stalls.

In many show schedules special classes are provided for cherries. The number per dish is usually fifty. In collections of choice dessert fruit, or in classes for hardy fruit, they are amongst the most attractive. The judges will look for large, well-coloured and clean fruits. All stems should be left on, though for convenience they may be shortened. Cherries are easily bruised and the bruised portion quickly turns brown. Such fruits should not be used. Care should also be taken to ensure the stems are not shrivelled.

Excellent cherries may be grown in pots. It was not unusual in the large gardens some years ago to see houses devoted to this purpose. With the changed conditions of the country, probably few cherries are now grown in this way. If grown in pots, and also in the garden, care must be taken to include compatible varieties for fertilization, for all sweet cherries are self-sterile.

The greatest difficulty in growing cherries in the garden is to keep the birds from them. At the very first sign of ripening, blackbirds, starlings and thrushes, among others, will immediately start on them and whole crops may be taken before they are ripe. In orchards of standard trees probably the few taken by birds do not matter so much; in gardens it is different. For this reason, cherries in many gardens are grown on walls, and it is unnecessary therefore to deal with the matter in any other way in this work.

The best fruits for exhibition are grown on walls, usually on fan-trained trees. In the case of sweet cherries, fruit is produced on young wood and on fruiting spurs formed on the older wood. New growths may be introduced periodically to replace the older branches, and in this way good crops may be obtained from the same trees for many years.

It is well known that cherry trees are susceptible to bacterial canker and gumming. Mr. Grubb, in his excellent book on cherries, recommends, as a partial control, spraying with Bordeaux Mixture twice annually—one application at leaf-fall and another shortly before blossoming.

For the summer treatment of sweet cherries, it has been the practice of the writer to pinch the young shoots at the fourth or fifth leaf, except those shoots required for tying in, as recommended for plums and apricots (see page 235).

Insect pests most troublesome to cherries are the cherry black fly and red spider. If the spraying programme recommended in these notes (see page 235) is carried out, both should be adequately controlled.

The following is a selection of standard varieties obtainable from most fruit-tree nurseries:

Bedford Prolific—July
Bigarreau Kentish—July
Bigarreau Napoleon—August
Bigarreau Schrecken—June
Early Rivers—June
Elton—July
Emperor Francis—late July
Géante d'Hedelfingen (Bradbourne Black)—August. This variety is particularly useful for August Shows
Governor Wood—July
Waterloo—July
White Heart—July

The following are among new varieties raised at the John Innes Institution. Several have been given the A.M. by the Royal Horticultural Society. Trees of these varieties will be available soon.

Merton Bigarreau
Merton Bounty
Merton Favourite
Merton Heart
Merton Premier

THE MORELLO CHERRY

This is the best of the acid culinary varieties. It differs from the sweet cherries in that it fruits almost entirely on wood of the previous season, as the peach and nectarine. It can be accommodated on north, east and west walls. It can also be grown on bush and standard trees for the birds are not as fond of it as the sweet varieties. There are various strains of Morello, some growing to a larger size than others. Trees should therefore be purchased from a reliable firm.

The Morello will make a useful contribution to exhibits of hardy fruit. Specimens should be large and of a rich, deep colour. The fruits need careful handling to preserve the bloom.

FIGS

Maximum Points 7

In collections of ripe dessert fruit, every effort should be made to include figs. In points value (seven) they are equal to apricots. The number to constitute a 'dish' is usually seven. The fruits should be of good size, according to variety, and it is an advantage if they are slightly cracked. They should not be picked till fully ripe. Figs are a popular fruit and their inclusion in a competitive collection will be favoured by the judges—all other points being equal.

For early shows, figs must be grown under glass. In the south, excellent fruits are produced out of doors from about the middle of August.

The culture of figs under glass is not difficult. The first crop is carried mainly on wood of the previous season's growth. These shoots should be tied in not less than six inches apart. Figs will stand a fair amount of forcing, but extremes of temperature should be avoided or the fruit will drop. When new growth is firm enough, it should be stopped at the fifth leaf and all surplus shoots removed. A second crop is obtained later in the season from the new growths.

Established trees under glass will respond to judicious feeding. This should be varied according to the crop. A good dressing of a compound fertilizer may be given before growth commences and another just as the fruit shows signs of ripening. A mulch of stable manure is beneficial and makes watering easier.

The ripening period of figs extends over several weeks. During this time the trees should not be sprayed and the atmosphere of the house should be kept drier. A gentle heat in the pipes during the night should be maintained.

Insect pests of figs under glass are not numerous or difficult to control. Mealy bug was at one time troublesome but is now easily kept under control by fumigating with DDT. Red spider may also appear but fumigating with azobenzene gives 100 per cent control.

Out of doors, figs are planted against walls. Often, through unintentional neglect, the trees are allowed to grow away from the wall, and such trees will fruit well. They can, however, be grown as fans and kept neatly tied in. In this case it is wise to plant the trees in concrete pits five feet square by three feet deep to prevent them becoming too gross. The shoots should be tied in in the same way as those under glass and stopped once, at the fifth leaf. All surplus growths should be removed and new shoots tied in where necessary. Trees grown in pits need frequent watering. Manuring is according to the crop and at the discretion of the grower. Trees grown by this method will give satisfactory results for many years.

Varieties for indoors

Brown Turkey
Brunswick
Negro Largo

Varieties for outdoors

Brown Turkey
Brunswick
White Marseilles

GOOSEBERRIES

Maximum Points 4

Classes for gooseberries are included in many of the late June and July shows. A 'dish' usually consists of thirty. Fruits for exhibition should be uniform in size and colour according to the variety. They should be left on the bushes as long as possible so that they have a fresh appearance when placed on the exhibition bench.

Good fruits for exhibition may be grown on trees trained as bushes, cordons or fans. It is important that all gooseberry bushes should be grown on a leg—i.e. have a clean stem rising three to six inches from the ground before branching. In training for bush specimens, care should be taken with the pruning. The green, unripe tips of the shoots should be taken off and the shoot cut back to a bud on the upper surface. The branches should be distributed thinly to admit light and air and to facilitate picking. Fruiting spurs will form on the older branches. Carefully selected new growths may periodically be encouraged from the base of the bush to take the place of the older branches. In this way new blood is being continually infused into the tree. The best fruits for exhibition will be found on the young wood.

Gooseberries trained as single, double, or triple cordons produce good crops. The gooseberry is an accommodating plant and is easily trained. Cordons may be grown on wires stretched across the garden, between other trees on walls, or on pillars, in fact any place where there is room for them. They are not particular as to aspect, and excellent fruit may be grown on walls facing north. When fan-trained, the branches should be evenly distributed and given sufficient space between to admit light and air.

These trained trees are grown on the spur system; they are pruned so that fruiting spurs are formed along the length of the branches. Many growers practise summer pruning about the end of June, when the new growths are cut back to five or six buds. A better method is to pinch the young shoots as soon as firm enough at the second or third leaf as recommended for trained trees of other fruits.

The gooseberry sawfly is probably the most troublesome insect pest. The caterpillars which emerge from the eggs of the sawfly may, if unchecked, defoliate whole bushes. Control may be attained by spraying with liquid derris. Another effective spray is nicotine and quassia, but the fruit should not be eaten for some days after this has been used.

The worst trouble of all is gooseberry mildew, which appears to have become more prevalent in recent years. Once established it is difficult to control and almost impossible to eradicate completely. The mildew usually appears first on the tips of the shoots, and then quickly on the fruits. The tips of the shoots should be removed and burnt, and the trees thoroughly sprayed. Lime sulphur (one part to ninety-nine parts of water) is recommended for this purpose, but it must be borne in mind that some varieties are sulphur-shy. These include Golden Drop, Early Sulphur and Leveller among others. A safer spray is washing soda, two pounds, and soft soap, half a pound, to ten gallons of water. This has proved effective but may check the growth of the bushes. The disease having once appeared, the trees should receive a good spray of lime sulphur before growth commences and one of washing soda and soft soap in a weaker form before any mildew is seen.

The following is a selection of the most popular varieties :

RED	YELLOW	GREEN	WHITE
Lancashire Lad	Leveller	Keepsake	Careless
Crown Bob	Broomgirl	Lancer	Whitesmith
Warrington			White Lion

GRAPES

Maximum Points varies according to Variety—See page 227

Grapes are the *élite* of all English fruit. Good, well-finished bunches, attractively displayed on boards, will claim the admiration of all who see them. Owing probably to the changed conditions throughout the country, they are not grown to such perfection now as in the past. Great interest was taken in the cultivation of grapes from 1900 to the outbreak of the first world war in 1914. Since that time there has been a gradual deterioration in the quality of the majority of those exhibited; only occasionally does one see first-class bunches shown.

No fruit needs such care and attention to bring it to perfection as the grape, but when he has attained his object, nothing will give the grower more pleasure and satisfaction.

In judging grapes, points are awarded according to variety (see scale of points, page 227). Colour and finish are the deciding factors. These qualities, combined with large, well-shaped bunches and even berries, form the ideal. Small bunches of good colour and finish will always be placed before large bunches of poor quality. The keen exhibitor will therefore show as many bunches as possible of those varieties which claim the highest number of points.

The choicest of all grapes are the Muscat of Alexandria and Canon Hall Muscat. These need a warm house to bring them to perfection. For this reason they are best grown in a house by themselves. If they must be with other grapes, they are best planted together at the warmest end of the house. It is helpful in mixed vineries to graft these muscats on to more hardy varieties such as Black Hamburg, Alicante, or Buckland Sweetwater. When on these stocks the grapes are easier to grow, but (with the possible exception of those on Buckland Sweetwater) will not attain such a rich amber colour as those on their own roots and in a house by themselves.

In private gardens, special borders are prepared for vines. Some are inside the house, others are half inside and half outside. Except for hard forcing, borders both inside and outside the house are to be preferred.

Commercial growers usually select a site where the land is suitable for grapes. The houses are then built and the vines planted inside, allowing the roots to go where they will. A large commercial house of Black Hamburg and another of Muscat of Alexandria known to the writer, were planted more than sixty years ago and still produce good crops of excellent quality.

To have grapes ready for exhibition in July and August, the vines should be started into growth during the latter half of January and in February. To allow sufficient light and air to reach the fruit, the fruiting spurs should be approximately eighteen inches apart and alternated on the rods as far as possible. One lateral only should be allowed to each spur. The shoots should be stopped at the second leaf beyond the bunch and all sub-laterals removed from the base to the bunch. Thereafter, sub-laterals should be continually pinched at the first leaf.

To attain that extra quality and good colour so necessary for exhibition work, the vines must not be over-cropped. Other factors, such as feeding, ventilation and heating contribute to this end, but correct cropping is the most important. Experienced growers can estimate the weight of the bunches and aim at approximately one pound of fruit per foot of rod.

Thinning is an important operation for exhibition work and should be done according to variety. For instance, Gros Maroc, Gros Colmar and Madresfield Court will need much more thinning than Black Hamburg and Mrs. Pince. Few berries will need to be taken from the top of the bunch—a perfect bunch of grapes is well covered over the top. All berries must be removed from the centre of the bunches and the remainder so left that the berries touch when ripe, but maintain their natural shape.

At the commencement of growth, a temperature at night of about 45° to 50° F. is sufficient. When the shoots are two or three inches

A corner of the Royal Horticultural Society's Autumn Fruit and Vegetable Show, showing some of the pear classes.

A class for four varieties of plum at the same show. Different methods of staging may be observed.

Left: Plums benefit from severe thinning when specimen fruits are desired. The stalks are left attached to the branch to avoid wounds. *Right:* Paper 'collars' will help to deter birds pecking ripening pears. Muslin bags are often also used.

long, the temperature should rise to about 60° F. at night. Careful ventilation of the houses is essential. Experienced gardeners know immediately they enter a vinery if the ventilation is correct. The beginner should watch the thermometer and when growth has commenced, begin to ventilate when the temperature has reached 68° F. to 70° F. More air should be admitted as the heat rises till the maximum is reached. When the temperature begins to fall, the ventilators should be lowered, finally closing the house to shut in some sun-heat.

Slight front ventilation may be necessary during hot weather before the grapes begin to colour. During the ripening period more air should be given and a little ventilation top and bottom admitted at night.

Good grape growers use as little fire heat as possible. They do, however, keep a little heat in the pipes at night throughout the season till the crop is cut.

The berries of some varieties of grape are liable to scald in hot, sunny weather during the period of about fourteen days before they begin to ripen, i.e. at the end of the stoning period. This applies especially to Madresfield Court and Lady Downes, and in a lesser degree to the white muscats. Extra care must therefore be taken with the ventilation at this time to ensure a circulation of air. Bunches that are exposed to the sun may be covered with a sheet of tissue-paper. Some successful exhibitors of muscats make a point of thus covering all their best bunches and keep the paper over them until they are cut.

Vines are gross feeders. A dressing of about four ounces per square yard of a compound fertilizer—preferably organic—may be given before the vines are started into growth, another when the crop has set, and a third when the fruit shows signs of ripening. A manure which has given good results is composed as follows: two parts hoof and horn, two parts bonemeal or superphosphate, one part sulphate of potash. The vines will also benefit from a mulch of stable manure after thinning is completed.

The two most troublesome insect pests of the vine are red spider and mealy bug. Many commercial growers control red spider by parathion smoke bombs. Others use azobenzene by the aerosol method. The writer has found the latter safe and effective. Mealy bug is controlled by fumigating with DDT when the crop has been harvested. It is also advisable, when this scourge is known to exist on vines, to throw the houses wide open during hard, frosty weather. This is usually 100 per cent effective.

When placing the bunches on the boards for exhibition, great care should be taken to place them so that they show to the best advantage, and to ensure that the 'bloom' is preserved intact.

The varieties of grape most commonly grown are:

WHITE	BLACK
Muscat of Alexandria	Alicante—late
Canon Hall Muscat	Appley Towers—mid-season
Mrs. Pearson—a small late muscat	Black Hamburg—early
Foster's Seedling	Gros Colmar—large-berried, late
Buckland Sweetwater	Gros Maroc—mid-season
	Lady Downe's—late, large berries, small bunches
	Muscat Hamburg—early to mid-season
	Madresfield Court — mid-season, the best black grape
	Mrs. Pince—a late black muscat

MELONS

Maximum Points 8

The melon is a popular fruit for exhibition. With peaches and nectarines it ranks next to the grape in possible points value.

In competitive collections of fruit, melons are of great importance. When shown they should be well netted and of good size and colour, according to variety. In single-dish classes for melons, the fruits are usually cut and tasted by the judges, prizes being awarded to those of the best flavour. To obtain fruits of good flavour, they should be allowed to remain on the plants till ripe. As much air as possible must be admitted to the house during the ripening period and the foliage of the plants kept free from insect pests until the fruit is ripe.

The span-roofed house is the best type in which to grow melons for exhibition, but lean-to structures or, in fact, any glasshouse that provides sufficient light and heat, may be used. Commercially, melons are grown mainly in large span-roofed houses.

Melons may be grown in pots, but the better and more usual method is to plant on raised beds, about fifteen inches in width and about nine inches in depth. Meadow turf of medium texture cut about four inches thick and stacked for a few months is ideal for the purpose. The turf should not be broken up but placed grass side downwards to form the beds. A small quantity of rotted manure and ground chalk may be placed between the turves and the whole made very firm.

To raise melon plants from seed, a temperature of about 70° F. is needed. After germination, the seedlings should be placed near the glass to prevent them being drawn. Though not actually necessary, it is wise to plant on small mounds of sterilized soil, and to place the plants so that the basal leaves are level with the soil. This minimizes the danger of canker. The plants should be twelve or fifteen inches apart, and one fruit only allowed to develop on each.

The plants should be grown unchecked until they have reached approximately six feet or the leader has reached its limit. The leader should then be stopped and laterals allowed to develop. The female flowers are produced on the laterals. They are easily distinguished by the embryo fruit at their base. Occasionally, when the plants are growing strongly, no female flowers appear on the laterals. Such laterals should be stopped, and the necessary flowers will then appear on the resulting sub-laterals.

Two or three flowers should be fertilized on each plant at about the same time. Should all fertilized flowers develop, the surplus fruits should be removed as soon as it is obvious which will be the best to leave. Generally, the best fruits are produced about the centre of the plant. The fruit-bearing lateral should be stopped at the second leaf beyond the swelling fruit and no other growths allowed. Other laterals may be pinched at the fourth or fifth leaf and the subsequent sub-laterals at the first leaf, continuing to do so according to the vigour of the plant. The fruits are supported by nets secured to the training wires.

The night temperature of the melon house during the growing period should be from 65° F. to 70° F. Ventilation should commence at about 75° F. according to weather conditions. Melon plants are very sensitive to draughts and great care must be taken to avoid them. The plants should be lightly syringed and the house closed early to shut in sun-heat. The temperature of the house may then reach 100° F. and the plants will revel in the heat and moisture. When netting is complete, the house must not be closed so early and a drier atmosphere should be maintained.

Melons require a fair amount of water when the fruits are swelling and until they are fully netted. It should then be gradually reduced until the fruit is ripe. Over-watering during the ripening period may cause the fruits to split.

A dressing of balanced fertilizer may be given immediately the fruits have set and another during netting. Weak liquid manure may also be given at frequent intervals, but all feeding must stop before ripening commences.

Melons for exhibition should be left on the plants until fully ripe. They should be cut with a portion of the lateral attached, and this should be fresh and firm when the fruit is on the show bench.

Timing of the fruit is important. As a guide, it may be stated that plants from seed sown in January or February should produce ripe fruit in fifteen or sixteen weeks from the time of sowing. Plants from seed sown in April, May and June should ripen fruit in twelve to thirteen weeks.

Melons will not keep in good condition long when fully ripe. If the exhibitor finds his fruits becoming too forward, a good plan is to wrap them, while still on the plants, in several thicknesses of tissue-paper. The house should be kept cooler and only sufficient water given to keep the plants from flagging. Melons so treated will keep in good condition for two or three weeks.

The most troublesome pest is red spider. This often becomes prevalent when the atmosphere of the house is kept dry for ripening. It is kept under control by an azobenzene aerosol. Canker may occur and cause some plants to collapse. It usually attacks the plants round the collar. It may be caused by too much water at the roots or a check to the plants by careless ventilation. Water should be kept away from the stems of the plants, and it is for this reason that planting on small raised mounds of soil is recommended. Planting to the first leaves also helps to prevent canker.

Melons should be shown singly on plates or in small baskets. A ring made of twisted tissue paper is helpful to hold the fruit in position. It should be so placed that the whole of the melon can be seen.

There are many varieties of melon. The following may be seen exhibited at the various shows:

White fleshed	Scarlet fleshed	Green fleshed
Hero of Lockinge	Superlative	Emerald Gem
	Sutton's Scarlet	Ringleader
	King George	
	Longford Castle	
	Blenheim Orange	

CANTALOUP MELONS

These are more hardy than the netted kinds and may be grown successfully in unheated frames or under cloches. In quality they are inferior to the netted varieties and in competition would be placed below good specimens of the latter kinds. They are, however, very useful in gardens where no glasshouse is available.

Seeds should be sown singly in three-inch pots in early May. For a six-foot by four-foot light or a dutch light, one plant only is needed. A mound of soil of similar composition to that recommended for indoor work should be placed towards the back of the frame and made firm. The seedling cantaloup should be planted in the centre of the mound and shaded for a few days. Careful ventilation is essential, and, except during very hot weather, the frame lights should be propped up some three or four inches only. The frames are closed early to shut in some sun-heat.

When the plants have made six or seven leaves, they should be stopped and two or three of the resultant shoots allowed to develop, according to the size of the frame. When these have grown the length of the frame, the growing points should be pinched out. The female flowers will appear on the sub-laterals and these should be fertilized when a sufficient number are open. Allow one fruit to each shoot—i.e. two or three melons to a plant. The sub-laterals should be pinched as recommended for the indoor varieties. The fruits should not rest on the bare earth. They should be placed on pieces of slate or tile. Another and better method is to place a melon net over the top of a seven-inch pot. This is plunged halfway in the soil and the fruit placed on the net.

As far as possible, the plants should be given similar treatment as regards watering and feeding to the indoor varieties. As soon as ripening commences, a crack of air must be left on the frames at night. From the time of seed-sowing till the fruit ripens is approximately sixteen or seventeen weeks.

Two varieties of cantaloup melon are Bellegarde and Paris.

NUTS

Maximum Points 3

Nuts may be exhibited in competitive collections of fruit, but it is only in exceptional circumstances that they are used. One pound constitutes a 'dish'. Nuts may be used with advantage in comprehensive non-competitive exhibits of fruit.

PEACHES AND NECTARINES

Maximum Points 8

Peaches and nectarines are among the most important fruits for the summer and early autumn shows. With melons, they are next in value to grapes. Many show societies provide classes for single dishes of peaches and nectarines, the number required usually being six. In competitive decorated tables of fruit and collections of ripe dessert fruits, the number is sometimes seven. In large collections of fruit and in non-competitive exhibits, peaches and nectarines are shown in market boxes. The boxes are lined with white paper and cotton wool placed over the inset. They may hold twelve or fifteen specimens according to the size of the fruits.

The colour of peaches and nectarines varies from brilliant crimson as in Peregrine, to creamy-yellow, striped red as in Duchess of Cornwall. Richly coloured, well-finished fruits are among the most attractive of all exhibits, and to attain perfection will test the skill of the grower.

Peaches and nectarines are easily bruised, and for this reason it is wise to hold cotton wool or wood wool in the hands when picking about two days before the show and when the fruit is not fully ripe. Fruits should be gently eased away from the laterals and placed immediately into the boxes. Cotton wool should be placed above and between the fruits to ensure safe transit. If all this is carefully done, they will be in good condition for the judges.

In gardens where there is an orchard house, peaches and nectarines may be planted out as standards or grown in pots, but the most common method is to train them as fans. They produce fruit on wood of the previous season's growth which should be of medium thickness and, when tied in during the winter months, should be not less than four inches apart.

Under glass, hives of bees are often placed in the house when the trees are in flower to assist pollination. Failing this, wood fans are sometimes used, or the flowers lightly brushed with a rabbit's tail. Peaches and nectarines are easily fertilized and a good 'set' presents no difficulties. The front ventilators of the house should be opened slightly during the day when the trees are in flower.

To ensure good, well-coloured fruit, the trees must not be overcropped. This statement applies to all fruit for exhibition, but especially to peaches. The fruitlets should be gradually thinned. Approximately one to a square foot is a good guide. To attain good colour the fruits require the maximum of light, and to obtain this the leaves round the fruit should be tucked under the laterals and a label or wad of cotton wool placed at the back of the fruit to hold it in position. Careful ventilation of the peach house is essential. Peaches require somewhat more air than grapes, but the same method of ventilating should be employed.

Before starting the trees into growth in the spring they will need a thorough soaking. Thereafter watering is at the discretion of the grower. Usually another good watering is required as the flowers begin to open, and when the fruit is swelling, once a week is not too often until ripening commences when watering is gradually reduced. But peach and nectarine trees must never be allowed to become dry. Often, with the stress of other work, they are neglected after the crop has been harvested, with the result that many of the buds drop. They should be kept well watered until the leaves have fallen, and the trees sprayed during dry and sunny weather.

A good dressing of concentrated manure as recommended for grapes may be lightly forked into the border after the trees have been pruned and tied but before the house is closed; another dressing after the fruit has set and a third when the fruit begins its final swelling before ripening commences, will be adequate. A mulch of stable manure is also beneficial when the fruit has set.

The most serious insect pests of peaches and nectarines, both under glass and out-of-doors, are the leaf-curling aphis and red spider. In glasshouses, both are easily controlled by fumigation. Immediately the petals have fallen, the houses should be lightly fumigated with nicotine and this repeated eighteen to twenty-one days later. This will give complete control of aphis. Red spider is controlled by azobenzene as advised for grapes.

In the south, excellent peaches and nectarines may be grown out of doors. They may be equal, or in certain cases superior, to those grown under glass. A southern aspect is perhaps the best, but they may also be grown very successfully on east and west walls. A glass coping to the wall is a great asset. It is seldom the trees suffer from leaf blister when they have the protection of a coping. It is also useful as netting may be hung from it in the early part of the year as a protection against frost. The trees require the same pruning and training as those grown under glass, and though possibly less water is required, care should be taken that the trees do not become dry. The trees should be sprayed with insecticide at petal fall and again at intervals of eighteen to twenty-one days as long as necessary. This will clean them from all insect pests.

A selection of recommended varieties:

INDOOR
Alexander—early
Amsden June—early
Barrington—late, large fruits
Bellegarde—mid-season to late
Duke of York—mid-season, excellent colour

A selection of recommended varieties (*cont.*):

Dymond—mid-season
Golden Eagle—late
Kestrel—mid-season
Lady Palmerston—late
Peregrine—mid-season, very rich colour
Solway—very late
Sea Eagle—late

The following have proved successful out of doors:

Amsden June
Barrington
Duke of York
Dymond
Kestrel
Lady Palmerston
Peregrine
Solway
Sea Eagle
Waterloo

PEARS

Maximum Points 6

Pears are exhibited from August to December. As with apples and plums, many of those seen at the August shows are grown in pots. First-class specimens of choice varieties may be seen at provincial shows during this month. Among those that have been noted are: Beurré Bedford, Beurré Superfin, Doyenné du Comice, Louise Bonne of Jersey, Marguerite Marillat, Pitmaston Duchess, and Williams's Bon Chrêtien.

Pears rank equal to apples, cherries, dessert plums and strawberries in the R.H.S. points classification. Exhibition fruits should be of good size and clean. A few varieties only colour well, of which mention may be made of Marguerite Marillat, Louise Bonne of Jersey, and Souvenir de Congrès. When showing such varieties, good colour will gain points. A 'dish' usually consists of six fruits.

Pears may be grown as bushes, cordons, espaliers, fan-trained or pyramids. It is seldom that exhibition fruit is grown on standards. Cordons, espaliers and fan-trained trees are trained to fences or other supports in the open garden, or against walls. Those grown against walls produce the cleanest fruit for exhibition.

The main branches of espalier trees should not be less than a foot apart; single cordons should be planted at two feet six inches. Branches of double and triple cordons and fan-trained trees should be so spaced that the maximum of light and air may reach the fruit. The same method of summer pinching is carried out as for trained trees of apples, sweet cherries and plums (see page 235).

Bush trees of pears are summer-pruned about the end of June or early in July, according to the vigour of the tree. If of normal growth, the shoots (except those needed for extension) are cut back to about the third leaf. This increases the size of the fruit, encourages the production of fruit buds and also improves the fruit by allowing additional light and air to reach it.

A dressing of a balanced compound manure may be given the trees before growth starts in the spring. After the fruit has set, a dressing of a nitrogenous manure may be given. This has proved very helpful to pears and may be given in the form of dried blood, Nitro-chalk or nitrate of potash. Trees bearing heavy crops of fruit will benefit by another dressing of the balanced compound in July. They will also benefit by a mulch of farmyard manure, especially those trees growing against walls.

It is seldom that trees in the open need watering. Those planted against walls will dry out quickly and will always need water during dry weather. The irrigation pipe lines now available will help considerably in this respect.

Scab is the worst fungus pest of pears. It is seldom troublesome on wall trees, especially if the walls have a glass coping, and it is usually unnecessary to spray such trees against scab. It is in the open garden that the disease is most prevalent. It may be controlled by spraying with lime-sulphur or Bordeaux mixture. The first spray is given just before the flowers open, and the second at petal fall. This is usually sufficient.

To obtain pears of first-class quality for exhibition, the fruit in a normal season will need thinning. If too many pears are left on the trees they will be small and of inferior quality. Thinning will also help to prevent biennial bearing. No hard-and-fast rule can be laid down as to the number to be left on the tree. It is a matter best left to the discretion of the grower. Much will depend on variety and vigour of the tree.

The correct time to pick the pears is also important. Each variety of pear has its normal season of ripening. The process may be hastened by picking a little earlier and storing in an air-tight box in a warm room, or delayed by leaving on the tree a little longer. In either case it can make only a little difference. If gathered too soon, the pears will shrivel and be unfit to exhibit. On the other hand, if left on the tree too long they become mellow and sleepy. If the fruits part easily from the tree it is a sign that they are ready for gathering. If force is needed, they should be left a little longer. The following are varieties recommended for exhibition with the approximate time of ripening:

LATE AUGUST-EARLY SEPTEMBER
Laxton's Superb
Williams's Bon Chrêtien
Clapp's Favourite

SEPTEMBER AND EARLY OCTOBER
Beurré d'Amanlis
Beurré Superfin
Fondante d'Automne
Marguerite Marillat
Souvenir de Congrès
Triomphe de Vienne
Beurré Bedford
Beurré Hardy
Pitmaston Duchess
Conference

OCTOBER AND EARLY NOVEMBER
Beurré Diel
Doyenné du Comice
Durondeau
Emile d'Heyst
Marie Louise
Thompson's

NOVEMBER AND LATER
Beurré Easter
Bergamotte d'Esperen
Charles Ernest
Glou Morceau
Joséphine de Malines
Santa Claus
Winter Nelis
Marie Benoist

PLUMS

Maximum Points—Dessert 6; *Culinary* 3

There is a difference in the points value of dessert and culinary varieties. The maximum for dessert kinds is six—culinary varieties are placed in 'any other fruit' for three. This must be borne in mind when showing in competitive collections of fruit. The usual number required for a 'dish' is nine.

For exhibition, plums should be large according to variety, of good colour and fresh. Every effort should be made to preserve the bloom intact. Plums, especially those of the gage section, often show a slight shrivelling at the base when shown late in the season. This is not considered a defect.

Good fruits for exhibition may be grown in pots, and many of those shown in August are produced in this way. They are also grown on fan-trained trees under glass—at the back of a peach house, or in any cool greenhouse. Some cordon trees known to the writer, planted at the back of a peach house, provided fruit for Shrewsbury show in mid-August for many years. These trees are now more than thirty years old, and are still producing crops of first-class fruit. The varieties are Laxton's Early Gage, Kirke's Blue, Jefferson and Coe's Golden Drop.

Out of doors the best plums and gages for exhibition are grown on walls; the fruit, being sheltered by the wall, retains the bloom better. The trees are usually fan-trained, though occasionally cordons are seen. East and west aspects are best suited for plums, but they may also be grown successfully on walls facing north.

When the trees have filled their allotted space the same system of summer pinching may be practised as for trained trees of apples, cherries and pears (see page 235). Grown by this method, trees will produce crops of first-class fruit for many years. In time the fruiting spurs become too long and extend too far from the wall. They may then be thinned out—a few each year. New growths will develop from the main branches and form new fruiting spurs.

In the open, plums are grown on bush and standard trees. The pruning of established trees is not difficult, consisting mainly in removing dead, diseased and overcrowding wood.

In most seasons the fruit will need thinning to produce that extra quality and size necessary for exhibition work. Small fruits from over-cropped trees are of little use on the show bench or for dessert purposes. No fruit responds more to careful cropping and good cultivation than the plum. The surplus fruits should be removed when they are quite small. No special rule can be made as to the quantity to be left on the tree; this must be left to the discretion of the grower.

A dressing of a good, balanced manure may be pricked into the soil before growth starts in the spring. Like black currants and pears, plums and gages appreciate a dressing of nitrogenous manure when the fruit is swelling. A mulch of manure or compost may also be given. A reminder may also be given here that trees growing against walls will need occasional watering during the growing period.

The worst pest of plums is the leaf-curling aphis, which, if allowed to become well established, may ruin or even kill a tree. For trees in the open a winter spray of tar oil or DNC is helpful. Trees planted against walls do not require the winter wash, but should be sprayed with an approved insecticide at petal fall. Thereafter they come into the summer spraying programme.

Some varieties of plum and gage are self-sterile and need the pollen of others for fertilization. In gardens where a collection of varieties is grown the fruit should set freely.

Fruits for exhibition should be left on the trees as long as possible. They should be fully ripe and picked with great care; if possible they should not be touched by hand but held by the stem, which is severed by scissors, and placed in the box for transport.

Varieties recommended in approximate order of ripening:

DESSERT	CULINARY
Laxton's Early Gage	Early Rivers
Oullin's Golden Gage	Belle de Louvain
Denniston's Superb	Victoria
Kirke's Blue	Pond's Seedling
Early Transparent Gage	Monarch
Jefferson	Giant Prune
Victoria	Warwickshire Drooper
Golden Transparent Gage (very shy bearer)	Late Duke
Coe's Golden Drop	Marjorie's Seedling
Coe's Violet	President

RASPBERRIES

Maximum Points 5

For exhibition purposes, raspberries should be large, of good shape and bright colour and be fresh. Special classes are provided for them in many of the summer show schedules, and they are shown extensively in collections of hardy fruit. The usual number of fruits required for a 'dish' is fifty. The fruit should be cut and shown with stalk attached.

Raspberries thrive best in a good, rich soil of medium texture. It must be borne in mind that the canes are surface-rooting. A moist position is therefore to be preferred and a mulch should be given during the summer months. To obtain first-class fruit for exhibition, efforts must be made to secure good, strong, sturdy and healthy canes. To this end plants from certified stocks only should be planted. They are planted two feet apart in the rows which should be six feet apart. After planting, the canes should be cut down to within six inches of the ground. About four of the new growths should be selected for fruiting and all surplus canes removed during the summer months. The old canes should be cut down as soon as fruiting is finished and the new ones tied in their place. These are mostly cut back the following spring to remove the sappy tips.

A dressing of a good, well-balanced fertilizer, such as is recommended for other fruits, should be sprinkled along the rows in the early spring. This, with the summer mulching, is sufficient manure for this fruit.

Raspberries are very prone to virus disease. This is identified by weak growths, mottled leaves and deformed fruit. All diseased stools must be grubbed up and burnt. The average life of a plantation is from eight to ten years. Insect pests are not usually troublesome. The raspberry beetle may do some damage and to control it two sprayings of liquid derris or nicotine and quassia may be given about ten days after flowering has commenced, and again about a fortnight later. Cane spot may appear, but with good cultivation should not do much harm. It is controlled by spraying with Bordeaux mixture.

Late-fruiting raspberries may be useful for the autumn shows. These varieties produce fruit on canes of the current season's growth. They are cut down to the ground in early spring, and the new canes carefully tended during the summer. Good fruit may be picked as late as November if the weather is suitable.

For exhibition, raspberries should be handled no more than is necessary. The fruits must be carefully selected, picked with some stem, and placed directly into the punnets or boxes for transport.

The following is a selection of popular varieties:

Malling Promise	Pyne's Imperial	AUTUMN FRUITING
Malling Landmark	Bath's Perfection	Hailsham
Newburgh	Yellow Antwerp	November Abundance
St. Walfried	Ringwood Yellow	Lloyd George

STRAWBERRIES

Maximum Points 6

Strawberries are the most popular of the soft fruits. They attract the attention of the exhibitor during June and July. Occasionally some fruits are produced in the autumn and are exhibited at the October shows. They are a popular entry in classes for 'Any other Fruit'. When exhibited, the fruits should be of a large size, of good shape and colour, and quite fresh. They should be shown on the stalk.

Good crops of strawberries may be grown in pots, and very fine exhibits of fruit so grown may be seen at the Chelsea Show. In large gardens special houses were used for forcing strawberries, and may still be in evidence today. Plants are also accommodated on shelves in vineries and other houses till ripening commences, when they are moved to the drier atmosphere of the plant houses. The plants are usually grown in six-inch pots and the fruits thinned to six or eight per plant. By judicious feeding very fine fruits are produced.

Early crops of strawberries are grown in frames, under dutch lights, and under cloches. In strawberry-growing districts many thousands of the latter may be seen covering the plants. Cloches protect the flowers from frost, keep the fruit clean and ripen it much earlier.

Strawberries thrive best in good, deep, rich soil. For planting, only clean, virus-free runners should be used, obtained from clonal stocks certified by the Ministry of Agriculture. The rows should be thirty inches apart, with about fifteen inches between the plants in the rows. Plantings made after September should not be allowed to fruit the first year, and all runners must be removed. Runners should always be removed from fruiting plants.

The finest fruits for exhibition are grown on good strong runners planted the previous July and August. Exhibition-standard strawberries are rarely produced on plants more than two years old. When grown especially for showing, the fruit may be thinned and given the protection of cloches.

A good dressing of a compound fertilizer should be given to the plants in early spring before growth commences, and the beds kept free of weeds. Another dressing may be given after fruiting, when the beds have been cleared. This will strengthen the crowns for the next season. Straw mats or a bed of clean straw should be placed round the plants for the fruits to rest on to keep them clean and to protect them from slugs.

For exhibition, strawberries must be picked with the stem, and when quite dry. They should be left on the plants as long as possible so that their freshness may be preserved for the judges. Each fruit should be placed in a leaf and handled no more than is necessary.

Probably the most famous varieties of strawberry are Sir Joseph Paxton and Royal Sovereign. The latter is still heavily planted and good crops are obtained from clonal-raised plants. Occasionally good crops of Sir Joseph Paxton are also seen. Early Cambridge is a strong, vigorous grower and is to be recommended. Other varieties largely planted are Perle de Prague, Oberschlesien, Tardive de Leopold, and Auchincruive Climax. The latter produces a second crop in the autumn and is proving a popular and successful exhibition variety.

Many new varieties have been raised at the Cambridge Horticultural Research Station. No reliable data are yet available for these varieties, which are still under number. Some are very promising and will doubtless be given a place with the most popular of the day. Cambridge 257 is similar to Royal Sovereign and may prove useful to the exhibitor.

PART THREE

Vegetables

By J. W. Tuffin

CHAPTER SEVENTEEN

Selecting and Staging Vegetables

People who wish to grow vegetables to show standard must have a considerable degree of enthusiasm and great tenacity of purpose if they are to be successful. Moreover, there must be a very real inclination to pay great attention to detail.

During the present century great progress has been made by seed firms in the matter of raising new varieties of vegetables which are of fine quality and appearance. I have recommended, in the following pages, varieties which I have proved to be excellent for exhibition, when grown in my own locality on soil which is of the old red sandstone type; it will, however, often rest with the grower to prove which particular varieties will best suit his own conditions of soil and locality.

Vegetables are treated individually in alphabetical order in the next chapter, and their culture to exhibition standard, choice of varieties and method of packing and staging are detailed. The staging of collections of vegetables is described on page 267.

Under the name of each vegetable is indicated the maximum points that it can gain when being judged in a collection. Thus it will be seen that onions, carrots and cauliflowers can each command a maximum of eight points, while more easily grown subjects such as cabbage and broad beans, even if perfect, could only gain six points, and radish and sweet corn only four points. This scale of points was drawn up by the Royal Horticultural Society, and is agreed by most show societies to be the basis upon which their judges shall work. Thus an exhibitor would be well advised to choose all those vegetables to which the most points could be given when deciding what to include in classes for a collection of vegetables.

The scale of points is given below for easy reference, and in the next table the number of each vegetable recommended by the Royal Horticultural Society for a dish is tabulated.

	Points		*Points*
Artichokes, Globe ...	6	Endive	5
Artichokes, Jerusalem ...	5	Kale	5
Asparagus	8	Leeks	8
Beans, Broad and Long-pod	6	Lettuces	6
		Maize	4
Beans, Runner and Kidney	7	Marrows	6
		Mushrooms	8
Beet	6	Onions	8
Broccoli or Cauliflower	8	Parsnips	6
Brussels Sprouts, stems	6	Peas	8
Brussels Sprouts, picked	6	Potatoes	8
Cabbage, Cooking ...	6	Radishes	4
Cabbage, Red	5	Salsify	5
Capsicums	4	Savoys	6
Cardoons	6	Scorzonera	5
Carrots	8	Seakale	8
Cauliflower or Broccoli	8	Shallots	3 or 4
Celeriac	6	Spinach	5
Celery	8	Tomatoes	8
Cucumbers	7	Turnips	6

In the case of any vegetables not enumerated above being shown, e.g. Pumpkins, Stachys, Witloof, Horseradish, small Saladings, Mustard, Cress, etc., not more than three points should be given.

Note on the Cabbage (*Brassica*) *Family.*—For exhibition purposes, the following are considered to be distinct kinds of vegetables: Cauliflower, Brussels Sprouts, Cabbage, Borecole or Kale, Savoy. Cauliflower includes Broccoli, and for exhibition purposes is not distinct from it.

Number of specimens to be shown:

	In Collections	*For Single Dishes*
Artichokes, Globe	9	6
Artichokes, Jerusalem	12	12
Asparagus	36	36
Beans, Runner, French	24	24
Beans, Climbing, French	36	36
Beans, Dwarf, French	36	36
Beans, Broad	24	18
Beet	6	6
Brussels Sprouts	50	50
Brussels Sprouts, stems	3	3
Cabbages	3	3
Cabbages, Savoy	3	3
Cauliflower or Broccoli	6	3
Capsicums and Chillies	24	24

Cardoons	3	3
Carrots, long	10	6
Carrots, stump-rooted	10	6
Celeriac	9	6
Celery, White...	6	3
Celery, Red	6	3
Couve Tronchuda	3	3
Cucumbers	2	2
Egg Plant fruits	12	12
Endive	6	6
Kale	3	3
Kohl Rabi	12	9
Leeks	9	6
Lettuce	6	6
Marrows	3	3
Mushrooms	12	12
Onions	12	6
Onions, Pickling	1 lb.	1 lb.
Parsnips	6	6
Peas	50	50
Potatoes	12	6
Pumpkin	1	1
Radishes, Bundle of	24	24
Rhubarb Sticks	—	3
Salsify	12	12
Scorzonera	12	12
Seakale	12	12
Shallots	24	24
Stachys	50	50
Tomatoes	12	12
Tomatoes, Cluster, Ornamental	3 Clusters	3 Clusters
Turnips	10	6

STAGING AND EXHIBITING COLLECTIONS OF VEGETABLES

Having grown good specimens, taken due care with the packing, and kept a watchful eye on them during transit, especially if a train journey has to be undertaken, it is of the utmost importance to stage to the very best advantage. In the case of collections of vegetables, points are often awarded for staging, and when the competition is very close, just that little bit extra put into the staging may well carry the day.

For staging collections some appliances, in the way of boards, battens for background, a stand or rings for fixing onions, and some exhibition baskets, will be needed. Black velvet is undoubtedly the best material for a background. The Royal Horticultural Society will permit only the use of green hessian, which they supply, for their shows at Vincent Square. Here they also supply boxes of various sizes which enable the various dishes to be raised to the desired height and plates on which to stage vegetables in the single-dish classes.

Dishes of such vegetables as potatoes, tomatoes, peas, brussels sprouts, and shallots, to mention a few, are best staged on plates; the larger subjects such as celery, leeks, cauliflowers and parsnips, are staged to best advantage directly on the table. At provincial and local shows the exhibitor is usually required to supply all his own requisites for staging; the society, of course, supply the tables.

When staging a collection of vegetables, it is well to plan an effective grouping beforehand, so that the desirable balance and contrast of colour in the various dishes is attained.

For an autumn show I recommend the following six subjects: cauliflowers, leeks, celery, potatoes, onions, and carrots or tomatoes. When staging such a collection as this, celery, cauliflower and leeks should comprise the back row, with these dishes raised, on a shelf or individual boxes, to something like fifteen inches above the table level. Cauliflower would occupy the central position, and it might be advantageous to raise this a few inches higher than the celery and leeks which would be staged on either side.

The cauliflower is best staged on a board, this being triangular in shape with six nails, five inches in length, driven through from back to front about six inches apart, three in the bottom row, then two across the middle and one at the top. There is usually some difference in the size of the specimens, therefore choose the three largest heads for the bottom row, the middle-sized ones for the second row, and the smallest one for the top. The stems of the cauliflower are fixed into the protruding nails; the spaces between are filled in with moss, and then the front covered neatly with parsley. Do not take anything off the depth of the heads by bringing the parsley out too far.

The celery and leeks should be perfectly upright when staged. They are usually shown on specially made boards which are roughly semicircular in shape. Nails should be fixed upright in these base boards at the appropriate distances according to the thickness of the specimens and the base of the leeks should be spiked on to these nails. Plait the foliage and then secure it with two or three ties of green fillis and if necessary tie this to a supporting pole fixed in the board.

Onions should occupy a central position in front of the cauliflower, and they may be staged on a large exhibition basket bedded with moss, or they may be made to sit on rings, or there is a special onion board with adjustable rings fitted. This 'dish' should be raised above table level a matter of some six to nine inches.

Potatoes and carrots should occupy positions on either side of the onions, rather more to the front, and raised about three inches above the table level. Potatoes are best staged on a round exhibition basket in the form of a flattened pyramid, with the rose ends of the tubers all pointing outwards. Carrots should be staged on a similar receptacle, in the form of a pyramid, with the root end facing to the front.

In the case of collections being staged with a greater number of kinds, the same three, viz. celery, leeks and cauliflowers should always occupy the back-row positions, and if such things as parsnips and long beet are introduced, they should occupy a position to the side of the onions, and those kinds which make up smaller dishes, such as peas, tomatoes, potatoes, cucumbers, beans and brussels sprouts, should be kept to the front.

Faults to avoid in a collection are flatness, and allowing any one dish to hide part of another one. Make good use of parsley for filling in any spaces between the specimens comprising a dish.

Long beet and parsnips are best staged in the same way as long carrots, as a pyramid, globe beet and turnips with their tails in the air and peas and brussels sprouts in the form of a flattened cone. Stage tomatoes in a single layer, stems downwards.

It may sometimes happen that only either celery or leeks is available, in which case I would recommend staging it to occupy the centre position in the back row, and, if using cauliflower, to stage this on an exhibition basket as one of the side dishes in the back row, with carrots on the opposite side; and then for the front row, onions in the centre, and potatoes and tomatoes on either side. This will maintain a well-balanced exhibit.

When staging cauliflower in a single-dish class, trim the outer leaves off level with the curd, but a few of the inner, small, fresh leaves may with advantage be left on. They should be staged with the curds to face the judges, and cabbage also should be staged thus. Single dishes of parsnips, carrots, long beet, celery and leeks, should all have their root ends facing the judges, and be staged neatly in the form of a pyramid. Potatoes should be staged on plates, and should be arranged with five on the plate with their rose ends outwards, and the sixth, the best specimen, resting on the top of the others.

Marrows and cucumbers should have the flower end facing the judges, although, when staged in collections, it is often better to stage cucumbers across, to show their length to better advantage. This also applies to runner beans and dwarf beans which should always be staged with all their stems at the same end.

All vegetables which will deteriorate if exposed to light should be covered with sheets of paper, as soon as they are staged; in the case of blanched vegetables, with brown paper. Tissue-paper coverings will suffice for such things as carrots, beet, peas, beans and marrows. Onions are about the only subject which will not derive benefit from being covered. The coverings should be left on until just before the time for judging to commence. It may be necessary to remove them temporarily so as to spray lightly subjects which need it.

Correct labelling of exhibits, is I think, very important, although it is not always made compulsory. In my opinion it is of great educational value to the visiting public and, of course, is always of interest to other exhibitors.

CHAPTER EIGHTEEN

Vegetables Described Alphabetically

CHINESE ARTICHOKES

Maximum Points 3

THIS VEGETABLE is fairly easily grown on a light warm soil. It is a low-growing plant producing small underground tubers which have a corkscrew-like appearance, and it is the tubers that are used for culinary purposes. They are only suitable for exhibition when included in an unlimited collection of vegetables.

To prepare them for exhibition, all that is necessary is to wash them in clean, cold water, using a sponge to remove soil from the crevices and not applying too much force as they quickly turn brown if bruised. They must also be kept from light as much as possible, before showing, to prevent them from becoming discoloured. They should be arranged in the form of a cone on a small exhibition basket.

GLOBE ARTICHOKES

Maximum Points 6

This vegetable is not often shown. It is in season for a relatively short time and it is always problematical whether it will be available in good condition just when needed.

The plants are perennial, so once established they are not much trouble to grow, but if needed for exhibition they will well repay applications of liquid manure when the heads are being formed. The best variety is Green Globe.

During spells of hot sunshine in summer, the heads of globe artichokes are likely to become scorched, therefore it is advisable to shade with some light material such as tiffany or butter muslin, to ensure maintaining a fresh green colour.

Six, nine, or twelve will be the number required for a dish. The heads may be cut some few days before they are required, as they will keep fresh for a short time if the stem is put in shallow water; the water should be changed fairly often.

JERUSALEM ARTICHOKES

Maximum Points 5

This vegetable will never be much in demand for show purposes, and the only place it is likely to be used is in unlimited collections. The white variety will be the best for this purpose, and if selection is carried out over a number of years, the shape and size of the tubers will, no doubt, be improved. There is no need to give any information on cultivation, as it will grow practically anywhere, but it will be much better if grown in good soil. When exhibited it should be staged in the same way as a dish of potatoes.

ASPARAGUS

Maximum Points 8

At one time the making of an asparagus bed was considered to be a very expensive and involved affair, but really this is not so. The ground should, however, be trenched and plenty of good farmyard manure worked in, as the crop will occupy the same land for a great number of years.

For exhibition purposes the varieties which produce large, stout sticks, should be chosen. Connover's Colossal is one of the best, and Giant French is also very good. Asparagus is one of the choicest of vegetables, and will be assured of high points from the judges if well grown, but it is in season too early in the year for most shows, and on that account is seldom seen on the show bench. During the months of April, May and June a dish of asparagus should always be included in a collection of nine or more kinds, and, of course, no collection of unlimited numbers would be complete without a good dish.

I shall not go into any details of cultivation. A bed well made, planted with the right variety, and well managed, and the plants fed generously year by year, will produce good sticks of asparagus over a long period of time.

When preparing the heads before a show, wash them carefully with cold water; usually just letting water run over them will suffice. Thirty-six sticks are required for a dish, and they should be tied neatly in one bundle, keeping all the tops level and cutting level the lower ends after bunching. The bundles should stand erect when staged.

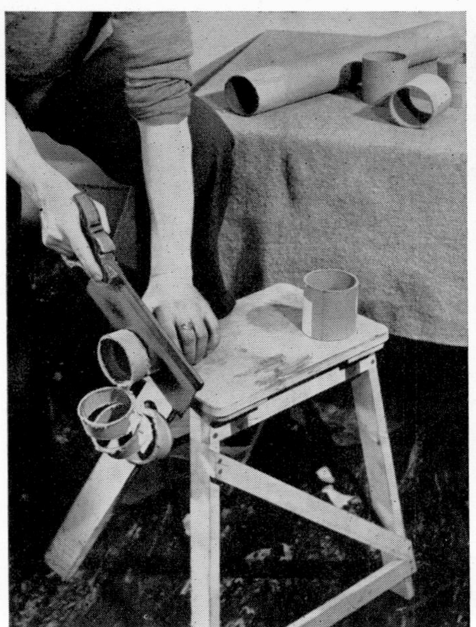

Left: Making useful rings on which to stage specimen onions. *Right:* Unpacking the box in which vegetables have been carried to the show; those needing the most protection are packed last.

Left: Arranging blocks to display a collection of vegetables to best advantage. *Right:* Plenty of fresh parsley should be at hand to use when staging.

Arranging different levels to display a collection of twelve vegetables impressively.

The completed exhibit, which was of superb quality and gained first prize.

Left: This exhibitor has put up some excellent savoys, but these are not highly pointed in a collection class. *Right:* A prize-winning exhibition tray showing effect of displaying celery and leeks upright.

Left: Beetroot and the other root vegetables should be washed gently with a sponge. *Right:* Even potato specimens are chosen and wrapped individually for packing.

Left: A good cucumber specimen is long and straight and the flower still attached. Pairs should be evenly matched. *Right:* Trimming and preparing an onion.

BROAD BEANS

Maximum Points 6

The season during which broad beans are exhibited is rather short, but there are usually single-dish classes for them at summer shows, and they may often be included with advantage in a collection of nine or more kinds.

The ground where they are to be grown should be trenched or well dug and generously manured. As an alternative method, trenches may be prepared about eighteen inches wide and deep, and a good layer of farmyard manure placed in them. At planting time, fork in a dressing of bonemeal and hoof and horn, or a good general fertilizer.

To have beans ready for a particular show it is advisable to make two or three sowings at intervals of a fortnight, or if more sowings can be made, so much the better. The usual number of pods asked for in a dish is eighteen to twenty-four, so that only a few seeds need be sown each time.

If the bean weevil attacks the young plants, spray with wettable DDT. Later on, if the black aphis puts in an appearance, spray with nicotine or a derris wash.

The early crops will not need much in the way of watering, but the later batches will probably need quite a lot of water to keep them growing freely, and occasional applications of liquid manure or a good fertilizer well watered in will be beneficial. To keep the plants growing upright, sticks should be put firmly in the ground and strings stretched along each side of every row.

When a good number of flowers are showing, the growing points of the plants should be pinched, as this will have the doubly beneficial effect of checking attacks of black aphis and encouraging greater size in the pods.

Varieties recommended are Aquadulce and Giant Seville for early use; Exhibition Longpod for mid-season and Sutton's Giant Windsor and Green Windsor for late summer.

Broad bean pods will not keep fresh for long, and should be gathered at the last possible moment, so that they do not become flaccid. They should be cut with a piece of stem attached, and handled carefully, as the pods are readily bruised. If they have to be gathered a day or more before a show, they must be kept in a very cool shed or cellar where there is no loss of moisture from the pods through evaporation.

The beans in the pods should be well developed, but with no sign of black-eye. The pods should contain, in the case of the longpod types from seven to nine beans, and the Windsors five beans.

When packing the specimens to carry to the show, the broad beans should always be in the top layer, with nothing else above them but a little wood-wool. They may be wrapped in tissue-paper (white) in about half-dozens, or in single layers on tissue-paper, with paper between each layer. Damp them with a light spray at the time of packing to keep them fresh and firm.

DWARF FRENCH BEANS

Maximum Points 7

This is a vegetable which is not shown a great deal except as a single dish at summer and autumn shows and in collections of nine or more kinds. It is shown in smaller collections occasionally as the points value is high, but a drawback is that the beans do not make a very imposing dish.

The ground where they are to be grown should be well sheltered, as they will not tolerate cold, windy conditions, and this especially applies to the early sowings. First sowings out of doors should be made not earlier than the end of April and successionally until July. Seeds should be sown for preference in a double row spaced about nine inches apart, the seeds themselves being planted at six inches apart, but thinned to twice this distance later on. Water and feed generously, and mulch the crop to conserve soil moisture. Spray the plants in the evening during hot dry spells.

To ensure production of fine straight pods, it is essential to keep the plants growing in an upright position, and this will necessitate supporting the plants with small twiggy sticks.

It is important that no pods be allowed to hang too long on the plants or the latter will soon become exhausted. Some of the best pods should be collected during the few days preceding a show, cutting them with a sharp knife or scissors, with a fairly long stem attached. If they are then placed stem downwards in a vessel containing a small amount of water, with care taken to keep the pods upright, and they are stored in a cool place, they will keep in perfect condition for several days. The chosen pods should be about nine inches long, flat and crisp. Thirty-six are usually required for a dish. One variety outstanding for exhibition is Sutton's Prince.

To carry to the show they should be wrapped in a damp cloth and have nothing heavy above them, in the top of the hamper.

RUNNER BEANS

Maximum Points 7

This member of the bean family is one of the most popular of summer vegetables and is universally grown, but it may not always be advisable to include it in a show collection of eight kinds or less, as it can only score a maximum of seven points, as against the eight points of several other kinds. It should, however, be included in collections of nine or more kinds at summer and early-autumn shows.

To ensure the production of really fine pods, the plot selected for the crop should be trenched and very liberally manured, or alternatively, trenches may be prepared, by taking them out about two feet wide and deep and incorporating plenty of good farmyard manure as the trenches are refilled. If the trenches are taken out during the winter or early spring, they may be left partly open for some time, for the soil to get well weathered. This is especially desirable when the soil is a heavy clay.

A double row of plants should be grown in each trench, with a space of about fifteen to eighteen inches allowed between the rows and also between the plants in the rows. They should be grown on the single cordon system, one plant to each stick. Side growths should be pinched at one or two leaves, and, if necessary, the main stem held to the stick with ties of raffia.

Near the date of the show, the pods should be thinned to the two most promising in each cluster and the stems tied to the sticks with raffia to prevent their bending downwards with the weight of the beans.

The plants at this time will need to be well supplied with water and liquid manure. Occasionally a light top-dressing of a good artificial manure should be applied and well watered in. Spray the plants overhead with clear water during the evening in hot sunny spells.

For supporting the plants, straight bean sticks about ten feet long should be used. These should be made secure by tying them to wires stretched tight on posts driven firmly into the ground.

Plants for an early crop can with advantage be raised under glass, the seeds being sown either in boxes, in which case they should be spaced four inches apart, or singly in four- or five-inch pots. The middle of April is a good time to sow. The end of May will be early enough to plant out after the seedlings have been well hardened off. If planted out earlier some protection should be afforded against cold winds or frosts at night. Protect also against slugs and snails. For successional crops the seed may be sown where the plants are to grow, from the middle of May to about the middle of June for the latest crop.

I think that Prizewinner is by far the best variety for exhibition purposes. By reselecting and sowing his own seed, a grower can work up a superior strain of his own and most leading exhibitors of this vegetable have done this.

It may be necessary to pick the beans as they attain the desired size, in order to make up the number required for a dish. They will keep fresh for several days kept in shallow water, standing upright in a cool shed. They should be cut with an inch or so of stem attached. The chosen specimens should be as long as possible, as much as eighteen inches long, but all of a uniform length, straight and fresh. There must be no sign of seeds showing in the pods, and no trace of stringiness. Eighteen to twenty-four is the usual number required for a dish.

For packing, it is a good plan to wrap them in a damp cloth, such as a piece of tiffany or linen, rolling them up and placing a layer of cloth between each two beans. This will keep them fresh, and also help to straighten them. These again should be kept in the top layer when placing in the box or hamper, and nothing heavy should be packed on top of them.

BEET

Maximum Points 6

The production of well-shaped round beet should present no difficulties on a light or sandy loam which has been well dug during the previous winter, but to which no farmyard manure has been added. A site which has been well manured the previous season for another crop, such as potatoes or celery, is very suitable. If the natural soil is of a rough, stony nature, or clay, it will be advisable either to take out small trenches or to make up a bed of prepared soil in a frame. The trenches should be about nine inches deep and filled with a light compost consisting of old potting soil, old hot-bed material, or leaf-mould and coarse sand, with a shovelful of wood ashes and a five-inch potful of bonemeal added to each barrowload of soil. A similar mixture may be used for beds in frames.

For really good, long beet, it will usually be necessary to bore holes. The holes should be made three feet to three and half feet deep with an iron bar, and filled with a compost as advised above. The soil should be well firmed in the holes, as filling proceeds.

Sowing of both types should take place from early April to the middle of May, and the seedlings, in the case of the long type, should be thinned at the earliest opportunity to the best one at each prepared hole. The round type growing in rows should be thinned to about nine inches apart.

Mice are sometimes most troublesome in eating beet seed, and also gnawing the tops of the roots at ground level later on. Traps should be set on the bed at sowing time, also under walls and in the mouths of any holes observed. Well-soaked dried peas are a good bait. The crop should be dusted lightly with old soot at intervals and the surface of the soil kept well stirred with the dutch hoe.

Of round varieties, Sutton's Globe and Carter's Crimson Ball are very reliable. Of long varieties Sutton's Black and Dobbie's Purple are to be recommended.

If frequent sowings have been made, it should be possible to lift suitable specimens of round beet at the time they are required for a show. In the case of long beet, they may be at their best some time before the show date, in which case they may be lifted and stored in an almost upright position, in moistened sand or peat litter, in a cool shed, the tops being trimmed back to about three inches. In either case the lifting must be carried out carefully, so that the tap root is intact and uninjured. If damaged, bleeding will occur with a subsequent loss of colour.

Beet may be washed a few days before a show without any loss of quality, and time is often very important near the show day when there are several things which must be left to be done at the last possible moment. The roots should be washed with a sponge and water, rinsing them afterwards in clean water. Any fibrous roots should be carefully trimmed with a sharp knife, but the tap root must be left intact.

The chosen specimens in the case of round beet, should be of medium size, perfectly round, with a good clean tap root, clean, clear skin, and, most essential of all, good colour. Unfortunately one is not able beforehand to determine if the root the judges cut is going to be of good colour.

In the case of long beet the specimens entered should be of good size and shape and quite long, with good round, clean shoulders and, of course, good colour. Six specimens are required for a dish.

For carrying, the specimens should be wrapped singly in tissue-paper, and packed carefully with wood-wool. They may be consigned to a position in the bottom of the box or hamper, and should be sprayed to keep them fresh.

BROCCOLI

Maximum Points 8

In classes for collections of vegetables which call for distinct kinds, it is not permissible to show both broccoli and cauliflowers, but they are of such value to exhibitors that one or the other should always be included in their season.

Provided broccoli is grown on soil which has been well dug and well manured, it is a crop which will more or less look after itself. It is a good plan about a month before the heads will be needed, to go through the bed and mark with a cane any promising specimens and continue to do likewise to within a few days of the show. These selected specimens may receive some extra attention in the way of watering and feeding. The fact of their being marked with a stick will make it easy to find them for future inspections and also should ensure that they are not cut for any purpose other than the intended one.

As the heads begin to turn in they must be protected from light to keep them white and clean. This may be done either by having the outer leaves tied loosely, by covering with some leaves broken from the outside of the plants, or by bending a few of the inner leaves over. If some of the heads turn in before they are wanted, they can be kept fairly well for a few days by lifting the whole plant with a fork and hanging it upside down in a cool, dark shed. To keep them fresh, the plants thus treated should receive a daily spraying with clean water.

Varieties are numerous, and it would be difficult for me to name the best. The self-protecting types are good for autumn. In south-west counties, where they can be grown successfully, varieties of the Roscoff type are excellent, but their territory is limited. I find Sutton's Peerless strain to be perfectly hardy in a normal winter and also of superb quality. There are varieties in this strain to cover the season from December to almost June.

The following remarks on preparing for exhibition apply equally to cauliflowers.

As the heads are not much spoilt if lifted early and hung in a dark shed, they may be cut in the ordinary manner during the three or four days immediately preceding a show. Trim most of the leaves off but leave just enough to protect the curd, which should have further protection by placing over it a piece of soft white tissue-paper, tucking in the edges of the paper between the leaves and curd. The leaves left on as a protection when packing, should be shortened but not too much.

Although I have mentioned saving heads for several days before a show, this should only be done from necessity, and not from choice. If enough good heads can be cut a day or two before a show, then they will look all the fresher when exhibited. Freshness is a great point with good judges.

Three specimens are required for a single dish, and usually six in a collection. Good medium-sized heads should be chosen in preference to over-large, coarse ones. They should be perfectly white and round, and showing not the least sign of blowing. Of course, they must be free from any damage by caterpillars or other pests.

The heads will stand no rough treatment, and they must be handled and packed with the greatest care. In addition to the covering of tissue-paper already mentioned, each head should be wrapped in a half sheet of brown paper, which will afford further protection, and also exclude light. They should be either packed with wood-wool in a box or hamper on their own, or consigned to a place near the top if they have to share with other occupants. Nothing heavy must be packed over them, and they should be kept dry. Do not cut the stems too short, as a fair length is needed when staging on a cauliflower board, and they can be adjusted to the right length at the time of staging.

BRUSSELS SPROUTS

Maximum Points 6

Brussels sprouts will usually be included in a collection of twelve kinds of vegetable at autumn shows and often in classes for smaller numbers. Their perfect hardiness ensures their being available at any time in season as also does their habit of producing sprouts in succession over a long period. To produce well-developed, firm sprouts by early autumn, seed should be sown in a greenhouse or frame in early February and the seedlings pricked off at an early stage into boxes or frames. They must be kept well up to the glass to prevent them becoming drawn, the aim being to keep them as hardy as possible all the time. For successional crops, sowings should be made out of doors from the end of February onwards.

The young plants should be set out in their final quarters from about the middle of April onwards, after being thoroughly hardened off, and should be well watered in if dry conditions prevail. A dressing of a good compound fertilizer should be worked in at planting time, and after the plants are well established a top-dressing of a nitrogenous fertilizer will boost them. Apply in rainy weather or water well in.

The plants should be spaced at least two feet apart each way and should be put out on ground which has been trenched or well dug and well manured, but made very firm before planting.

Precautions must be taken to ward off attacks of the cabbage root fly, the grubs of which in some seasons play havoc with these early plants. DDT powder should be dusted on to the roots at planting time and several applications of four per cent calomel dust should be made, commencing a couple of days after planting out, to the surface soil close round the stems of the plants. Later on a watch must be kept for attacks of white fly and cabbage aphis, as both these pests will deposit a lot of filth on the developing sprouts, and render them unfit for show purposes. To destroy these pests, the plants should be sprayed very thoroughly with a nicotine and soap wash.

If the plants are inclined to rock in the wind, a stick or cane should be put to each one and the plants made secure to these with raffia ties. For some weeks before the sprouts are needed, the plants should be helped along with water and liquid manure. The surface of the soil must be kept constantly stirred with the hoe.

For large sprouts, the variety Fillbasket is very good, but Universal is a favourite with many exhibitors, the sprouts being very firm, not over-large and of a pleasing dark-green colour.

The collecting of exhibition sprouts will consist in carefully going through the bed, and having decided on a standard, selecting them all as near as possible to this standard. They are best severed from the plants with a sharp knife.

They should be perfectly clean and free from any filth caused by cabbage white fly or cabbage aphis. They should be shown as gathered, and no outer leaves removed, or the appearance of the sprouts will be spoilt, and the green colour lost. It is a good plan to drop them in a bucket of water to wash them. They will drop into any odd corner in the hamper when packing. Fifty specimens are usually required for a dish, but very often fewer are asked for at local shows.

CABBAGE

Maximum Points 6

Cabbage is not often in demand for collections of vegetables. However, there are times at summer shows when it is necessary to include a dish, three being the number usually required. There are classes for single dishes in most schedules and often separate classes for a round-headed variety, a pointed variety and a red variety.

The general cultivation of the cabbage is so well known that very little need be said on the subject here, and there is not a great deal in the way of extra treatment which may be provided. One or two top-dressings of a quick-acting compound fertilizer, during the growing season, will prove of benefit. Young plants put out during the spring and early summer, will need watering till they get well established. It is essential to keep the plants free of insect pests, as the leaves should be quite clean and free of holes caused by caterpillars of the cabbage white butterfly.

It is a good plan to mark with a stick a few weeks before they are needed, the plants which are likely to be selected, as this makes it easy for the grower to keep an eye on them, and may be the means of preventing their being used by the housewife.

For spring and early summer, Flower of Spring is a very good choice of variety as one of the larger type. Winningstadt is about the best for a March sowing to heart in the autumn. Earliest is a good variety to sow in spring to turn in during the summer. The foregoing are pointed varieties.

Of round-headed varieties for summer cutting, Primo is about the best and for autumn, Improved Christmas Drumhead. Large Blood Red is the best red cabbage for show.

The chosen specimens should be cut as near the show date as possible. They should be cut near to the ground where the stem is hard, since there will then be less loss of sap from the leaves, and the cabbage will be fresher when exhibited. No washing should be necessary. Choose specimens of a good medium size, with really firm hearts, and clean outer leaves, which should still be attached for showing. Keep them well sprayed with clean water up to the time of judging.

They travel well when packed in a large box that will take a single layer of heads, with a sheet of paper wrapped round each one. Three is the usual number for a dish, but often only a pair are required at local shows.

CARROTS

Maximum Points 8

To the exhibitor carrots are of such great value that every effort must be made to have them in fine form for all occasions. A good, light loam or sandy soil (provided the latter is not too hot and dry) will best suit this crop, but if special provision be made the crop can be grown successfully on less kindly types of soil.

For shows from the end of May till July, I prefer to grow in brick pits. The bed may be made up either on a hotbed or without. A good depth of finely sifted soil will be needed, in the case of long carrots, from two and half to three feet, so that the tap root may grow straight down. For the short types a depth of at least one and half foot must be provided. In any case the surface of the soil should be kept well up to the glass. This compost should be good, consisting of old potting soil, leaf-mould, old hotbed material if available, some coarse sand, and wood ashes with a little bonemeal added. Moreover, it should be made fairly firm in the pits.

The first sowing should be made in early January. In the case of long carrots a long season of growth is needed for full development of the roots; somewhere about six months is the average. The short types will develop in about four months under favourable conditions. After sowing the seed in drills about one foot apart, the frames should be kept closed till germination has taken place, when a little air should be admitted on the mornings of favourable days, but the lights closed early in the afternoons. The plants should be given a spray with tepid water if conditions warrant it.

As growth develops and the weather gets warmer, the amount of air should be increased and about early April the lights may be removed in good weather. Warm rains at this time will prove very beneficial. Growing under these conditions, watering must be carefully attended to and must be done thoroughly when needed.

Thinning out must be attended to at an early date and the long types should be finally spaced about eight inches apart, Favourite about six inches and the small-type shorthorns about four inches. Some of the later thinnings may be made use of in the kitchen. From about the middle of May a top-dressing should be added, to prevent the tops of the roots becoming green through exposure to light; this should take the form of finely sifted old potting soil, old leaf-mould or anything else of a similar nature.

The plot selected for the outdoor crop should be well dug during the winter, but no farmyard manure added. A site which has been well manured for a crop the previous season is the best. The first sowing out of doors should be made about the middle of March, followed by later ones till the end of April.

In the case of long carrots, it is usually necessary to bore holes with a crowbar and fill them with finely sifted soil composed of old potting soil, leaf-mould and old hotbed material, with the addition of bonemeal, wood ashes and coarse sand. In addition some National

Growmore or other suitable compound fertilizer may be added, a suitable amount being a five-inch potful to each barrowload of soil. The holes should be made at least three feet deep for long carrots, and should be made as perfect in shape as possible, tapering gently all the way. The soil should be well firmed in the holes as filling proceeds. They should be spaced a foot apart and, if more than one row is put in, the rows should be eighteen inches apart. If the holes are prepared some time before sowing the seed, mark the centre of each with a small cane.

Short carrots may be grown in a similar manner but, of course, the holes need not be nearly so deep. Another good method with short types is to take out a small trench about nine inches deep and fill it with the same compost as recommended for long carrots.

Care should be taken to sow the seed in the centre of each hole or trench, and thinning must be attended to as soon as the seedlings are large enough to handle, leaving the best one in the centre of each hole or spacing trench-grown plants at least six inches apart.

During the growing season frequent light dustings of old soot should be given, but it is most important to apply this in the early morning or late evening, as if left till the sun is high, scorching will result. I am a great believer in old soot for the dusting of kitchen garden crops in general and if applied regularly and persistently I believe this will go a long way towards warding off or checking a host of pests, especially carrot, onion and celery fly. Avoid using it on leeks, however, as it gets down inside the outer skins and causes discoloration.

Keep the surface of the beds well stirred with the dutch hoe. I am still old-fashioned enough to believe in this tool and that constant surface cultivation is of some value to the plants.

If greenfly should put in an appearance in the carrot bed, it must be dealt with by spraying with nicotine and soap or other suitable insecticide.

Be sure that the tops of the roots do not become exposed to light. Soil should be pulled over the crowns with the fingers as necessity arises. Mulching the beds from the end of May onwards will also serve this purpose, as well as being of benefit in conserving moisture in the soil. Suitable material for this purpose is old hotbed material, old potting soil, material from the compost heap, old manure in a crumbly state, or lawn mowings.

An occasional top-dressing of a good compound fertilizer should be given and liquid manure may be applied. Damping over the plants in the evening during hot weather will be beneficial, and if watering can be done thoroughly I would recommend this in dry spells.

From outdoor sowings, exhibition long carrots should be available from the beginning of August and short types from an earlier date.

For very early use and especially for sowing in frames, Champion Scarlet Horn is excellent, as also is Early Gem. For later use, and still in the short class, Favourite is invaluable. In the long class, New Red Intermediate is unsurpassable. The two last-mentioned varieties may be grown satisfactorily in frames when they are required for early shows.

Carrots for exhibition will be best if they can be left growing in the ground, until a few days before they are required. If, however, it is found that the crop is ready some time before it is needed, then the roots should be lifted and stored as advised for long beet (page 281). The washing of the roots should be done a day or two before the show, using a sponge and clean water, but must not be done at all roughly or scratching of the tender skin may result. No oil or similar substance should be used on the skins to make them shine, as good judges look with disfavour on this practice, and it would probably lead to disqualification.

About two inches of neatly trimmed green top should be left on and the long thin tap root left intact. With a good specimen of long carrot, one should be able to put a foot rule down its length and touch all the way. When washed the specimens should be laid out on a piece of clean tiffany, and covered with similar material till they have dried. This latter practice applies to all root vegetables which it is desirable to have dry for packing.

The specimens should be wrapped singly in sheets of white tissue-paper, and packed with wood-wool in the bottom of the box or hamper.

Six specimens are needed for a single dish, and ten for a collection, but at local shows, six for a collection is often all that is asked for. The specimens should be as large as possible consistent with good quality, but above all they must be free from blemish. The markings caused by the grub of the carrot fly are one of the chief faults, as also are green tops to the roots and cracked shoulders.

CAULIFLOWERS

Maximum Points 8

With the necessary planning, cauliflower may be had from outdoors from the end of May till well into November, and as it is an all-important item to exhibitors of collections of vegetables, every effort should be made to have it available for any show falling within this period. It will be a good test of a grower's skill to produce this vegetable to perfection during spells of hot summer weather.

Cauliflowers have a habit of all bursting into head at the same time; therefore to have good heads available when needed, it is necessary to make frequent small sowings. For late spring and early summer use, seed should be sown either in the autumn or in gentle heat in January or early February. For the autumn sowing in the south, seed should be put in at the end of August and through September, either in boxes placed in a cold frame or in a sheltered spot out of doors. Keep growth sturdy and the plants as hardy as possible. For over-wintering the seedlings should be pricked off into frames in not too rich soil which contains some lime. Allow three inches between the plants. Do not coddle the plants at all, but protect them from severe frost. During March, transfer them to open quarters on land which has been really well enriched. Lift the plants carefully with as much soil as possible attached to the roots and plant with a trowel in shallow drills at a distance of eighteen inches. Water them in well and see that they never suffer from lack of moisture, as this will most likely lead to premature formation of the hearts.

Treat the plants liberally in the way of water and plant food, and heads of the finest quality should be available for cutting from the end of May onwards. If the variety All the Year Round is included, there should be some good heads available till well into July.

If the method of sowing the seed in January or February is favoured, then the seed should be sown in pans or trays, germinated in gentle heat and the seedlings pricked off either into boxes or in frames. The young plants will need a little nursing at the start, but as they begin to grow freely they should be hardened off gradually and planted out in their final quarters about the middle of April.

During March and early April some seed of the early types (and the variety Early Giant should be included in this sowing), should be sown in a sheltered spot out of doors to give plants to follow those brought forward under glass. If well looked after, these outdoor-sown cauliflowers should give good heads in late July and August.

For producing heads to cut in late summer and autumn, seed of suitable autumn varieties should be sown, from the end of March till early May. Sow on a well-prepared seed bed, and as soon as the seedlings show through the ground keep them dusted with DDT to control flea beetle.

Get the plants put out into their final quarters before they become too large, as, if they are left too long, the result may be premature heading. The distance for these later crops should be two feet between the rows and at least one and half foot between the plants.

If the weather be dry at planting-out time, water the plants in well, but once well established this crop, in marked contrast to the early cauliflower, will almost look after itself, provided it is put out on really well-manured ground.

Cauliflowers, in common with other brassicas, especially those put out during April and May, are very susceptible to attacks by the cabbage root fly, and the necessary precautions must be taken to ward it off, as advised previously for brussels sprouts (page 284).

In the case of the autumn cauliflower it is advisable to look through the bed some few weeks before a show and to mark the most promising plants with a cane. This will enable the grower to keep a watchful eye on them and give more generous treatment in the way of feeding and watering. As soon as the heads start to form it is imperative to exclude light from the curds, and this may be accomplished by covering with a few leaves from plants which have been cut, or by turning in a few outside leaves, snapping them but not breaking them off completely.

If some turn in before required they may be kept for about a week if they are lifted with roots attached and hung upside down in a cool, dark shed, as advised previously for broccoli. They will need to be sprayed with clean water daily, to keep them fresh. The time to lift the plants or cut the heads is the early morning when fresh with dew, and when the moisture content of the plant is at its highest. The method of packing for carrying to the show and of staging is described under *Broccoli* (page 283).

It is necessary to grow the varieties which are suitable for the particular season when curds are required. Thus for spring and early summer Purity, Harbinger, Sutton's Improved Snowball and All the Year Round, which is the latest of this group, are recommended. For late summer and early autumn the variety Early Giant is good and for autumn, Autumn Mammoth and early and late stocks of Autumn Giant. All the foregoing I have proved to be of excellent quality and appearance.

CELERIAC

Maximum Points 6

This vegetable is very seldom seen in competitive collections where fewer than twelve kinds are asked for. It would be included at autumn shows in unlimited collections, and there are sometimes classes for single dishes.

It should be grown on well-manured ground, on the flat, and not in trenches as celery. Plenty of water and liquid manure should be given during the summer. The plants should be grown as large and as cleanly as possible and washed and trimmed clean of roots for showing, with a small tuft of green leaves left on the top. Nine or six heads will be required for a dish in competition. They should be shown on a plate or exhibition basket, just sitting.

CELERY

Maximum Points 8

When well grown and well blanched, celery makes an imposing dish for the back row in a collection of vegetables at late summer, autumn and winter shows. It is the perfect opposite number to leeks. In collections of six or more kinds we must regard it as being very desirable, in fact almost indispensable. If celery is to be brought to perfection very generous treatment is necessary; plenty of farmyard or stable manure should be given and water applied without stint every day in hot sunny weather.

Celery for exhibition is best grown on the flat or on slightly raised beds and not in trenches as for the ordinary crop. It must be realized that, grown thus, the plants will need more in the way of watering and feeding with liquid manure, but provided this is forthcoming, the extra light, warmth and air available to the plants will ensure that they grow to a greater size. For July and August shows I prefer to grow in frames. The self-blanching types are very suitable for this purpose, but, if a heated house is available for raising the young plants and growing them on early, I prefer to grow Solid White as this gives a larger and heavier stick and is of superior quality. It can be produced in good form by the end of July.

Seed should be sown at the end of January or early February for the earliest crop. As soon as the seedlings are large enough to handle they should be pricked out in boxes filled with a compost consisting of good fibrous loam, leaf-mould and well-rotted stable manure in equal parts, with enough coarse sand to make it open and a small amount of bonemeal and hoof and horn added.

About the end of March the plants should be ready for removal to a frame which should be kept fairly close for a time. By early April the plants should be planted in their final stations in the frame. The lights should be kept on for several more weeks, but plenty of air given on hot sunny days. Early in June the lights may be removed altogether.

See that the plants never suffer from lack of water. When they are growing freely feed occasionally with weak liquid manure water or soot water, and at intervals give a light application of a good fertilizer well watered in. The planting soil for the frames should consist of well-decayed turfy loam or good garden soil, and stable manure in about equal parts.

Keep slugs and snails at bay always by having small heaps of Meta and bran near the plants. Examine the plants often and carefully for insect pests in general; earwigs and woodlice are often troublesome. Every precaution should be taken to keep the stems free from blemishes. Frequent light dustings of old soot during the time the celery fly is on the wing, should ward off this pest, but this soot must be applied in the early morning or late evening. If applied when the sun has power, scorched foliage will result. A nicotine wash may be employed instead of soot if preferred (it is cleaner to use); applied against the maggots after they have started their leaf-mining activities, it is again a deterrent rather than a cure.

Blanching takes from about five to seven weeks; stiffish brown paper, the darker the colour the better, should be used, bound round the stems. Cut the paper into six-inch-wide bands, each long enough to encircle a plant at least three times. Fasten them in position with raffia ties, but not too tightly or buckling of the growing centre will result. A length of from fifteen to eighteen inches of blanched stem should be aimed at, additional paper bands being applied as the plants grow. During the period of blanching the paper bands should be removed at least every twelve days, so that an examination for insect pests may be carried out and side growths and any decaying leaves removed. The paper should be replaced immediately as each plant is finished, for greening will occur very quickly.

For autumn exhibitions the seed should be sown in early March and the plants pricked out in boxes or frames as soon as large enough to handle and grown on, ready for planting out at the earliest opportunity when the plants have reached a good size.

It is essential to keep the plants growing in an upright position, and with this crop out of doors it may be necessary to support with canes and raffia. Blanching by the paper-band method is best, and other routine jobs will be the same as for the frame plants.

For early use in frames, a self-blanching type or Sutton's Solid

White may be used, and for the main crop outside, Solid White, Giant White, Monarch White, Giant Red and Superb Pink are all first class. It is a good plan to grow one of the coloured varieties as well as a white celery, as in some seasons it will prove more successful than the white.

To prepare for exhibition, the plants should be carefully lifted, as late as possible, and most of the roots trimmed off, but the paper left on. They must not be exposed to light more than is absolutely necessary, until left for the judges. It is a good plan to place the sticks in a bucket of water as lifted. They should be taken in to a cool shed and examined, and the chosen sticks carefully washed in clean water, after any necessary removals of marked or insufficiently blanched outer stems. Following this, tie the stems together again with raffia or green fillis twine, to prevent breakages. The leaves should be left intact, and sprayed often to keep them fresh. Keep the sticks covered with tiffany after washing.

A long box will be needed for packing. Each stick should be wrapped first in white tissue-paper, and then in brown paper to keep out all light from the blanched stems. Any light subjects may be packed on top, but nothing heavy. Three heads are required for a single dish, and six for collections.

CHILLIES AND CAPSICUMS

Maximum Points 4

Chillies and capsicums are hardly ever exhibited, except in an unlimited collection of vegetables, where they are of immense value because of the colour they introduce. Their unusual shapes also add greatly to their decorative value. When shown they are usually arranged on pyramidal cones, being fixed by means of wreath stubs.

Their cultivation closely follows that of tomatoes in their young stages, the seed being sown in pans or boxes, and germinated in a temperature of about 60° to 65° F. The seedlings are potted off into three-inch pots, and then into their finals. For this, pots of five-inch or six-inch diameter will be quite large enough.

The plants may be grown all the summer either in a house, or in a cold frame, and brought into warmth in the autumn. They may even be ripened successfully out of doors in a warm border, in a hot summer. Red spider is one of the chief enemies, and frequent syringing with clean water will be necessary to keep this pest in check.

CUCUMBERS

Maximum Points 7

The cliché 'As cool as a cucumber' gives no indication of the cultural requirements of this subject, for, to grow them to perfection, cucumbers need a high temperature, not less than 60° F., with ample humidity in the atmosphere.

By far the best method of producing exhibition cucumbers is in a heated house with the plants trained on wires or on a suitable trellis framework under the roof glass. With a moderate amount of heat at command, from two to three months should be allowed from seed sowing to the time the fruits are required. Of course the plants will go on producing good fruit over a considerable period of time, if they are kept in a healthy state, and to ensure good health the plants must at no time be overtaxed by allowing them to carry too many fruits at once.

Seed should be sown in three-inch pots, in a light compost and germinated in a close case with bottom heat of 70° F. When established the young plants should either be potted on into five-inch or six-inch pots, or planted direct into the prepared ridges. Prevent them becoming hard and starved in pots.

The soil for the ridges should consist of equal parts of roughly chopped turfy loam, fresh stable manure and beech or oak leaves, collected the previous autumn. Add a five-inch potful of a good compound fertilizer to each barrowload of the compost.

The plants must be shaded from direct sunlight and should never suffer from lack of moisture at the roots; when growing freely they will need copious supplies of water. An arid atmospheric condition must be avoided, as it will almost certainly lead to an attack of red spider. This will entail much overhead syringing, but the fruit needed for exhibition should not be syringed after the flowering period.

Feeding of the plants must be attended to regularly and about every ten to fourteen days they should be top-dressed with suitable compost, such as that recommended earlier for planting in, and with the addition of a suitable fertilizer.

It may be necessary to help the fruit to grow straight and there are glass tubes for the purpose which may be fixed to the wires and into which the fruitlets may be pushed after setting. The high humidity in these tubes encourages rapid growth and straight, well-coloured fruits result. Gently straightening the fruits with the hands each morning will also prove effective.

If no house is available in which to grow the plants, and they have to be put in a frame, they must be kept well stopped, and the growths thinned out. Keep an eye on the development of the fruits needed for show right from their earliest days. They will probably need a little encouragement to grow straight, and it will help the fruits in becoming green all round if they are raised on slates or flower pots, well up to the light.

For exhibition those varieties which have smooth skins, short necks, and perfect shape are the best. Everyday, Model and Delicacy fill these requirements most admirably. Improved Telegraph is also still very good, if a good strain is secured.

Cucumbers do not require very much in the way of preparation, but are shown as grown, and if possible with the flower still attached. Cut carefully and do not handle except by the stems, as the appearance will be spoilt if the bloom is rubbed off. Pack carefully in tissue-paper, in a shallow box, which may be packed again in a larger box or hamper.

Two fruits are needed for a dish. They should be as alike as twins, with a short handle, and not at all old. An ideal length is eighteen inches.

RIDGE CUCUMBERS. There are often single-dish classes for these at summer shows. Seed should be sown at the end of April under glass, in three-inch pots. A bed of leaves and long stable manure should be made up in an open sunny position and a covering of soil, using a mixture as recommended for indoor varieties, should be placed on top. A frame should be placed in position over the top and the plants put out about the third week in May or a little later.

They should be afforded the protection of a light for about a month, but allowed a fair amount of air so that the plants do not become soft. Towards the end of June the services of the lights may be dispensed with, but the frames left in position, as the protection afforded from wind will be much appreciated by the plants.

Recommended varieties are King of the Ridge and Long Green.

EGG PLANT (AUBERGINE)

Maximum Points 3

The fruit of the egg plant is not often used for culinary purposes in this country, but dishes of both the white and purple forms would be an additional attraction in an unlimited collection of vegetables.

Cultivation in the young stages is the same as for tomatoes, and the pots for the final potting should be seven or eight inches in size. One of the most successful cultivators of this vegetable used to grow them planted out in a bed in a warm house. They are very susceptible to red spider, therefore frequent syringing of the plants is necessary.

ENDIVE

Maximum Points 5

Sometimes at shows there is a class for a single dish of endive, and at autumn shows it could be included in a class for collection of salads and, of course, in a comprehensive group. There are two kinds, the curled and the large-leaved Batavian.

Cultivation is fairly simple, although this crop does prefer a dry sandy soil, well enriched with farmyard manure, and supplied with ample water in dry weather. The curled type should be grown at least a foot apart, and the Batavian at least fifteen inches.

Endive, to be fit for the table, or for exhibition, must be well blanched. To effect this several different methods may be employed. For the smaller-growing types, inverted flower pots may be used, covering the drainage hole to exclude all light. A frame and lights or large cloches may be placed over a batch of plants, and covered with frame mats, or bags, or any other suitable materials. Or the plants may be lifted, accommodated in boxes or pots in soil, and placed in a dark shed or cellar. The blanching will take probably about three weeks, and the plants must be used as soon as blanching is completed, as decay will quickly set in. They look attractive when staged on a rectangular exhibition basket.

KOHL RABI

Maximum Points 3

To the exhibitor this vegetable will only be of service in an unlimited collection, as there are very seldom single-dish classes for it. It is quite useful in a collection, however, as it is distinct in form from any other vegetable. The green, white, and purple forms will make attractive dishes, arranged in a cone shape on a round exhibition basket.

Cultivation is similar to that of turnips. This vegetable is particularly useful in a hot, dry season, as it withstands dry conditions well.

LEEKS

Maximum Points 8

Leeks, with glistening white, blanched stems, some fifteen or sixteen inches in length and two inches or more in diameter, make the perfect opposite number to celery, standing up like guardsmen in the back row of a collection of vegetables. They are undoubtedly one of the most difficult subjects to produce to perfection.

The method of raising young leeks and growing them on under glass follows much the same lines as that employed for onions. They need a long season of growth to be fit for late summer and autumn shows, so an early start must be made. Seed should be sown under the same conditions as for onions (page 304) from the middle to the end of January, in a good rich compost which should not be made over-firm. It may be sown in either pans or seed trays. As soon as large enough to handle the seedlings should be potted off singly in small pots or pricked off into boxes and grown on in gentle heat in a position near the roof glass where possible. Alternatively, the seed may be sown directly in three-inch pots, about four seeds in the centre of each, and thinned to one as soon as the seedlings are large enough to handle.

When a shift is required, pot on into five-inch or six-inch pots in a good compost consisting of turfy loam, leaf-mould and rotted stable manure, with some coarse sand and bonemeal added. Grow them on in the house for a while and about the third week in March they should be fit to be moved to a cold frame, to be gradually hardened off. They should be ready for planting out in their final quarters about the middle of April. As the young plants develop it is a good practice to remove the tip of each leaf, as this tends to make the plants more sturdy.

It is the usual practice to grow exhibition leeks in trenches prepared as for celery. This method helps to get the necessary size of stem in a comparatively short time and calls for generous treatment. Plenty of well-rotted farmyard manure should be incorporated as the trench is made up and if the top layer can be of old potting soil with which some bonemeal and hoof and horn have been mixed, this will ensure the plants having a good start. Plant firmly and give a good watering-in. Keep the young plants growing freely by watering and feeding with liquid manure and damping overhead in the evenings of hot summer days to freshen them up. This also helps to keep thrips in check for these are pests which sometimes attack the foliage in dry weather.

Blanching must be started very soon after planting out. Land-drain pipes of two-and-half-inch or three-inch diameter may be used for the purpose, placing them over the plants and pulling a little soil up to the base to prevent them toppling over; they should be made secure with a cane and tie if necessary. When the leaves have emerged well through the tops of the pipes, light must be excluded from the stems by filling in the top of the aperture with moss or wood-wool.

This method of blanching is very successful for it allows the ready application of water and food to the roots, which is not the case when the plants are earthed up with a wide bank of soil.

The best method of blanching by earthing up is to use stiff brown paper collars about six inches in width and at each earthing up to draw the collars a little higher until the required length of blanch is obtained.

Prizetaker is a most excellent variety, and a good strain of Improved Musselburgh or The Lyon will produce excellent stems.

Leeks will need to be carefully lifted with a spade and the white fibrous roots should be left on, although if too long they may be shortened. Any soil adhering should be worked out with the fingers.

As lifting proceeds keep the stems covered for, as with all blanched vegetables, it is essential to keep the light from them. The green top should be kept its full length and, to prevent it breaking, should be tied with raffia.

Take the stems along to a shed for washing as soon as lifted. Wash carefully with a sponge and clean water, and wash all soil from the fibrous roots. Usually the one outer skin will need to be removed. Renew the ties on the green tops with new raffia.

Leeks must be packed in a long box. The blanched part of each one should be wrapped in white tissue-paper; they are then packed in the box with wood-wool. They could share a travelling box with celery. Nine specimens are required for a collection, and six for a single dish.

LETTUCE

Maximum Points 6

Lettuce is one of our most popular vegetables, being the foundation of most salads. It does not often become necessary to include a dish in a collection of vegetables, but single-dish classes will be included in most schedules of summer and autumn shows, and some spring shows. In a collection of salad vegetables, lettuce should, of course, always be included. This vegetable will grow more or less satisfactorily on most soils and, as it appreciates good living, a good coating of farmyard manure should be worked in when the ground is being dug. Material from the compost heap would also help to improve the soil and encourage the production of good hearts.

Manure for this crop should be kept fairly near the soil surface, say about five inches under. The roots will then find it when the plants are about half grown and need it most. It will also ensure that the plants do not suffer distress during drought periods and stand well without bolting.

Lettuce will do well as a catch crop, and suitable positions are on the ridges between celery trenches and between the rows of peas and beans, provided the rows are spaced well apart. It is a good plan during the hottest part of the summer to grow cos lettuce in prepared trenches, but these need be only quite small.

To ensure having a good supply at all times, frequent small sowings must be made. For all summer and autumn crops the seed must be sown *in situ* and thinned when very small, to one foot apart in the case of cabbage varieties and fifteen inches for cos. For winter and early spring crops, sowing the seed in beds or boxes and transplanting is the normal method.

The soil in which lettuce is to be grown is best made moderately firm, as on a loose soil the plants tend to be flabby and do not heart firmly. The best present-day varieties of cos are self-blanching and do not really need any aid in this direction, but if the grower thinks it might improve matters to tie the plants, this should be done about ten days before they are required for exhibition. Tie the plants quite loosely with a broad band of raffia, when they are perfectly dry.

There are many excellent varieties suitable for exhibition, Cos Superb White and of summer cabbage varieties, Improved Trocadero, Ideal and Improved Unrivalled are all first class. Imperial is an excellent white variety for outdoors, while for frames and houses, Cheshunt Early Giant and Golden Ball are good.

Lettuces should be lifted at the last possible moment before the show. They should be lifted with their roots attached and not cut, as this method will prevent undue loss of sap. Wash all soil cleanly from the roots, and if necessary wash the outside of the lettuce leaves by carefully letting clean water run over them. Wrap them in paper—a sheet of newspaper will do if economy has to be studied—and either place them in the top of a hamper, or pack them separately in a strong cardboard carton. It is a good plan to tie some damp moss or cotton wool on the roots, as an aid to keeping the specimens fresh. Six heads are required for both single dishes and collections.

MAIZE (SWEET CORN)

Maximum Points 4

Maize or sweet corn has gained enormously in popularity during recent years, and often now in show schedules there are classes for a single dish. When used in a large unlimited collection of vegetables, it can be highly ornamental.

The cobs when shown should be well developed, but not to the point of hardness. Some of the layers of the outside covering should be removed completely, and some of the inner ones left on but pulled down so as to reveal the corn; the silky threads should be left intact. It is important that the cobs are perfectly fertilized, so that the corn is evenly developed along the whole length, and not at all gappy. This perfect pollination may be ensured by planting in a block, rather than in one or two long lines across a plot.

Cultivation does not demand a lot of attention. The plants will appreciate rich soil, and some water in dry spells. Seed may be sown towards the end of April *in situ*, or plants may be raised under glass, sowing the seed in April, and planting out in early June. A warm, sunny, sheltered spot should be chosen for this crop.

In a competitive class six cobs will usually be required for a dish, and they look best when staged in an upright position, standing in a bed of parsley.

MUSHROOMS

Maximum Points 8

Mushrooms are one of the delicacies of the vegetable kingdom, appreciated by most people, but not often grown on private establishments, and by amateurs, at the present day owing to the difficulty of obtaining suitable stable manure.

I do not intend to go into the matter of cultivation of mushrooms, as the same methods would be employed to produce exhibition mushrooms, as would be for an ordinary crop, and it is a somewhat lengthy process to explain. To the exhibitor, mushrooms might well be included with advantage, in a collection of nine kinds or more, but they would have to be of the best quality. Twelve is the usual number required for a dish, a class for a single dish being sometimes included in a show schedule.

The chosen specimens for exhibition should be of a fair size and of good substance, the underside a bright flesh pink which indicates freshness, and the stalks when trimmed, must show no sign of injury by maggot. Mushrooms should not be gathered until the last

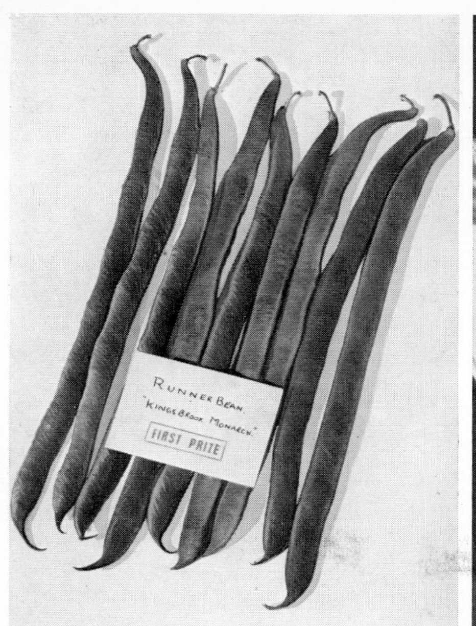

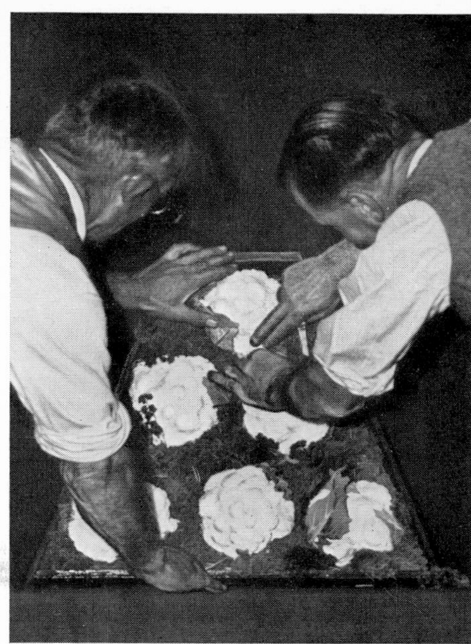

Left: A first-class exhibit of runner beans, long, even in size and not coarse. *Right:* Bedding cauliflower-heads in parsley. The leaves will be trimmed and the board removed.

Left: Perfectly matched carrots, variety New Red Intermediate. *Right:* Full-hearted celery with long, blanched stems. Note how the base is trimmed and the foliage bunched together.

Left: Boring holes for exhibition parsnips or carrots with an iron bar. These are filled with good compost. *Right:* Long straight parsnips, variety Smooth White.

Left: Perfect, even-sized specimens of King Edward potatoes. *Right:* A good dish of single-bulb shallots staged on parsley.

possible moment before a show. For travelling, pack them in a shallow box in a single layer, with some soft material round them to prevent any movement.

MUSTARD AND CRESS

Maximum Points 3

These two members of the salads group are of service to exhibitors in a collection of salads, or in an unlimited group. They are best shown in punnets or small flat baskets, in cones, or on shallow seed trays and may be produced quite easily at any time of the year.

ONIONS

Maximum Points 8

The large specimen onions which are seen at great and small horticultural shows all over the country, always form one of the principal attractions to exhibitors and the visiting public alike. In the kitchen garden a bed of the big fellows growing is always assured of being one of the chief centres of attraction to visitors. To produce these large bulbs, which weigh about three pounds each, it will be appreciated that liberal culture must be the keyword.

The best results can only be obtained as a result of much experience and there will no doubt be some disappointments to growers new to the game. Success in the growing of exhibition vegetables generally has to be arrived at largely by the process of trial and error, but perseverance in the right way will lead to success.

I was one of the members of a brains trust recently, at an Allotments Societies' Rally, and one of the questions was, 'Is digging necessary?' I am sure the person who submitted this question was not a grower of exhibition onions. Deep and very thorough digging of the onion plot is absolutely essential if best results are to be hoped for, but fortunately this crop may be grown on the same piece of ground for a number of years without detriment, unless of course, an attack of white rot should affect the bulbs. The plot chosen for the crop must be fully open to all light and air available, to ensure firmness and ripeness of the fully developed bulbs.

Farmyard manure should be dug in liberally; a barrowload to four square yards will not be too much. In the case of light and medium loams and sandy soils, cow manure is to be preferred, as this will greatly improve the moisture-holding properties of the soil. On heavy clay soils, stable manure will be preferable, as this helps to improve their texture and also helps to warm them up earlier in the spring.

This question of improving the mechanical condition, or texture, of the soil is important. On all light soils, it is preferable to trench early in the autumn, working the ground from two feet to three feet deep. It must be left to the man on the spot to decide whether his bottom soil is in a fit state to bring to the surface, or whether bastard trenching is more suitable. If drainage is thought to be at fault, some coal ashes, coarse sand, small gravel and some long, strawy stable manure should be dug into the bottom of the trenches as the work proceeds, and this should improve matters somewhat.

In the case of clay soils it might be advisable to leave the trenching till early spring. This will be for the grower himself to decide; he should know how best to deal with an intractable soil. After digging leave the surface of the bed rough and lumpy so that as large a surface as possible may be subjected to the sweetening and pulverizing influences of the weather. A good coating of soot may be spread over the surface when trenching is completed. Soot is a splendid thing for onions, and when it is spread on the surface of the soil it has the effect of darkening the soil, thereby absorbing more of the sun's rays and raising the temperature during winter and early spring.

About the middle of March, when the soil is in suitable condition, the bed should be forked over to a depth of about six inches and a dressing of wood ashes and a good balanced fertilizer, or bonemeal, worked in. If the soil needs lime, this should be spread on the surface during February.

A long season of growth is essential for the production of large, well-ripened bulbs, therefore the seed should be sown at the end of December or early in January. It is absolutely essential to obtain seed of a first-rate strain of a suitable variety.

Some good growers prefer to save and grow their own seed, not only with onions but with other vegetables as well. This practice has a lot to recommend it. A start must be made with a good strain, then by constant reselection, the best specimens only being saved for seed, a really good strain may be worked up.

Various methods of raising seedlings exist, governed, of course, by the facilities at the grower's command. Seed may be sown early in January in heat (about 55° F.) in boxes or three-inch pots, or on a hotbed covered with a few inches of rich soil made up in a frame, or they may, from about the middle of January, be sown in a cold frame—but naturally, under the latter conditions, growth will be much slower.

If the seed is sown in three-inch pots, put three seeds in each, and when the seedlings are well up, thin to the best one. When they have made sufficient headway they should be potted on into five-inch or six-inch pots. Seed may be sown in boxes and pricked off into other boxes or, if time presses, they may be spaced about two inches apart and grown on in the same boxes till they are planted out in their outside quarters.

The soil for sowing should consist of decayed fibrous loam two parts, leaf-mould one part, and decayed stable manure one part, with the addition of a good dash of coarse sharp sand and a three-inch potful of superphosphate, and a little lime if necessary, to each barrowload of the mixture. It should all be passed through a half-inch sieve. The soil in the boxes should be made quite firm and the seed covered only slightly, the soil for covering having been passed through a quarter-inch sieve.

The seed should be watered in and covered with glass and paper, or only paper, until germination has taken place. To build up a sturdy growth the seedlings must be kept growing fairly near the roof glass, and air must be admitted with care as outside conditions warrant it. Spray the young plants on sunny days.

If pricking off is needed, the seedlings will be ready for this operation about the middle of February, and it is essential that the soil for their reception be nicely warmed. Space them about three inches apart, water well in and grow on as before.

Plants that have been growing on in a heated house will be ready for a move to cold frames about the middle of March. For the first week they should be kept fairly close and if the weather is sunny the plants sprayed with tepid water and the lights closed early in the afternoon. Gradual hardening off must then follow so that the plants are completely hardened and ready for planting out by the middle of April.

The beds for planting should take four rows of plants with alleys two feet wide between if there is more than one bed. This will facilitate the operations of watering, hoeing, top-dressing, etc., without damaging the plants. Overcrowding is disastrous, and a space of from fifteen to eighteen inches should be allowed between the plants.

When lifting the plants from the boxes, retain as large a ball of soil as possible round the roots. Plant with a trowel, firmly and shallowly.

Showery weather is the best time to choose for this operation, but if the weather is dry, water the plants in well and damp over daily with a fine-rosed can until they are well established.

About the end of May mulch the beds with old stable manure or other suitable material, if possible passed through a three-quarter-inch sieve. When top-dressing with artificial manure, it will be best if mixed with some sifted soil, as this makes for easier distribution and is less likely to burn the roots.

Ample water must be applied during very dry spells, and it will be all the better if exposed to sun and air for some time before use. Frequent light dustings of soot, in addition to its manurial value, should serve to keep away the onion fly.

Keep a sharp look-out for onion mildew, which is devastating in some seasons, and take measures to prevent it by dusting the plants well with sulphur powder, or a proprietary fungicide suitable for the job.

About the middle of August in the south and midlands, partially lift the bulbs with a fork to hasten ripening. After this they must be protected from rain, for a heavy shower would result in much splitting of the best bulbs.

When collecting the bulbs to take under cover, have plenty of wood-wool in the receptacle used to carry them. If bruising is allowed, rotting of the bulb will surely follow.

The final ripening of the bulbs is best carried out under glass, either on the staging of a greenhouse which has become empty, and in which no watering has to be performed, or, failing this, in a frame under lights. In either case ample air must be admitted and a light shading of tiffany or similar material will be necessary if the sun is very warm. The bulbs must always have a good layer of soft wood-wool to rest on, and when ripening is completed a dry airy room will be suitable to accommodate them until the show date.

For exhibition purposes, I know of no better variety than Selected Ailsa Craig, and Premier is also excellent. For early summer shows, autumn-sown Ailsa Craig or one of the flat-bottomed Tripoli type is to be recommended, and also the variety A.1.

If the drying and ripening process has been successful, the bulbs should be prepared for exhibition by carefully taking off any pieces of loose skin, till the one perfect well-ripened skin is reached. The dried roots should be cut off neatly close to the bulb, and the dried top should be cut down to about two inches, bent over and tied neatly with raffia. Each specimen should be wrapped in a sheet or two of newspaper, and packed carefully in a box or hamper, with plenty of wood-wool between so that there is no chance of bruising. Six is the number for a single dish, and twelve for a collection, although for local shows probably a smaller number will be needed for a collection.

PARSLEY

Parsley is always of great value to the exhibitor of vegetables for garnishing purposes, and he should always be sure of having a good supply on hand. It is indispensable in the staging of collections of vegetables, for such purposes as the setting of cauliflowers on a board, the covering of the bases of celery and leeks, and as a bed on exhibition baskets, for carrots, beet, potatoes, tomatoes, and many other subjects.

By sowing at different times, a supply of young leaves should be ensured throughout the year. The first sowing may be made under glass in heat during early February, pricked off, and planted out during April. This should give a supply from June for some time onwards. A sowing may be made out of doors during March, which will give a supply from July on through the summer, and a successional sowing in April will give a supply well into the autumn. From a sowing made in July a supply will be forthcoming for the later autumn, winter, and early spring, but the protection of a frame will be necessary from late autumn to ensure the early supply.

A class for a collection of herbs is sometimes included in show schedules, and in such a collection parsley should always be included, owing to its widespread use in cooking. One of the better varieties should be chosen, such as Giant Curled, or Imperial Curled.

PARSNIPS

Maximum Points 6

To grow good exhibition parsnips it will be necessary to bore holes with an iron bar and fill these with finely sifted soil. The method will be the same as for carrots, but the holes will require to be made deeper, down to about four feet, and larger—four inches—in diameter at the top.

To get good exhibition roots by August or September, it will be necessary to make a first sowing at the end of February, and I would recommend at least one later sowing from the middle to the end of March. I like to make a further sowing towards the end of April.

In a dry season the first sowing will probably produce the best specimens, but in a wet season these will most likely be attacked by canker and the later sowings will be the most profitable. The best variety I know for exhibition work is Tender and True.

To be sure of getting a dozen or so good roots it is as well to prepare about four times the number of holes. The same applies to long carrots and long beet. There will always be a few wayward ones, which will not keep to the straight line of the bored hole.

If possible, the site chosen should be one where the soil has been well manured and trenched for a crop the previous season. The ground should be double-dug but no fresh manure added. The holes should be bored eighteen inches apart and the rows, if more than one, should be twenty-one inches apart.

A suitable compost for the holes is as follows: old potting soil two parts, leaf-mould one part, coarse sand half a part, and a shovelful of wood ashes to each barrowload of the compost. Fill the holes and sow the seed as recommended for carrots (see page 286).

Parsnips must be lifted at the last possible moment before exhibiting, and sometimes this is a very strenuous job. It is best accomplished by digging the soil well away from one side, examining the top of the parsnip to see if the crown is clean of canker and, if so, then working enough soil clear of the top half of the root to get a good grip. By using a twisting and pulling movement the parsnip may usually be harvested with a long length of root thong. The ease or otherwise with which they may be lifted depends to a large extent on the amount of moisture in the ground. If there has been a lot of rain they come easily, but if the ground is dry the task can be laborious, to say the least.

The lifted roots should be kept covered with bags or sacking and when lifting is completed, should be taken and washed straight away. This should be done with a sponge and clear water in a large bath, where the roots can be kept in the water while the washing proceeds. Cut the tops down neatly to about three inches, but take care to preserve the long whip-like tap root intact, as, in addition to adding to the appearance of the dish, it is regarded by good judges as a sign of good culture.

Lay the roots out to dry on a piece of tiffany as they are washed, and then pack by wrapping each one first in a sheet of white tissue-paper, and then a sheet of brown paper, to keep out the light. They quickly turn brown when exposed to light. Six roots are required for both single-dish and collection classes.

PEAS

Maximum Points 8

Peas are an important item in collections of vegetables. They are held in the highest esteem for culinary purposes and they form a most attractive dish when well staged. They must be exhibited in a perfectly fresh 'pea-green' state when the pods have reached perfection, and they must be carefully gathered and staged, so that the bloom is not removed. It greatly detracts from their good appearance to exhibit them shiny and polished.

Peas may be produced in first-class form over a very long season, from May till November, and a collection of vegetables at any time in this period will gain by having a good dish included.

Ground preparation for this most valuable crop should be very generous and thorough. The plot chosen should either be trenched and plenty of farmyard manure dug in, or trenches may be prepared for each row as for celery, and a good dressing of manure put in the bottom. Space the rows well apart, and if necessary intercrop with something of a low-growing habit, such as lettuce, spinach or radish.

As peas should always be exhibited in as fresh a state as possible, fairly frequent sowings should be made throughout the season, and thus a regular supply should result. A selection of varieties to provide a succession will also help to supply good pods when they are needed.

If peas are wanted on a particular date for a show, but a succession of varieties cannot be accommodated, it will be advisable to make three sowings, allowing for one to mature over a normal period, and then making one sowing about ten days early and one ten days late. For autumn shows, frequent sowings will not be necessary, but one should be made in early June and a later one about the middle of the same month. In the autumn, peas will hang for some time in good condition on the plants.

For really first-class pods, the cordon system of training should be adopted as in the case of sweet peas. Cane supports will be needed, spaced about six inches apart in a double row and tied to a wire stretched between firm end-posts. The peas may be sown *in situ*, or they may be sown singly in three-inch pots, and planted out; the latter is probably the better method. They must be kept growing to the one main stem, all side growths being taken out as they develop and after the fourth flower the plants should be stopped by taking the growing point out of each one. This will direct all the plant's energy into the four pods and first-class specimens should result.

Peas have several enemies. In the early stages of growth the pea weevil can be very much of a nuisance. I find that spraying the plants with wettable DDT as soon as they are through the ground will deal effectively with these pests, and if there is a recurrence blast them again with the same medicine. Thrips are often troublesome in hot weather at a later stage in the plant's life, about the time that the pods are forming. Nicotine and soap insecticide applied in the evening will effectively control this pest. During hot spells in the summer, spraying the plants in the evening with tepid water will do much to keep thrips in check. The pea moth is also an enemy to be reckoned with on late sowings, but DDT applied seven to ten days after the first flowers open will control this pest. Maggoty peas are no good on the show bench; one maggot discovered by an inquisitive judge, and the exhibitor has 'had it.'

For mid-season and late varieties, mulching with strawy manure or other suitable material will be of value to the well-being of the crops. Mildew is often in evidence on late crops and steps must be taken to combat this by dusting the plants with green sulphur, or applying some other suitable deterrent. Dryness at the roots is one of the most usual forerunners of mildew.

As with all exhibition subjects, choice of varieties is most important. There are some large-podded kinds which, when well filled make a very imposing dish, but the snag is they are so often not well filled, but merely bags of wind which are looked upon by judges with disfavour. A medium-podded variety, which can always be relied upon to be well filled, is always to be preferred for the show bench.

For an early variety I would recommend Early Giant. For second earlies Sutton's Evergreen, Prizewinner and Selected Duke of Albany are all excellent. A good dish of the last named should win in any company, the quality being of the highest. For a late variety I recommend The Gladstone as being the most reliable, but it is somewhat lacking in quality.

To be sure of their being exhibited in good condition, peas should be left on the plants until as late as possible before a show. They should not be picked in the ordinary way, but cut carefully with a pair of scissors, with a good long foot-stalk and only handled by this stem so that the bloom on the pods is preserved.

A large flat basket or box lined with white tissue-paper should be

Left: Tomatoes are best displayed flat not piled for single-dish classes. They are covered until the judging time. *Right:* The judge will cut into a specimen turnip to test for coarseness.

A first-class exhibit of onions, the exhibitor's own selection of Ailsa Craig. Note the ripe skin and absence of 'neck.'

A class for three specimen marrows. Good table specimens of even size gain points over coarse-over-large fruits.

A dish of sprouts. These should be even and unblemished and not severely 'peeled.'

at hand, and the gathered pods laid in this in a single layer only, with the stems all one way. They should be packed for travelling in this manner, either in a shallow box, or as the top layer in a box or hamper containing other vegetables. Nothing else should be packed on top of them, but the lid should be padded with some very light packing.

Fifty pods is the number required for both a single dish and a collection, and these should be as nearly as possible all the same size. Local show schedules will often ask for a smaller number of pods.

POTATOES

Maximum Points 8

The potato is one of our staple articles of diet; I suppose we might say it is our most important vegetable, and therefore a dish of potatoes should feature in a collection of vegetables, no matter what time of the year it is exhibited.

Tubers suitable for exhibition may be turned out without special treatment from some soils; for instance, light and medium loams and sandy types containing no stones. But usually the grower has to adopt special means to ensure shapely, clean specimens. Ideal tubers are of medium size and good shape, with shallow eyes and a clear skin, and must be free from all blemishes and typical of the variety. It is astonishing how many really bad dishes of potatoes are staged at the present day and how very few good dishes are seen.

The chosen plot must be fully open to sun and air and should be double-dug, or at least very thoroughly dug one spit deep, during the winter. The soil surface should be left in a rough state, so that the top six inches of soil becomes really well weathered by planting time. Some stable manure or other suitable material should be dug into the bottom of each trench and a good dressing of wood ashes spread over the plot as it becomes vacant during the winter.

Planting should be done from the middle of March to early April, the seed having been previously sprouted. Plenty of room between the rows must be allowed, a distance of two feet nine inches or three feet is not too much, and one and half foot to two feet between the sets. The sprouts should be disbudded to one or at the most two. Take out trenches about six inches deep, with either a mattock or a spade. These should be filled with a special light material, put through a half-inch sieve; either leaf-mould alone, or peat litter where it has been used for stables, or a mixture of leaf-mould and old hot-bed material may be used. A light dressing of a potato fertilizer may be dusted in the trench. When the trench has been made up with the material, cover it with a little fine soil.

The sets should be planted five inches deep, which will be almost at the bottom of the special material, and this will ensure the young tubers developing in it. When the haulm is up and growing, thin out superfluous shoots if they arise, and it is a good plan to support the haulm in an upright position. Spray with a copper fungicide in the summer to prevent potato blight disease affecting the crop, for, if this malady has been present, it will often develop in the tubers after they have been stored.

As soon as growth is completed, cut off the tops and lift carefully, without in any way bruising the tubers. Select the best specimens as they are lifted and place them in a Sussex trug basket or something similar, lined with a soft material. It is very important to whisk the chosen tubers out of the sunlight with all possible speed, as the less light they see before being shown the better.

It is very important to lift early, probably as soon as the first week in August, for the tubers quickly deteriorate if left in the ground, a lot of the best tubers becoming overgrown and misshapen. Also slugs may spoil them by eating into them.

The selected specimens are best put in a box of dry sand, finely sifted leaf-mould or peat, or a mixture of these, and stored till required in a cool, dark shed, making sure they are safe from attack by mice and rats. Keep the different varieties in separate boxes and label them.

Show schedules often include a class for a collection of potatoes and may ask for as many as six varieties; the R.H.S. include such a class at their autumn fruit and vegetable show. If the object of the grower is to show in such a class it will be advisable to grow at least eight varieties.

Here is a list of varieties recommended as being especially suitable for the exhibition table. Arran Comrade, Arran Banner, Arran Signet, Dunbar Standard, King Edward, Red King and Catriona for maincrop; and Redskin, Di Vernon, Home Guard and Sharpe's Express for earlies. One of the best exhibition potatoes is The Bishop but it is now almost unobtainable. The general favourite for inclusion in collections of vegetables is Arran Comrade, and is usually the one used by all the best exhibitors at late summer and autumn shows, and Di Vernon is very popular for the same purpose at early summer shows.

For summer shows it is usual to dig the tubers straight from the ground as required, and washing them is then a very easy matter as the soil will not have had time to dry on them. Clean water, with a little yellow household soap rubbed in, is admirable for washing, but the tubers should be rinsed in clear water. A sponge or soft light material such as tiffany should be used for the washing, and care must be taken not to damage the skin.

For autumn shows, the tubers will be selected from the store. These will need a little harder and longer rubbing to obtain a nice clean skin, but again be careful not to cause damage. As they are washed the tubers should be laid out on tiffany to dry and kept covered from all light. It is a good plan to wash several more tubers than will be needed for each dish, and then select the most suitable to make up a uniform dish. It is always a good point to bear in mind that the more specimens one has to choose from the better will be the chosen dish.

The tubers should be quite dry when packed, each one being wrapped in a piece of tissue-paper, and they may be packed with wood-wool in the bottom layer of a hamper or box. They will suffer no harm from having other vegetables packed on top of them, provided plenty of wood-wool is used between the layers.

Six tubers are required for a dish for potato classes and twelve in a collection of potatoes. Where, say, six varieties are asked for, make a nice balance by showing two dishes white round, two dishes white kidney, and two dishes coloured; the latter will usually be kidney varieties.

RADISHES

Maximum Points 4

Radishes are not indispensable to the exhibitor, but they are of use in a collection of salads, and there are often classes for a single dish. When a collection of an unlimited number of kinds is being staged they are of very great value with their various forms and colours. For display they are usually staged in the form of pyramids on cones, being fixed on with wreath stubs, and very beautiful they are in the various shades of scarlet and rose, with here and there a contrasting one in white, icy cold in appearance.

To grow them well, radishes need a good rich soil, where they will grow and mature quickly. They do not need a deeply worked soil, but it is a good plan to have four inches of half-rotted stable manure covered with three inches or so of fine soil to make a bed in which to grow them. To keep them growing well, they will need a good damping over each day during dry weather in the summer. For the first supplies, sowings should be made in frames during January and February and from March onwards out of doors. If, during the heat of the summer, a situation not too hot and dry can be found for the crop so much the better. The number for a dish in competition is usually a bundle of twenty-four.

There are quite a large number of varieties from which a selection may be made, but French Breakfast is as good as any, for general purposes. For winter use we have Chinese Rose, and Black Spanish, but in my opinion they are more useful as objects of interest than as articles of diet.

RHUBARB

Maximum Points 5

Rhubarb for exhibition may sometimes be in demand for use as a single dish, and a dish or two will be quite an attractive addition to a comprehensive collection, especially in spring and early summer. The sticks chosen will usually be drawn from the permanent bed, and quality may be improved by watering occasionally with liquid manure. Rhubarb for exhibition should be as long and straight as possible, of a good colour, and still young enough to snap easily. The leaves should be trimmed off neatly fairly close to the stem, say a matter of about three inches. For a competitive dish, three or six sticks is the usual number asked for, and they are best staged lying flat.

SEAKALE

Maximum Points 8

Seakale, although one of the most choice and highly pointed vegetables, is not often seen staged in competitive classes. This is because it is in season during winter and early spring, when there are not many shows with competitive classes for vegetables.

When shown the heads should be perfectly blanched, not over-drawn, but as stout as possible.

To ensure it being absolutely clean, lightly wash with a sponge and clean water. Keep from the light till the last possible moment before judging, as blanched seakale will go green very quickly when exposed to light.

Twelve is the number of heads required for a competitive dish, and they should be tied in a bundle, and staged standing upright in a round exhibition basket or on a plate or other suitable dish.

SHALLOTS

Maximum Points 3 *or* 4

Shallots are widely grown and shown by cottagers in single-dish classes. They usually top the bill for number of entries and are often a headache to judges. They are of no value in a collection of vegetables, being so badly pointed.

When grown for exhibition a little extra care should be taken in the cultivation of the crop. The site chosen should be an open and sunny one. Medium-sized bulbs should be selected for planting, and should be set one foot apart. The bulbs chosen for exhibition should be well ripened, very firm, and with a perfect outer skin, of a nice nut-brown colour.

A dish for competition might comprise any number from twelve to twenty-four. They should be staged in a single layer on a plate, and it is a good plan to set them up in dry, clean sand.

Some of the shallots one sees exhibited at local shows are enormous, but the Royal Horticultural Society favours the old English cluster type, which are quite small. This is the true *Allium ascalonicum* and may receive up to four points, whereas the large Russian or red shallot, which is a hybrid from *Allium Cepa*, may earn a maximum of three points.

SPINACH

Maximum Points 5

Spinach will not often be needed in a competitive collection of twelve or less kinds, although sometimes at a summer show it may be necessary to include a dish in a collection of twelve kinds. A class for a single dish is often included in schedules.

Cultivation does not present many difficulties, but the crop will appreciate some well-rotted manure dug in the plot where it is to grow, and water should be applied in very dry weather.

The leaves chosen should be of a good size, fresh and of a good green colour, and free from blemishes, such as are caused by caterpillars, slugs, and snails.

It will be necessary to leave the picking until as late as possible before the show. Spray well with clean water when packing, and again at the show, up to the time of the judging, to prevent the leaves from becoming flaccid, or alternatively, with the same object in view, place the leaves with the ends in water in a vase or other suitable receptacle.

Twenty-five is the usual number of leaves asked for and they should be staged by laying them flat on a plate or other suitable dish, arranged in an orderly manner.

TOMATOES

Maximum Points 8

Tomatoes are of the greatest value to exhibitors, and they should be included whenever possible in any collection of six or more kinds and, of course, are indispensable in a collection of salads. The effect which a dish of well-coloured tomatoes introduces to the scene is unique, and this subject is of very great value on that account alone. The treatment which will grow good tomatoes for general use will produce some good specimens for the show bench.

If facilities exist for raising and growing on tomato plants in the early months of the year a start should be made by putting in the first batch of seed in early January. A night temperature of about 55° F. should be maintained. The seed should be sown in pans or boxes, and germinated in a temperature of 60° to 65° F. Pot the seedlings off singly into three-inch pots while still in the seed-leaf stage.

If a house with pipe heat is available for the final planting, whether in beds, boxes or ten-inch pots, they may be planted in early March. If the grower has to be content with a cold house or protection by frames, or large cloches, the middle of April will be the earliest safe time to plant. Whichever method is adopted the soil should be well warmed beforehand.

If really fine tomatoes are to be hoped for, the final soil must be good, and a compost I have found suitable consists of turfy loam four parts, enriched with good stable manure one part, the latter in preference to cow manure. If cow manure has to be used it should be in a well-rotted state, fairly dry and crumbly. If neither horse nor cow manure is available, then material from a compost heap should be used as a substitute. To each barrowload of soil add two shovelfuls of coal ash (passed through a half-inch sieve), a five-inch potful of bonemeal, a four-inch potful of hoof and horn, a four-inch potful of sulphate of potash, and a good shovelful of wood ash.

See that the soil is well firmed before planting, and get the plants into their final quarters before they become pot-bound or drawn. When they are well established in their final quarters, they must never be allowed to suffer from lack of moisture at the roots or from lack of plant food; either shortage would cause hardening and thinning out of the main stem, with detrimental effect to the production of big, well-ripened and well-coloured fruit.

It is of the utmost importance to give the plants ample space, so that light and sun are able to reach every part of each individual plant. A very good method of spacing is to set a single row of plants eighteen inches to two feet apart along the front of a house, and train them under the roof glass, tied to wires or strong string.

The best fruits for exhibition are almost invariably produced on the first and second trusses, due to the fact that after this point the plants often contract one or more of the very numerous diseases or pests which tomato growers know only too well, and which lead to a weakening of the plant's vitality and subsequent loss of size and quality in the fruit. If the plants can be kept perfectly healthy and growing strongly, then there is no reason why the higher trusses should not produce fruit of exhibition standard.

Some thinning of the fruit trusses is advantageous and should consist in taking off any misshapen big fruits, and the small ones at the end of the truss.

The early batch of plants will produce the best fruit during June and July; for August shows a sowing should be made in early March, and a further sowing about the end of April.

Although vast numbers of tomatoes are grown out of doors during the summer, they do not produce fruit good enough to win in keen competition. They are always lacking in quality when compared with those grown under glass. If the plants are grown against a wall or fence, or if frame lights are fixed over the tops of the plants for some two months before the fruits are needed, then there will be a marked improvement in quality. It is protection overhead that is all-important.

In my opinion the best variety for exhibition is Sutton's Best of All. There are numerous other good varieties, nearly every firm of repute having a speciality of their own. Growers may like to improve their strain by saving seed from the best fruits.

If it is necessary to do so to get sufficient numbers, tomatoes may be picked some time before they are needed for a show; they will keep quite well if laid on cotton wool in a box, and kept in a cool, dry room. But the nearer to the date of the show they are gathered, the fresher they will look when exhibited. They must always be picked at the first joint with the green sepals still attached to the fruit.

The fruits should be as large as possible, provided they are perfectly round, of a deep, red colour throughout, and with no sign of greenback. They must be perfectly ripe without being 'watery', or flabby to the touch.

When packing for travelling, each one should be wrapped in a piece of tissue-paper, then packed in a shallow box, with cotton wool or soft wood-wool between each two fruits. Twelve specimens are required for both single dishes and a collection of vegetables.

TURNIPS

Maximum Points 6

In a collection of vegetables needing ten or more kinds, turnips may be included with advantage, though not as a rule for preference. When well grown they can make quite a telling dish, especially when they are difficult to produce in good form, that is, during hot, dry spells in the early summer. During August and onwards, when the nights are cooler, they are easier to grow, as the night dews are especially beneficial to them.

The plot where they are to be grown should be in good heart, but not recently manured with farmyard manure. There should be several inches of good tilth, so that the roots may develop to a perfect shape, but the lower soil should be firm. This crop is fond of wood ashes, so a good dressing should be added before sowing, and a dusting given about once a fortnight with the same material. A well-balanced fertilizer should be applied to the soil at the time of sowing the seeds, and an occasional top-dressing should be well watered in during the growing season.

The plants should receive a good damping over daily with tepid water, applied with a rosed can in hot summer weather, for, to produce sweet juicy turnips, they must be grown quickly and not allowed to suffer from drought. Frequent dustings of old soot will be beneficial, and the surface of the soil should be constantly well stirred with the hoe.

As turnips do not remain in their best condition for very long, it is wise to make several small sowings. Thinning of the seedlings should be effected at an early date in two operations, leaving them spaced finally at twelve to fifteen inches apart.

The turnip flea beetle will almost surely be a nuisance, and to counter this pest the seedlings should be kept dusted with derris or DDT.

As a selection of the various types I would recommend the following: Early Snowball, as being the best of the early round types; Red

Globe, as being excellent in hot dry weather; and Golden Ball. Manchester Market is a good variety of the green-top type.

Turnips should be lifted when required for a show, and washed at once, then laid out to dry. The chosen specimens should be free of any blemishes caused by the turnip maggot, or by galls or any pests or diseases. The green tops should be trimmed back neatly to about two and half inches, and the tap root, if not too straggly, left intact, but if need be it can be shortened back to about two inches. They should be wrapped in paper, and may be consigned to one of the lower layers in hamper or box, when packed for travelling. Six is the number required for a single dish, and ten in a collection of vegetables.

VEGETABLE MARROW

Maximum Points 6

Vegetable marrows are widely cultivated, since they give a good return for labour and time expended on them. They will grow satisfactorily on the flat or on a mound. The site often chosen is a bed made up of a heap of fresh leaves and stable manure, or a bed of rotting straw. A little soil should be put on top to plant in. Another method is to take out a trench or holes about two feet deep and give these a good coating of farmyard manure covered with soil.

The seed may be sown *in situ* or, what I think to be the better way, the plants raised in pots and planted out. They will pay for a little nursing in frames or under cloches at the start, for they have a tender constitution. The chief requirements of the plants will be ample supplies of water and occasional feeding with liquid manure, or a good vegetable manure, well watered in.

They should be shown as they should be eaten, in a young state. It is fatal to further production if fruits are left to grow old on the vines. Sometimes the schedule asks for three to a dish, and sometimes two, and as these should be as much alike as peas in a pod, it is often more difficult to obtain a good match than to grow the fruits.

Marrows are often of service in collections at early summer shows, but should not be included later on in the season.

There are a great many different types and different colours, but the medium-sized ones are the best always for exhibition, and the white or cream-coloured ones are often favoured by the judges. Two of the latter type which are very good are Moore's Cream, and The Sutton. Another very good variety is Table Dainty, striped pale green on a darker ground.

It is advisable to look through the plants several times during the fortnight before a show, so as to ensure getting a dish of three marrows all the same size. It may be necessary to cut them on different days, but they will keep quite well for a few days in a cool shed or cellar, with the ends of the stems in shallow water.

The chosen specimens must all match exactly for size, colour and age, and should be of medium size. The judges will test for age by pressing with the thumb, when the nail should enter the skin with the greatest of ease.

Keep them sprayed over to keep them fresh, before and after packing, and again till the time for judging. They should be wrapped in white tissue-paper, and may be packed anywhere in the hamper where room can be found. Three are required for a dish, but often at local shows only a pair is asked for.

Index

The illustrations in this book have not been indexed. A full list of the illustrations in the various sections will be found at the front of the book on pages 7-10.

THE SHOW SCHEDULE **pages 13–22**

ANNUALS **pages 25–34**

ANNUALS—*continued*

BORDER CARNATIONS **pages 35–45**

PERPETUAL CARNATIONS **pages 46–51**

CHRYSANTHEMUMS **pages 52–72**

DAFFODILS **pages 73–84**

DAHLIAS **pages 85–117**

GLADIOLI **pages 118–129**

PANSIES and VIOLAS **pages 130–137**

HARDY PERENNIALS **pages 138–156**

HARDY PERENNIALS—*continued*

ROCK PLANTS **pages 161–166**

ROSES **pages 167–181**

SHRUBS and TREES **pages 182–189**

SWEET PEAS **pages 190–207**

DECORATIVE CLASSES **pages 208–220**

FRUIT **pages 223–262**

VEGETABLES **pages 265–322**